Understanding
HUMAN
RIGHTS

Understanding HUMAN RIGHTS

An Exercise Book

Elisabeth Reichert
Southern Illinois University, Carbondale

SAGE Publications
Thousand Oaks ■ London ■ New Delhi

For information:

Sage Publications, Inc.
2455 Teller Road
Thousand Oaks, California 91320
E-mail: order@sagepub.com

Sage Publications Ltd.
1 Oliver's Yard
55 City Road
London EC1Y 1SP
United Kingdom

Sage Publications India Pvt. Ltd.
B-42, Panchsheel Enclave
Post Box 4109
New Delhi 110 017 India

Printed in the United States of America

Library of Congress Cataloging-in-Publication Data

Reichert, Elisabeth.
Understanding human rights : an exercise book / Elisabeth Reichert.
    p. cm.
Includes bibliographical references and index.
ISBN 1-4129-1411-6 (pbk.)
  1. Social service. 2. Human rights. 3. Cultural relativism.
4. Social service—Problems, exercises, etc. 5. Human rights—Problems, exercises, etc. 6. Social service—United States. I. Title.

HV41.R435 2006
323.02′43613—dc22

2005030921

This book is printed on acid-free paper.

06 07 08 09 10 9 8 7 6 5 4 3 2 1

Acquisitions Editor:	Arthur T. Pomponio
Editorial Assistant:	Veronica Novak
Production Editor:	Kristen Gibson
Copy Editor:	Mary L. Tederstrom
Typesetter:	C&M Digitals (P) Ltd.
Cover Designer:	Candice Harman

Contents

Introduction   **vii**
    Why Human Rights and Social Work?   vii
    Human Rights and Law   ix
    Purpose of This Book   x
    Outline of Book   xi
    Teaching Human Rights and Social Work   xiii

1. What Are Human Rights?   **1**
    Definition of Human Rights   2
    Three Sets of Human Rights   3
    Human Rights Terms   12
    Enforcement of Human Rights   13
    Exercises   13

2. Beginnings of Human Rights   **19**
    Evolution of the Human Rights Framework   21
    The Universal Declaration of Human Rights   23
    Social Workers and Development of Human Rights   27
    Exercises   28

**3. Building the Foundation: Universal
Declaration of Human Rights**   **39**
    Opening Statement   40
    Summary of the Universal Declaration of Human Rights   50
    Exercises   51
    Taking the Human Rights Temperature of Your Community   54

4. Beyond the Universal Declaration of Human Rights   **59**
    International Covenant on Civil and Political Rights   60
    International Covenant on Economic,
        Social and Cultural Rights   65
    Conclusion   68
    Exercises   69

5. **Human Rights and Vulnerable Groups**   **77**
     What Is a Vulnerable Group?   78
     Women as a Vulnerable Group   78
     Children as a Vulnerable Group   82
     Victims of Racism as a Vulnerable Group   85
     Persons With Disabilities as a Vulnerable Group   86
     Persons With HIV-AIDS as a Vulnerable Group   87
     Older Persons as a Vulnerable Group   88
     Gays and Lesbians as a Vulnerable Group   88
     Conclusion   89
     Exercises   89

6. **Cultural Relativism**   **103**
     Guidelines for Analyzing Cultural Relativism   104
     Cultural Relativism—This Era's Fascism?   109
     Exercises   111

7. **Human Rights and Ethics**   **119**
     NASW Code of Ethics   120
     IFSW and Ethics   120
     Human Rights and Ethics   122
     Exercises   127

8. **Social Work Practice and Human Rights**   **137**
     Preliminary Foundation for Applying Human Rights   137
     Exercises   144

9. **The International Side of Human Rights and Social Work**   **153**
     International Human Rights Issues   155
     Exercises   162

Conclusion   **171**

Appendixes   **173**

References   **257**

Index   **263**

About the Author   **271**

Introduction

Human rights. These two words receive great attention from lawyers, politicians, and other government leaders, but usually only limited consideration from social workers. Within the United States, social workers have yet to embrace human rights in a consistent and unified manner. The social work approach to human rights has, so far, been one of distance, as if human rights belong more to the domains of law and government than the less rarified world of social work. Nothing could be further from reality.

Recent policy statements by the Council on Social Work Education (CSWE) and the National Association of Social Workers (NASW) emphasize the need to educate social work students and professionals about human rights. For example, CSWE, the organization responsible for accrediting schools of social work in the United States, has issued educational standards that require social work curricula to integrate social and economic justice within the context of human rights (CSWE, 2003, pp. 34–35). An NASW policy statement maintains that human rights and social work are natural allies and urges social workers to promote human rights, especially as they relate to vulnerable populations (NASW, 2003, pp. 205–217). Certainly these organizations recognize the importance of human rights to the social work profession.

While human rights currently occupy a major role within social work in respect to educational standards and policy statements, actual knowledge of human rights among social work educators and professionals appears limited. Few social work academics have written on human rights and social work, and social work educators are only beginning to integrate human rights into university curricula. If, however, the social work profession truly intends to incorporate human rights into its policies and practices, the profession needs to ensure that students learn principles of human rights and how to apply those principles to social work.

Why Human Rights and Social Work?

Social work is a dynamic and fundamental edifice upon which societies are built and managed. The primary mission of the social work profession is to enhance human well-being and help meet the basic human needs of all people, with particular attention to the needs and empowerment of people who are vulnerable, oppressed, and living in poverty (NASW, 1999). A historic and defining feature of social work is the profession's focus on individual well-being in a social context and on the well-being of society.

Social workers play major roles in protecting children and other vulnerable populations; they perform numerous counseling roles; they carry out international relief work and occupy the frontlines of disaster assistance; they assist in delivery of social services to all populations—in other words, without social workers, the world would enjoy a less hopeful and welcoming environment.

But while the social work profession can draw upon its history and accomplishments to trumpet its importance, the profession must also prepare for future challenges and needs. The profession must adapt to changing social movements and respond effectively.

What does this mean exactly? Let's review the recent development of "welfare reform" that has occurred in the United States. In 1996, the U.S. federal government enacted major laws that restricted the years an individual could receive federal welfare assistance (Reichert & McCormick, 1997, 1998). In many cases, a person is no longer eligible for welfare assistance after having received assistance for five years during his or her lifetime. Also, the federal welfare laws contained incentives to require recipients to obtain employment. The general idea behind the welfare laws was to reduce government assistance and require welfare recipients to become more self-sufficient, especially through employment.

The new welfare laws no longer viewed public assistance as an entitlement. In effect, the rationale behind welfare reform sent a clear message: either find employment or other legal means of earning a living or expect only limited help from government. In theory, not a bad principle. Why should government always have to shell out money for people who could work and earn their own living? From a social work perspective, some hesitation has arisen in wholeheartedly embracing welfare reform (NASW, 2003). But, once again, if people can earn their own way, then so much the better.

The problem with this seemingly reasonable analysis is that it fails to view welfare reform from a more humanistic or human rights approach. What are the underlying reasons behind the distribution of welfare assistance? Why does a person not have employment, or why cannot everyone earn enough to live self-sufficiently? And, just as important, what about the human rights aspects of welfare reform? Does a welfare recipient have a human right to receive food, shelter, medical care, and other basic necessities? If a social worker adheres to the bare legal rules of welfare reform, then nobody has a human right or any other right to receive such assistance. This sounds unduly harsh, even cruel. Yet, that's what the law intends, and social workers must follow the law. Under human rights principles, though, an individual does have a *right* to adequate food, shelter, medical care, and other necessities (United Nations, 1948, art. 25).

The reality is that social work finds itself aligned with human rights principles much more than the legalistic and stern dictates of current welfare laws. Social work principles would never allow someone to go without shelter, food, or medical care if that person truly needed those items. To simply label someone as lazy or undeserving because they do not have employment or sufficient income to cover basic needs contradicts everything social work represents. Yet, welfare laws in the United States provide minimal leeway in dealing with economic circumstances of lower income individuals.

Human Rights and Law

The previously mentioned example concerning welfare reform illustrates why the law does not always satisfy human rights or social work principles. In other words, a purely legal approach to human rights can be inadequate to meet social work principles. The law simply is not a sufficient guideline for social work, and it may even conflict with human rights.

Unfortunately, one likely reason why social workers have kept their distance from the study of human rights is that they may perceive human rights to be a purely legal concept and only indirectly related to social work. Certainly, the legal profession has a worthwhile tradition and history of promoting and protecting human rights. In the United States, legislatures and courts have established legal frameworks for supporting and enforcing some human rights. However, these legal frameworks have their own set of deficiencies:

The Adversarial Nature of the U.S. Legal System. Human rights should not be pursued on an adversarial basis. Human rights require discussion and a search for consensus. To award or not award human rights on the basis of the most argumentative or persuasive lawyer devalues human rights. The adversarial nature of the court system can actually traumatize someone if their circumstances are degraded or ruled to be sufficiently unimportant to warrant notice. Loopholes abound within the law, and legal procedures often work against the search for realization of human rights.

The Pick and Choose Nature of Identifying and Enforcing Human Rights. In the United States, laws clearly favor political and civil human rights over economic and social human rights. Laws in the United States generally support a person's right to exercise free speech, vote for public officials, choose his or her religion, demand fair and open trials, have recourse against discrimination, and enjoy many other civil and political benefits. However, laws in the United States generally do not value economic and social rights to the same extent as political and civil rights. A prime example of this distinction is health care. The United States does not guarantee anyone the right to health care, which a social worker might view as equally important to the well-being of an individual as the right to free speech. Both free speech and adequate health care are listed as human rights within the Universal Declaration of Human Rights, a document agreed to by the United States. This selective legal treatment of human rights occurs everywhere and depreciates the overall value of human rights.

The Expense of Undertaking Legal Action to Enforce Human Rights. The economic cost of any legal enforcement of human rights can easily deter many people from even considering this avenue. The cost becomes especially relevant when trying to oppose a well-endowed employer or institution, which can easily afford to spend thousands of dollars fighting any adverse claim. This fact alone would deter many individuals from even considering legal action to enforce human rights.

While human rights and the law may seem ideal companions, the reality can be different. Human rights will often conflict with established laws and cultural norms. While an important part of realizing human rights, the law can also work against establishment of human rights principles.

Purpose of This Book

By illustrating the importance of human rights to the social work profession, this book highlights why social workers should integrate human rights into policies and practices. Social workers should embrace the concept of human rights, which is clearly more than a legal concept.

The purpose of this book is to provide social workers (and others) with guidance in

- identifying human rights,
- recognizing the value of human rights,
- analyzing human rights, and
- taking action to realize human rights.

By learning these four aspects of human rights, social workers will be in an excellent position to apply human rights principles to the social work profession.

Identifying Human Rights

The first step in any approach to human rights is identifying or understanding the meaning of human rights. Much of the literature about human rights simply assumes that everyone knows what human rights are and therefore assumes that there is little to be gained by defining them. *Not true.* Without a thorough understanding of specific human rights, using actual documents—especially the Universal Declaration of Human Rights—as a starting point, it simply is not possible to apply human rights to social work practice. Subsequent chapters will discuss the importance of human rights documents in understanding the full scope of human rights.

Recognizing the Value of Human Rights

After obtaining knowledge about the meaning of human rights, social workers should recognize why human rights are valuable to any society. Human rights are not restricted to certain groups or individuals. Human rights have great importance to everyone and every society. Too often, human rights principles may seem relevant to only vulnerable individuals or others in need. This is not the case.

As Amnesty International, a well-known human rights organization, has stated: "Human Rights belong to everyone, or they are guaranteed to no one."

In this book, the reader will learn that human rights principles do support the singling out of individuals or groups for special treatment. However, the primary foundation behind human rights concepts is that everyone has basic human rights and human dignity. For instance, a basic human right is that of adequate shelter and food. Everyone has a human right to receive shelter and food, not simply those who can afford it or those who qualify for government assistance. Recognizing the value of human rights to all levels of society forms the second part of the overall approach in applying human rights to social work.

Analysis of Human Rights

The third step necessary in applying human rights to social work involves analysis. Simply knowing how to define human rights and recognizing their value does not get the social worker very far in actual practice. Because human rights can conflict with established laws, such as the earlier example of welfare reform, or cultural norms, social workers should develop techniques to analyze and critique potential conflict within human rights concepts. Cultural relativism, the general notion that culture determines what is important for a society, not universal rules of conduct, also enters into any analysis of human rights. Ethical considerations also play a role in the analysis—do ethical standards always conform to human rights principles?

This book includes discussion and exercises on cultural relativism and ethical dilemmas within human rights. Social workers should recognize the importance of cultural relativism and ethics when applying human rights to practice.

Taking Action to Realize Human Rights

The final stage in applying human rights to social work practice and policies involves the development or planning of action to bring about relevant human rights. The first three steps have enabled the social worker to define, evaluate, and analyze human rights. The fourth and final step is that of realizing human rights. How does the social worker develop the means to ensure that agencies and other places of employment respect human rights? How does the social worker help ensure that clients and other individuals with whom they are professionally involved enjoy human rights? This book provides numerous examples in making the connection from social work to human rights.

Outline of Book

The use of this book will introduce students and nonstudents to human rights concepts, with the primary goal of making those concepts real and adaptable to everyday consumption. The format of each chapter aims to make the study of human rights and social work a more compelling topic. The format presents a discussion of a major human rights theme followed by numerous exercises that assist students in understanding the concepts discussed.

Learning about human rights can be compared to learning a language. Without understanding the application of human rights in the everyday world, social workers will only obtain an imperfect knowledge of human rights. This book is designed to generate true enthusiasm about human rights and leave students with a working knowledge of this all-important topic. Exercises within the book form the crux of the learning experience, with the text serving primarily as introductions to the exercises. Only by performing the exercises can the student of human rights adequately grasp the critical thinking skills necessary to link human rights to social work.

The first chapter will discuss the development and history of human rights, which is a relatively recent term. However, the concept of human rights has existed for centuries. Social workers have been at the forefront of human rights issues, such as the important historical figures Jane Addams, Elizabeth Ross Haynes, Ida B. Wells-Barnett, Alice Salomon, and Eglantyne Jebb.

The second chapter will address the definition of human rights. References to specific human rights documents will provide the reader with context and a better understanding of human rights.

The third chapter examines the Universal Declaration of Human Rights, the most important of all human rights documents. Every country within the United Nations agrees in principle to respect the Universal Declaration of Human Rights. As the reader will discover, promises to respect human rights are not always followed with action.

In Chapter 4, the reader will go beyond the Universal Declaration and encounter subsequent UN documents on human rights, including international agreements on political and economic human rights. While the United States has approved the agreement on political and civil human rights, it refuses to accept the agreement on economic and social rights. This promotion of political rights over economic rights is a recurrent theme within the United States. Too often, discussion of human rights omits economic human rights, which should occupy the same importance as political and civil human rights. As previously stated, this ignoring of economic rights is particularly prevalent within the United States.

Chapter 5 concerns itself with specific groups referred to as vulnerable populations, meaning groups that are more likely to suffer human rights abuses than others. Human rights apply to everyone. Yet, some individuals, like children, persons with disabilities, older persons, and women need specific attention to ensure promotion of their human rights. This chapter addresses those vulnerable groups.

A major criticism of human rights is that they are a Western creation and do not adequately consider differing cultures. Chapter 6 tackles this legitimate issue and argues that "cultural relativism" frequently parades as an excuse to ignore human rights. After all, why should some universal rules dictate and control what goes on within a particular society or culture? Human rights should respect various cultures, but cultures should also examine their own practices in terms of possible harm to others.

Chapter 7 addresses social work ethics within the context of human rights. Many ethical themes mirror human rights principles. An exercise in this chapter will examine ways to perform an ethics and human rights audit of organizations and companies.

To illustrate how prevalent human rights principles are to social work practice, Chapter 8 will examine well-established social work cornerstones, including strengths perspective, oppression, empowerment, ethnic sensitive practice, feminist practices, and cultural competence.

Chapter 9 addresses international concepts, such as globalization, in relation to human rights principles. Discussion of the roles social workers play within the international community aims to encourage social workers to comprehend the far-reaching importance of the social work profession.

Overall, this book aims to introduce social work students to human rights in a practical manner. The primary purpose is to familiarize social work students with human rights and prepare a base for further study. The hope is that the students will go far beyond this book in tackling the many dilemmas and challenges contained within applications of human rights.

Teaching Human Rights and Social Work

Social work educators and students who concern themselves with human rights will undoubtedly present their unique views on how to teach and learn about human rights and social work. Some may insist on an extensive overview of the history, theory, and morality giving rise to human rights. A primary concern from their perspective is "How can you truly understand human rights if you do not understand history and social currents behind those rights?" This mostly makes sense, except that, in many cases, an understanding of human rights does not necessarily require extensive study of historical and social backgrounds. The creation of the Universal Declaration of Human Rights is a case in point. That document came about primarily as a reaction to the horrific circumstances perpetrated by Nazi Germany with its genocidal and racist policies against Jews and other groups, including Gypsies, Slavs, homosexuals, and others who did not fit within defined societal guidelines. Does an understanding of the Universal Declaration truly require an extensive study of social theory, morality, and culture? Certainly, detailed knowledge about human rights can only enhance the overall comprehension of this area of study. However, a brief overview of Nazi policies is probably sufficient to instill an appreciation for the motives behind the Universal Declaration.

Human rights have obviously not arisen out of a vacuum. A student of human rights could spend an entire course on nothing more than history, morality, culture, and other important aspects of human rights. Yet, without diminishing the relevance of these aspects, a student should also be able to obtain an important overview of human rights without extensive background study. As in any area of teaching and learning, educators and students can differ as to the approach they take.

Most importantly, unless students first appreciate the importance of human rights to social work, any significant study of human rights will be unlikely. This book aims to be a social work student's first step toward developing an appreciation and understanding of human rights. With this book, social work students can quickly gain an understanding of how human rights principles play an important role in the social work profession.

CHAPTER 1

What Are Human Rights?

For human rights to have any impact on social work, those within the profession need to develop a relevant understanding of human rights. Too often, social workers encounter references to human rights only within a political or legal context. Viewed within the confines of politics or law, human rights might appear to have only slight relevance to social work.

The unfortunate restriction of human rights to political situations, especially those in other countries, has served to demean the importance of human rights to social work. For instance, when U.S. politicians speak of human rights, they typically do so in the context of a country far away and less economically developed than the United States. "This African country needs to respect human rights before we send them aid," a politician might say. What does that mean, though? To which human rights is the politician referring? Clearly the politician assumes that we all know what he or she is talking about and would readily agree: countries must respect human rights before our government will assist them.

In addition to politicians muddying the waters about human rights, lawyers also contribute to the murkiness of this topic. Lawyers often present human rights in legalistic language that has more application to the courtroom or some academic treatise than everyday life. No wonder social workers frequently find the topic of human rights vague and better suited to politicians and lawyers whose explanations about the topic appear divorced from social work. Yet, human rights have great relevance to the social work profession. The restriction of human rights to political and legal fields can only depreciate the importance of human rights to social work issues. A careful study of human rights exposes this parochial view. Social workers have at least as much claim to the exercise of human rights principles as do politicians and lawyers. Social workers such as Jane Addams and Alice Salomon have a long history of infusing human rights concepts into their profession.

Definition of Human Rights

Human rights encompass a wide variety of political, economic, and social areas. Human rights define needs but also present a set of rights for each individual, no matter where that individual resides. The concept of human rights can generally be defined as follows:

> Human rights are those rights, which are inherent in our nature and without which we cannot live as human beings. Human rights and fundamental freedoms allow us to fully develop and use our human qualities, our intelligence, our talents and our conscience and to satisfy our spiritual and other needs. (United Nations, 1987)

Of course, this definition is quite general and raises questions about whose "nature" is being defined.

Americans might feel that having access to electricity and running water is inherent in their nature, while some Africans might feel that simply having enough to eat is enough to live with dignity. Whose nature prevails? Are some people entitled to greater human rights than others because they possess the means with which to obtain or purchase valuable resources? Certainly not. Every individual is entitled to the same human rights. The difficulty arises in allocating resources to achieve human rights. A fundamental issue concerning human rights lies in constructing policies by which human rights apply to all, not simply select individuals and groups (Reichert, 2003). By classifying certain rights and freedoms as human rights, all governments recognize a common goal of creating conditions to guarantee those rights and freedoms. Obvious difficulties arise, though, in actually ensuring those rights and freedoms.

Another difficulty with the definition of human rights relates to the emphasis on "rights," which may seem overbearing. If everyone has a "right" to something, does that person also have an obligation to conduct herself or himself in a certain way? Should not the granting of human rights be connected to human obligations? If someone has an opportunity to work and earn a living but refuses to take that opportunity, why should that person have a right to public assistance? This question poses a dilemma concerning the exercise of human rights. The humane treatment of prisoners requires that they receive adequate medical care or food during their stay in prison. Yet, within the United States, those not serving time in prison have no guarantee to adequate medical care or food. This inconsistency of treatment appears to contradict human rights principles. Why is someone who has perpetrated a crime against society entitled to a social benefit that others are not? From a human rights perspective, regardless of circumstances, everyone is entitled to a basic existence encompassed by human rights principles. Aside from deficient social policies that allow inequitable situations, everyone shares a common humanity, whether that person is a priest, prisoner, teacher, or social worker.

Possibly the concept of a common humanity presents the most illusive and contested aspect of human rights. However, to carve out exceptions would destroy this essential foundation: human rights are inherent to the human existence.

Three Sets of Human Rights

The previous definition of human rights contradicts the notion that human rights refer only to political and civil rights, such as freedom of speech and religion, freedom to conduct democratic elections, and freedom from discrimination. Just as important within the previously given definition of human rights would be the right to food, housing, water, health care, employment, safety, and other rights necessary to the human existence. Also included within the meaning of human rights is the need for intergovernmental cooperation in resolving world issues. These three categories of human rights, generally referred to as sets or generations, cover a wide spectrum of items necessary for the human existence.

First Set of Human Rights

The first set of human rights lists political and individual freedoms that are similar to what U.S. citizens view as human rights. Political and civil human rights include the right to a fair trial, freedom of speech and religion, freedom of movement and assembly, and guarantees against discrimination, slavery, and torture (United Nations, 1948, arts. 2–15). Some might describe these rights as "negative," in that they restrict the role of government. In other words, government or other authority shall refrain from doing a certain act. This "shall not" set of guidelines emphasizes noninterference by government, or a negative position.

Second Set of Human Rights

The second set of human rights goes beyond political and civil rights. This set of rights attempts to ensure each resident of a country an adequate standard of living based on the resources of that country. Under this second set, everyone "has the right to a standard of living adequate for the health and well-being of himself and of his family, including food, clothing, housing and medical care and necessary social services." In addition, "motherhood and childhood are entitled to special care and assistance," and everyone has the right to a free education at the elementary level (United Nations, 1948, arts. 16–27). This set of human rights is frequently referred to as "positive" rights, in that government and individuals must take action to preserve or satisfy these rights. In other words, government shall provide these rights.

While many in the United States applaud themselves for their strong commitment to the first set of human rights, it is within the second set of rights that Americans frequently come up short. Compared to many other countries, the United States fails to fulfill its obligation to promote positive human rights (Press, 2000; Reichert & McCormick, 1997). For instance, not providing health care to all residents in the United States violates human rights principles just as prohibiting free speech violates those principles.

Third Set of Human Rights

A third and final set of human rights involves collective or solidarity rights among nations. This set of human rights is the least developed among the three types of human rights. Under this set of rights, everyone is entitled to a social and international order in which human rights can be fully realized (United Nations, 1948, arts. 28–30). Essentially, promotion of collective human rights requires inter-governmental cooperation on world issues, such as environmental protection and economic development. One group of countries should not dictate conditions to another group when these conditions would inhibit the growth or prosperity of the other group. Industrialized countries should not take advantage of less economi-cally developed countries by exploiting resources.

Viewing human rights in terms of three sets may inhibit uniformity in promot-ing human rights. With three different sets of rights, a logical response might be to favor one set of rights over another, as the United States does. Are political and civil rights more important than economic, social, and cultural rights or international solidarity? The purpose of sorting human rights into sets is not to establish dis-tinctions or preferences but to assist in the understanding of human rights. Ideally, there would be no distinction or preference between sets of rights. However, coun-tries and individuals continue to emphasize some human rights over others.

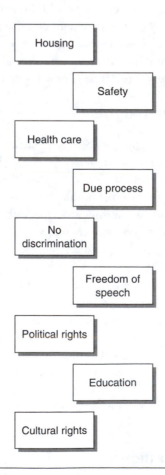

Figure 1.1   Human Rights

For this reason, knowledge of the different sets can assist in understanding different treatment often given to particular rights.

Social Work and Human Rights

Based on established concepts and definitions of human rights, social workers can readily identify a connection between human rights and their profession. The social work profession concerns itself with helping people (NASW, 1999). Human rights cover an entire range of political, economic, and cultural needs required to form a humane society. By any measure, social work and human rights have much in common. While a social work practice based on human rights is no panacea for discrimination, inequality, poverty, and other social problems, knowledge of human rights can help the profession better understand its role as a helping profession.

The social work profession has an obligation to advocate for human rights, with the first step being recognition that human rights play an important part of social work policies and practices. Unfortunately, a primary obstacle in integrating human rights into the profession is the adherence to social justice as the guiding principle of social work. While important to social work, social justice by itself does not provide a concrete set of guidelines for social workers to follow (Reichert, 2003). Social justice sounds nice but remains vague. The International Federation of Social Workers has taken a major step in moving beyond social justice by high-lighting its adherence to human rights within its code of ethics (IFSW, 2005). The recognition that social justice needs to incorporate human rights education is a first step toward fulfilling the goal of making social work a human rights profession.

Universality and Indivisibility

Two concepts crucial to understanding human rights are known as universality and indivisibility. Social workers should comprehend the importance of these concepts when relating human rights to policies and practices.

Universality

The framework for carrying out human rights requires that human rights apply to everyone, with no exceptions. Every individual has the right to enjoy human rights, wherever the individual resides. In many cases, this basic premise of universality presents little or no disagreement within cultures or governments. Few persons would disagree that everyone is entitled to adequate nutrition, medical care, and housing as basic human rights. While these items may be more abundant or affordable in some areas of the world, governments everywhere accept the universal need that people have to adequate nutrition, medical care, and shelter.

This universality principle differs from many social programs within the United States that are restricted to certain individuals, especially those with low income. For instance, many parents in the United States who do not have employer-based medical care may qualify for a government provided "medical card," based on the income of the parents. In some instances, the program only covers children of low-income parents, as if the parents have no corresponding need to have medical coverage. Parents who earn too much income do not qualify for any coverage, including coverage for their children. Yet, the cost of private health coverage will frequently be beyond the means of those individuals who do not qualify for the medical card. This exclusion of some individuals from health care coverage violates the universality principle inherent in human rights. The United States stands alone among industrialized countries in the lack of a plan to provide health care to all its residents. While most people in the United States probably agree that everyone should have health care, the reality is quite different.

The notion of universality may clash with particular cultures, laws, policies, or morals that fail to even consider the human right in question (Reichert, 2003). For example, the human right to be free from discrimination and to enjoy human dignity should obviously apply to everyone anywhere in the world. However, some countries allow discrimination against women because of cultural or religious norms that frown upon women performing certain acts reserved for men, such as voting or driving a car. The United States still allows capital punishment for individuals who are 18 or older, which violates established human rights principles (www.unhchr.ch/html/menu3/b/a_ccpr.htm). Other countries carve out additional exceptions to established human rights.

Human rights principles require sensitivity to culture and religion, and cultural and religious norms often prevail. This dilemma of universality raises the question "Which should prevail, the cultural or religious norm or the human right?" Obviously, if human rights apply to everyone, then the human right to be free from discrimination or capital punishment for juveniles must take precedence over sensitivity to culture and religious norms. Yet, a human right also exists to be free to carry out cultural and religious practices. In these circumstances, cultural and religious beliefs will often prevail simply because the powers that be determine the priority of human rights. In many instances, universality of human rights will be tempered by local practices. No easy resolution of this conflict exists. However, if the vast majority of countries throughout the world have accepted a particular human right, cultural, religious, or other authority for contradicting this right should be carefully examined.

Indivisibility

The second crucial concept in understanding human rights is that of indivisibility. The concept of indivisibility refers to the necessity that governments and individuals recognize each human right and not selectively promote some rights over others.

The absence of a guarantee to everyone of adequate health care within the United States highlights the importance of indivisibility among human rights. Opponents of universal health care might say that, even without an entitlement to health care, everyone receives adequate care—all they have to do is show up at the emergency room of a public hospital. By law, that hospital must treat the patient. Why should government go any further than that in providing this human right?

The problem here is that simply receiving treatment at an emergency room does not ensure adequate medical care. An individual without medical insurance may fail to attend to an illness that becomes life threatening or debilitating. Emergency room treatment would not even cover many situations that are chronic or cannot be dealt with as an emergency. Impaired health reduces an individual's enjoyment of other human rights, such as the promotion of family or employment. Impaired health could even affect the will or ability of an individual to participate in an election or other activities viewed as political human rights. Consequently, the denial of, or the refusal to recognize, one human right can easily impact the enjoyment of other human rights and directly or indirectly deny those rights. For this reason, indivisibility plays a key role in the exercise of human rights.

While the promotion of one human right over another should not occur, the reality, as with the concept of universality, becomes murky. Certainly not every country can afford to provide all the economic rights defined by the United Nations as human rights. Should not this excuse that country from recognizing or promoting those rights? Is it not more important to ensure elections, free speech, and religion and other political rights than attempt to satisfy economic rights? Even without sufficient funds to promote economic and social human rights, countries should still make efforts to fulfill these rights. Cooperation and assistance among countries becomes essential when facing such catastrophic situations as HIV-AIDS.

Certainly countries and organizations with limited resources will be selective in allocating funds to various activities. However, by understanding the importance of all human rights, social workers can advocate for the use of funds to be more targeted toward human rights policies than might otherwise be the case.

Differences clearly exist in definitions or interpretations of human rights, especially in respect to conflicts with universality and indivisibility. Who, then, decides whether to recognize a particular human right that the United Nations has included within the Universal Declaration of Human Rights or other document? Refer back to the discussion on health care in the United States regarding the provision of medical care. Based on the Universal Declaration, everyone is entitled to adequate medical care, with this right holding the same importance as any political or civil right. The United States, however, does not view the situation within a human rights context. Why not? To examine the process of how a country defines human rights, social workers should ask the following questions.

Who Defines a Human Right?

In many cases, the United Nations, acting through its various committees, issues documents on specific human rights. Member countries then decide on whether to adopt or enforce these rights. Within the United States, government leaders, with input through individuals and nongovernmental organizations, influence the defining of human rights. Other countries may define human rights differently than the United States, but the common factor is that, regardless of any UN document on human rights, the definition remains localized. This country-by-country, culture-by-culture method of defining human rights clearly chips away at the universality concept.

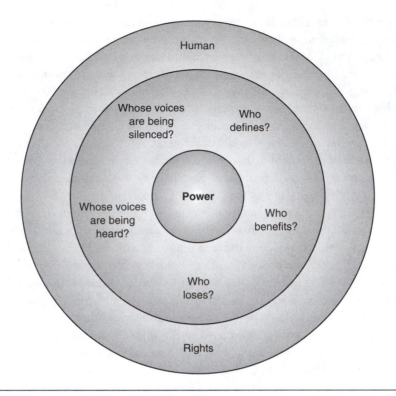

Figure 1.2   Human Rights and Important Questions

The United States, along with every member country of the United Nations, has agreed to respect human rights specified in the Universal Declaration of Human Rights, which includes the right for *everyone* to have adequate health care (United Nations, 1948, art. 25). Yet, in practice, the United States does not fulfill this promise to provide everyone with adequate medical care. The U.S. definition of adequate medical care omits any entitlement to health care. This refusal to recognize that everyone has a human right to adequate health care stems primarily from cultural and government traditions against "socialized medicine" or government intervention in health care systems (Mintz, 2004). The established practice that employers, not the government, provide health care to working adults accepts gaps within health care coverage. No law exists requiring employers to provide health care to employees, and many small employers cannot afford to offer this benefit. Self-employed persons must pay for their own medical coverage, with the cost of premiums often exceeding what they can afford. Unemployed adults usually have little or no access to medical coverage and must fend for themselves. The elderly, persons with disabilities, and children of low-income parents generally have the best possibility of qualifying for government-provided medical coverage.

Attempts to introduce universal health care in the United States have simply not succeeded. From a human rights perspective, those who define this human right are legislators, as influenced by individuals or groups, including the wealthy, insurance companies, and the American Medical Association. While legislators would never admit to violating a human right, the absence of a universal health care system can hardly be justified under human rights principles agreed upon by the United States. A disconnect between relatively clear human rights principles issued through UN committees and the actual definition of these principles as practiced by individual countries appears frequently.

Who Benefits From the Definition?

To better understand why a particular country defines a human right differently from the United Nations or another country, social workers need to examine those who benefit from the definition. Using the example of health care in the United States, those benefiting from a restrictive view of adequate health care would be taxpayers who do not want to pay additional taxes to cover the uninsured. Politicians can keep taxes lower because less public funding is needed for covering the uninsured. Lower taxes may benefit all taxpayers, but the greatest benefit of lower taxes generally goes to those who pay more taxes, the wealthiest. Doctors may object to universal health care because they believe the government would then control their working environments and rates of compensation. Health care corporations and insurance companies benefit from a private system of health care that enables them to charge higher prices for medical services or coverage to increase profits. Some individuals may also feel they benefit from a private system of health care because the current system allows them to choose their own doctor, although with the introduction of so-called managed care, choice of doctor is not always available.

Clearly, many individuals and groups perceive advantages from not fully extending health care benefits to everyone. The influence of these individuals and groups has always been sufficient to prevent legislators from instituting a health care system that would provide adequate care to everyone.

Who Loses From the Definition?

In the case of not providing everyone with adequate health care, obvious losers are those who do not receive the care. They must either forego care or incur bills for care, knowing that they cannot pay the cost of the services. However, other groups also lose from this definition. Hospitals may provide services to the uninsured but fail to collect the cost of these services. As a result, hospitals bill patients with medical coverage more to cover the cost of treating those who have no coverage. Doctors may also bill paying clients more to cover unpaid services. Employers who provide insurance to their employees may also find this cost increasing because of the overall cost increase in coverage simply to fund unpaid medical bills. Therefore, in a convoluted manner, some of those who benefit from the failure to cover everyone's health care may also find themselves losing because of additional costs.

Because the most obvious losers in the health care debate are individuals without insurance, many of whom are unemployed and possibly do not vote, legislators may not feel sufficiently pressured to recognize this segment when defining the human right of adequate health care. Only when the losers become more prominent and their voices more powerful will legislators consider revising the definition of this human right to include everyone.

Whose Voices Are Heard in Enforcing Human Rights?

Continuing with the health care example, the voices of those without medical coverage appear to be extremely weak, while the voices of the health care providers are extremely strong; the voices of those who speak against "socialized medicine" carry much more weight than the voices of those who want universal health care.

The previous three questions examine the process of how countries and groups define a specific human right. Essentially, the definition and carrying out of human rights remains a local affair, even within the context of universality. This cultural or local view of many human rights generally encounters little opposition from other countries.

However, situations may arise when local definitions of human rights create disagreement between different countries. A recent example of this clash between countries is the situation in Iraq. The United States accused Iraq and its head, Saddam Hussein, of human rights violations, including torture and genocide. Did the United States and its coalition of countries have a right to remove Hussein on the basis of these violations? The questions that examine the process of defining a human right are equally relevant in examining whether allegations of human rights violations by one country give another country the right to intervene within the internal affairs of that country. Where the voices defining the human right and benefiting from enforcement of that right are louder or more powerful than those voices not benefiting from enforcement, the more powerful voices may decide to take action. This action may consist of economic and other sanctions and, in situations perceived to be serious, military activity, as was the case in Iraq.

Social workers need to understand the process of defining human rights and the weaknesses of this process. In theory, everyone in every country should enjoy the same human rights. The reality is different, with cultural, historical, legal, and other types of factors contributing to the skewed definitions of human rights encountered in different countries. Yet, even with the less-than-perfect practice of defining particular human rights, general agreement on the definition of many human rights does exist. Domestic violence is an area where more and more countries and cultures are recognizing that women, as well as men, should enjoy freedom from violence within the household (Reichert, 1998). Other human rights that have gained stature and a more commonly agreed upon definition include prohibitions against torture, children's safety and welfare, freedom of speech, and many other political and economic human rights. The need to define human rights coherently stands out as an unfulfilled challenge in the realm of human rights principles.

Cultural Relativism—Justification for Ignoring Universality?

The concept of universality within human rights frequently clashes with the concept known as cultural relativism. In short, cultural relativism refers to the notion that cultural traditions or norms have priority when a particular human right conflicts with those traditions or norms. In many cases, cultural relativism plays little or no role in the promotion of human rights. After all, except in rare circumstances, cultural norms would never sanction the denial of adequate food or medical care to those in need. Culture generally does not condone torture or genocide. Nor does culture accept the physical or mental abuse of the elderly.

However, cultural traditions do condone many practices, which clearly violate human rights principles. For instance, physical abuse of spouses or children may very well be tolerated within some cultures. Some societies may totally suppress freedom of speech, relying on a much narrower definition of free speech than that espoused by the United States. Should these and other apparent violations of human rights be downplayed because they are the "cultural" norm? A strong argument exists against this use of culture to justify what are truly human rights violations.

Consider the following: Heshu Yones was just 16 when her father slit her throat because of her choice of boyfriend. Sahjda Bibi was 21 when a cousin stabbed her to death in her wedding dress for marrying against family wishes. Rukhsana Naz was strangled by her brother and mother for getting pregnant by a lover. The slaughter of a succession of young women by their male family members in recent years has alerted Britain to a problem that has migrated to Western Europe along with growing minority communities from South Asia, Africa, and the Middle East: these are known as "honor crimes."

For their perpetrators, these crimes have "honor" because they fulfill tribal custom to redeem the shame that some women have supposedly brought upon their families (Rice-Oxley, 2004). The problem of "honor killings" raises the precise issues that cultural relativism brings to the area of human rights.

> Honor killing, say activists, is just the tip of an iceberg of abusive practice toward women that also includes forced marriage, genital mutilation, domestic imprisonment, prescriptive dress codes such as *hijab,* and barred access to education and the workplace. . . . The effort to combat the brutal treatment of women in certain ethnic minorities raises a delicate question: How do authorities crack down on unacceptable practices without offending minority culture? . . . Feminists say the law often puts culture ahead of the safety of women. Communities say their culture is sacrosanct, inalienable. (Rice-Oxley, 2004, p. 6)

Should cultural relativism prevail in these circumstances? By most standards, the answer is no. Culture is not static. If worldwide trends—and not simply in the Western world—move toward greater respect for women's and children's rights, then cultural relativism must reflect these trends. Using culture as an excuse for what many know is wrong within the contemporary world should not be tolerated.

Of course, cries of cultural relativism come not simply from non-Western communities. Take into account the recent events of prisoner abuse by Americans in Iraq and Afghanistan. Until these episodes were made public and roundly condemned from allies of America, many U.S. officials might have considered these actions as part of the new landscape made necessary by the attacks on the World

Trade Center on September 11, 2001. To accept torture as a means of interrogation can only be viewed as culturally regressive. Culture does change, but in this case, the change would be backward. The United States has been in the forefront of promoting the human right prohibiting torture or inhumane treatment. To now tolerate these acts as culturally necessary would violate established human rights principles. The same view should apply to detaining prisoners without any right to legal counsel or knowledge of charges and the opportunity to defend against those charges. Fortunately, sufficient voices have opposed these actions by the United States to at least limit a backward tilt into cultural relativism.

Human Rights Terms

The language of human rights contains some terms that social workers should master as part of their own vocabulary.

Declaration. The most common document referred to within the area of human rights is the Universal Declaration of Human Rights, which this book covers in the next chapter. What does *declaration* mean? In respect to human rights documents, a declaration presents a formal and solemn nonbinding statement listing general principles and broad obligations (Human Rights Resource Center, 2005). While the Universal Declaration lists significant principles of human rights, no country is obligated to enforce those principles. Yet, because every country that becomes a member of the United Nations agrees to recognize the Universal Declaration as a model, this declaration does have importance. In other words, while a country has no obligation to enforce a declaration it has signed, by failing to comply with that declaration, the country is indicating bad faith and may lose respect within the world community.

Covenant. A covenant on human rights principles serves as an agreement between two or more countries that they will enforce provisions of the covenants with specific laws (Black, 1968). In contrast to a declaration, a covenant agreed to by a country does impose an affirmative obligation to enforce provisions within the covenant.

Convention. A convention refers to an international agreement that contains provisions to promote or protect specific human rights or fundamental provisions (Human Rights Resource Center, 2005). As with a covenant, a country that signs a convention has an obligation to enforce provisions within the convention. For instance, in discussions about prisoner abuse by U.S. military within Iraq and elsewhere, references to the Geneva Convention seem inevitable. These conventions obligate those countries that have approved them, like the United States, to respect human rights of prisoners (Holtzman, 2005). Yet, even though the United States entered into the Geneva Conventions, some U.S. officials have advocated the bypassing of these human rights principles because of the war on terror (Holtzman, 2005, pp. 20–24).

The key distinction between declarations and covenants or conventions is that of obligation. Countries approving a covenant or convention intend to bind themselves to the provisions of the document. Countries approving a declaration merely indicate their intent to follow provisions within the declaration. The language of a covenant or convention generally requires a country to undertake action to ensure specific human rights, whereas the language of a declaration focuses more on the need to recognize particular human rights. For that reason, a covenant or convention often follows a declaration.

Enforcement of Human Rights

Within the United States, enforcement of specific human rights has been highly selective. Court decisions rarely refer to human rights, and legislators may ignore human rights principles in drafting laws that involve human rights (Davis, 2000; Reichert & McCormick, 1998). Unfortunately, this neglect of human rights principles by judges and lawmakers does little to encourage or promote a more pervasive system of human rights within the United States.

Some European countries are subject to the European Court of Human Rights, which actually allows an individual to bring a case of an alleged violation of human rights before it (European Court of Human Rights, 2005). This avenue does provide some relief from specific violations of human rights, which include both economic and political rights.

Ideally, governments everywhere would take seriously all provisions within the Universal Declaration of Human Rights and do their best to enforce those rights. However, even though enforcement of human rights remains deficient in many countries, social workers can be advocates for change and encourage better enforcement. By better understanding the meaning of human rights, social workers will be at the forefront in the effort to bring about a society and culture that truly respects the importance of human rights.

Exercises

Exercise 1: Human Dignity and Rights

Consider the following statements by Eleanor Roosevelt:

Where, after all, do universal rights begin? In small places, close to home, so close and small that they cannot be seen on any maps of the world. Yet they are the world of the individual person; the neighborhood he lives in; the school or college he attends; the factory, farm or office where he works. Such are the places where every man, woman, and child seeks equal justice, equal opportunity, equal dignity without discrimination. Unless these rights have meaning there, they have little meaning anywhere. Without concerned citizen action to uphold them close to home, we shall look in vain for progress in the larger world. (Roosevelt, 1948)

Now consider the mission statement for U.S. social workers as cited in the NASW code of ethics:

> The primary mission of the social work profession is to enhance human well-being and help meet the basic human needs of all people, with particular attention to the needs and empowerment of people who are vulnerable, oppressed, and living in poverty. (NASW, 1999)

Part A: Human Dignity

Keeping in mind the statement by Eleanor Roosevelt and the NASW mission statement, consider the concept of "human dignity." On one side of a sheet of paper, list "qualities" necessary to fully develop and define humans, and on the other side list "rights" needed to develop or protect those qualities. For example:

Qualities	Rights
a. Ability to reason	a. Freedom of speech
b. Desire for spiritual growth	b. Freedom of religion
c. Need of food, health care, education, and other social needs	c. Guarantee of food, medical treatment, education, and promotion of family life

After completing your lists, discuss or reflect upon the following questions:

- What does it mean to be fully human? How is that different from just "being alive" or "surviving"?
- Based on your lists, what needs do people have in order to live in dignity?
- Are all humans essentially equal? What is the value of human differences?
- Under any circumstances, can or should any of the listed human qualities be taken from us?
- What are possible effects on both the individual and broader society when a person or government attempts to deprive someone of something that is necessary to human dignity?
- What would be the effect if you had to give up one of the human qualities on your list?

Part B: Rights

Discuss the different meanings of *right*, such as correct, opposite of left, just. Make a list of these meanings. What is the meaning of *right* when we speak of human right?

Relying on what you now know about the term *human rights*, create your own definition of this term. List different possibilities.

Consider the following statement: Human rights belong to all people regardless of their sex, race, color, language, national origin, age, class, religion, or political belief. They are universal, inalienable, indivisible, and interdependent.

What is meant by universal? Inalienable? Indivisible? Interdependent? Use a dictionary to obtain initial definitions.

Compare the following sets:

Survival: Subsistence

Human Dignity: Conveniences/Luxuries

Discuss the relationship of these sets within the context of human rights. For example, should conveniences be classified as human rights?

After discussion of the two sets, refer to the chart/lists made in Part A of this exercise. Place each of the items listed as a human quality under as many of the headings you believe appropriate. For example, if health care was listed as a human quality in your list, determine whether health care is necessary for survival or subsistence. Is health care necessary for human dignity or is it more of a convenience or luxury?

Items to discuss:

- Should human rights address only what a human being needs to survive? Why or why not?
- Should human rights also protect those things you classified as "conveniences and luxuries"? Why or why not?
- Some people in the world have only what is necessary to survive (if even that much) and others have luxury and conveniences. Is this situation just? Is it a human rights violation?
- Can something be done to equalize the enjoyment of human dignity? Should something be done? If so, how? And by whom?
- Discuss the relationship between human dignity and human rights.

Adapted from Flowers, Nancy (ed.) *Human Rights Here and Now: Celebrating the Universal Declaration of Human Rights*. Human Rights Resource Center (1998). http://www.umn.edu/humanrts/edumat/hreduseries/hereandnow/Default.htm

Exercise 2: Standing Up for "Rights"

This exercise requires a group of about six people and a facilitator. If done in a large class, separate the class into groups of six or seven.

- A facilitator asks each person in a group to remember a time when he or she stood up for his or her rights or the rights of other people. For example, a person may remember a time in childhood when the person supported a friend against a bully or a false accusation.
- After a few minutes of reflecting on an incident of standing up for rights, each member of the group relates the circumstances of the incident to another member. At this point, the group can separate into smaller numbers of twos or threes.
- After the exchanges of incidents, all members of the group come back together for general discussions. Each person in the group should have available the following information:

1. The time when I "stood up" for rights.
2. What happened.
3. Where it happened.
4. The motive: Why did I stand up?
5. Who or what were my sources of support?

- The facilitator now asks each member of a group to tell his or her story, keeping closely to the previously listed five points. After each member of the group has related his or her incident, the facilitator now raises the following points for discussion:

1. Were your experiences similar/different to those of others in the group? For example, did they happen in public/private, at home/work?

2. Did the place of the incident involve both positive and negative aspects? Did the persons involved react in ways both positive and negative?

3. Did anyone mention the law or authorities as a source of support? Why or why not?

4. How did you feel when you remembered the incident of "standing up"?

5. Were these positive experiences? Why or why not?

6. How many members of the group experienced support or solidarity from friends/colleagues/family? Do you believe this type of support is useful when we stand up for human rights?

7. Using the information in this chapter about human rights, did members find their experiences related to human rights principles?

Adapted from Flowers, Nancy, Marcia Bernbaum, Kristi Rudelius-Palmer, Joel Tolman. *The Human Rights Education Handbook: Effective Practices for Learning, Actions, and Change.* Human Rights Resource Center (2000). http://www.umn.edu/humanrts/edumat/hreduseries/hrhandbook/toc .html

Exercise 3: Social Workers and Human Rights

This exercise can be done with a group or individually as an assignment.

1. Using *only* information and human rights concepts presented in this chapter, list five social work issues that involve human rights.

2. What human rights are involved with each of the issues? Are those rights political/civil rights or economic/social?

3. Do you believe that some of the rights related to the social work issues have more importance than others? How would you rank the importance of the rights involved, using a scale of 1 to 10, with 10 being the most important?

4. How do you believe that human rights play an important role in social work? Discuss.

Exercise 4: Enforcement of Human Rights

This exercise can be done with a group or individually as an assignment.

1. Explain the difference between a "declaration" and a "covenant." List these differences either on a board for every member of the group to see or on paper if doing the exercise alone.

2. Should countries that support a human rights declaration be required to enforce provisions of that declaration? Why or why not? List reasons.

3. As a social worker, would you support the human right that requires respect for individual cultural traditions when one of those traditions may harm others (e.g., circumcision, domestic violence)? If not, what reasons would you give for refusing to respect the cultural tradition? List those reasons. If you believe that cultural traditions should always be respected, list reasons for allowing the harm done to others by respecting the cultural traditions.

4. Can there ever be universal enforcement of human rights? Discuss.

Exercise 5: Using the Media

The purpose of this exercise is to use the media (e.g., television, newspapers, Internet, movies) to become familiar with human rights issues.

1. Based on information gathered through the media, list a human rights issue that relates to your local community. Discuss how the media source reported the human rights issue. Did they describe the issue as one involving human rights?

2. Based on information gathered through the media, list a human rights issue that relates to the United States as a nation. Did they describe the issue as one involving human rights?

3. Based on information gathered through the media, list a human rights issue that relates to regions outside the United States. How was this issue described by the media? As a human rights issue?

4. After listing the human rights issues, how do you see those issues relating to social work?

Adapted from Flowers, Nancy (ed.) *Human Rights Here and Now: Celebrating the Universal Declaration of Human Rights.* Human Rights Resource Center (1998). http://www.umn.edu/humanrts/edumat/hreduseries/hereandnow/Default.htm

Exercise 6: Universality

The purpose of this exercise is to discuss the meaning of universality within a human rights context.

Analyze this statement from Amnesty International: "Human Rights belong to everyone or they are guaranteed to no one."

In your response, discuss the following:

- Can everyone realistically have the same human rights considering the different levels of income, different governments, and different cultures?
- Do you believe that even if some groups do not enjoy human rights, others have no guarantee of human rights?
- Do those who enjoy human rights have a social responsibility to ensure that everyone else can obtain human rights?
- How does the Amnesty International statement relate to social work values?

Exercise 7: Indivisibility

The purpose of this exercise is to discuss the meaning of indivisibility within a human rights context.

1. Should political and civil human rights have priority over economic, social, and cultural human rights? For instance, is freedom of speech more important than adequate health care?

2. List ways in which political and civil rights are dependent upon economic, social, and cultural human rights. List ways in which economic, social, and cultural human rights are dependent upon political and civil rights.

3. Do you believe that social work values have more relevance to one set of human rights than another? Give reasons.

CHAPTER 2

Beginnings of Human Rights

The specific phrase "human rights" has only existed for about sixty years. Its initial use occurred after the end of World War II in 1945 (Morsink, 1999). Why did this concept appear just at that time? Consider the catastrophic effects of World War II. Hardly any corner of the world escaped the immense destruction and loss of life arising out of that conflict. After the war, much of Europe, especially Germany and Russia, lay in almost total ruins. Cities resembled mountains of rubbish piles.

The unparalleled loss of life loomed larger than the destruction of property in the thoughts of postwar residents.

> The dead in World War II have been estimated at 15 million military personnel of which up to 2 million were Soviet prisoners-of-war. An estimated 35 million civilians died, with between 4 and 5 million Jews perishing in concentration camps, and an estimated 2 million more in mass murders in Eastern Europe. (Alexander, Isaacs, Law, & Lewis, 1998, p. 732)

All together, total loss of life from the war approached 50 million people. That would be more than one-sixth of the entire population of the United States today, or one-third of the U.S. population in 1945. The enormity of this loss of life can hardly be imagined, and it clearly left impressions on survivors that would never be erased.

In addition to the stark number of lives lost, another factor loomed large in postwar thinking about the type of societies people wanted to create out of the smoldering ashes: the maniacal attempt by German leaders to eliminate particular groups and individuals, including Jews, Gypsies, and people with disabilities, who they considered to be inferior to others.

The Holocaust, with its estimated 7 million deaths at the hands of German leaders and their supporters, received the most attention. German race laws enacted during the regime of dictator Adolf Hitler after 1933 attempted to "purify" German society and rid it of non-German elements. A primary target, for historical and cultural reasons, was the Jews, many of whom had incorrectly believed that they had fully assimilated into German society. Jews ran businesses, occupied esteemed positions as lawyers, and generally played a significant role in pre-Hitlerian German society.

> They were all children of an enlightened, imperial Germany, born at a time of Jewish emancipation and social mobility. In the forty-two years separating the births of the oldest—Max Warburg, in 1867—and the youngest—Hans-Joachim Schoeps, in 1909—the Jews of Germany would rise from being second-class citizens, denied the right to practice their religion freely, barred from many professions, and treated as pariahs, to a degree of equality and acceptance unknown to many Jews in other parts of the world. They grew up in an era when the complicated, symbiotic German-Jewish bond became as close as it ever would, as the aspirations and outlooks of the Jews and their fellow Germans merged, as the kaiser's Germany itself entered the modern world. They were offspring of a Jewish "golden age," marred only by sporadic, isolated anti-Semitism that seemed more the residue of an older, dying Germany than the harbinger of a holocaust. (Dippel, 1996, p. 1)

Many Germans associated with Jews and openly embraced the inclusion of Jews into German society. What happened to German society that it began to target Jews for discriminatory treatment and eventual genocide? It would be too easy and even incorrect to simply say that Germans always hated Jews and had no qualms about getting rid of them. A more critical analysis would have to take into account the factors leading to this egregious discrimination.

Perhaps the underlying theme behind any discrimination, whether or not it culminates in genocide, is the labeling of others as bad, inferior, or simply different. This is essentially what German leaders did to instill antipathy among the German populace against Jews and others. The German government blamed the Jews for their defeat in World War I, another horrific incident in the pages of history. Some Germans blamed Jews for predatory business practices, supposedly causing "pure" Germans financial difficulties. The list of grievances against Jews escalated, with the German government actively supporting this hate campaign. Finally, the German government began to isolate Jews and then kill them. This "final solution" was the ultimate form of discrimination. German citizens may have claimed that they had nothing to do with such a drastic stage in the discriminatory campaign against Jews, yet, in a realistic view, every German bore some responsibility for what happened (Goldhagen, 1996).

Are the Germans bad people? Look at German society today, with its democratic institutions and generous welfare benefits. Many foreigners reside in Germany today without fear of the government or German residents destroying their property or rounding them up as they did the Jews. How could this society, with its many freedoms today, have committed the horrors that it did? Countless books have explored this topic, with no definitive answer.

Americans may feel that they could never do what the Germans did in World War II. After all, have not Americans created a society where these types of abuses could never exist? Yet, with the extermination of indigenous peoples during the early settlement of the United States, colonial Americans were clearly capable of committing what some might view as genocide. During the segregation period in the Deep South, lynching of African Americans certainly occurred. Also, what about the abuse of Iraqi and other prisoners in the "war on terror," with some abuses apparently leading to deaths? What about the deaths of civilians caused by U.S. attacks in Iraq? While the U.S. government claims that it has made every effort to minimize abuse and civilian deaths in Iraq, the treatment of Iraqis by the United States raises the question of cultural superiority. Is it all right for the United States to harm others because Americans believe their culture and way of life is better, and everyone will benefit in the long run by U.S. actions? From a human rights position, this logic or reasoning does not justify the harm.

The unfortunate reality is that no country or group appears immune from the perpetration of horrific acts of discrimination and similar violations. After World War II, the guiding belief that the world must do better or possibly face annihilation the next time around served as the foundation for erecting a human rights framework. Something had to be done to help prevent future occurrences of rampant discrimination against others. If the Holocaust had not occurred, the notion of universal human rights would likely have been raised but would have also likely remained as a discussion point. World War II was horrific, but the exposure of an attempt to exterminate an entire people imparted urgency to the human rights movement.

Evolution of the Human Rights Framework

While World War II provided the impetus for a worldwide effort to create an effective framework that would prevent another Holocaust, the concept of human rights goes back many centuries and involves many different cultures (Ishay, 2004).

Since ancient times, philosophers have written about equality and justice. These great thinkers, including Plato and Socrates, more than two thousand years ago explored the realm of basic, inalienable rights of man, which at that time in history literally meant "man" (Wronka, 1998). Women's rights came much, much later (Reichert, 1996, 1998). In the year 1215, a cornerstone of human rights came into existence when English nobles, bishops, and archbishops forced the then reigning King John to end the abuses against his subjects. The subjects drafted a document known as the Magna Carta, which King John signed. The Magna Carta prohibited a sovereign from taking property without due process and from detaining his subjects without a legal judgment by their peers—the forerunner of trial by jury. The document also highlighted the importance of family and provided for safety from abusive treatment (Reichert, 2003).

The concepts of natural law and natural rights also made important contributions to the establishment of contemporary human rights. Natural law holds that a certain order in nature provides norms for human conduct (Hall, 1992, p. 581). During the seventeenth century, European philosophers advocated what they viewed as the natural rights of citizens—the idea that people by their nature have certain basic rights that precede the establishment of any government (p. 590).

Uprisings in the late eighteenth century against government and royalty in France and the American colonies engendered considerable discussion as to how nations should treat their citizens (Reichert, 2003). Until this period, privileged males occupied center stage in the discussion about concepts of human rights, with most if not all such rights understood as being limited to men. However, in 1787, Olympe de Gouges drafted a treatise on the rights of women, holding that women had the same "natural rights" as men (Staub-Bernasconi, 1998). In response to this revolutionary act, French authorities sent de Gouges to the guillotine.

The war fought by the American colonists against England led to important human rights developments (e.g., the Declaration of Independence and the U.S. Constitution [1787, as amended]). The Declaration of Independence borrowed from natural law and rights theories, with its famous holding of certain rights—notably life, liberty, and the pursuit of happiness—as being "self-evident." The U.S. Constitution provided further concepts of human rights through the Bill of Rights, which consists of the first ten amendments to the constitution. The Bill of Rights specified certain civil and political rights, but was silent on guarantees of economic and social needs. Another revolution of sorts became necessary to focus on these aspects of the human existence.

In the late eighteenth and early nineteenth centuries, the age of industrialization began in England, Europe, and the United States. In these parts of the world, people left their agricultural-based activities to find work in factories, often working long hours in unsanitary conditions. Factory owners frequently exploited their workers, paying them little for their efforts. While many people accepted these circumstances, opposition also emerged. In the middle of the nineteenth century, Karl Marx and Friedrich Engels produced the *Communist Manifesto* (1848) in opposition to what they saw as exploitation of the working class by owners of factories and other means of production (Wronka, 1998). The manifesto outlined the class struggle against capitalists and the eventual takeover of the means of production by workers. While many of the predictions of Marx and Engels never came about, the underlying theme of their writings resulted in greater attention to the less economically fortunate of the world.

In the early twentieth century, World War I and its aftermath brought greater attention to humankind's interdependence. A shared desire to condemn warfare and develop institutional frameworks for international cooperation took form. Establishment of the League of Nations and the International Labor Organization and the inception of social welfare organizations reflected this new mood of international, regional, and national collaboration (Reichert, 2003). Among social workers, the establishment of intergovernmental organizations such as the International Committee of Schools of Social Work and the International Permanent Secretariat of Social Workers paralleled this collaboration. During this period, social work organizations began to establish the basis for a social work profession and create social work values for their practice. This international promotion of social work formed the key concept that social work could transcend borders. However, while concepts of human rights underpinned the value base of social work, no formal teaching on human rights issued occurred (Center for Human Rights, 1994).

The relative ineffectiveness of world institutions, such as the League of Nations, contributed to events leading to World War II. Budding international organizations faltered owing to limited support and the lack of real enforcement powers. The League of Nations encountered obstacles from the start, mainly because the United States withdrew its membership (Alexander, 1996). The league became little more than a forum in which European countries could discuss world issues. It remained unable to enforce its decisions.

Meanwhile, Germany began to take advantage of its newly found muscles, led by Adolf Hitler. The course of events that gave rise to Germany's invasion of Poland in 1939 and its attempted conquest of all of Europe make for fascinating and troubling reading (Shirer, 1959, 1960). After World War II, nobody wanted to second-guess the possibility of another Adolf Hitler.

The Universal Declaration of Human Rights

The enormous consequences of World War II provided world leaders and peoples with a rare opportunity to propose universal principles that would hopefully prevent the occurrence of another Adolf Hitler. Devastation from the war was so horrendous that, at its end, individuals and governments from every corner of the globe realized another such global catastrophe would probably spell the end of humankind. The search for universal principles of conduct now began in earnest (Reichert, 2003).

In June 1945, in San Francisco, the United States, the Soviet Union, France, Cuba, Chile, Panama, and many other countries laid the groundwork for the creation of a United Nations (Morsink, 1999). Guiding principles for the United Nations pledged the organization to reaffirm faith in fundamental human rights, with article 1 of the UN Charter "promoting and encouraging respect for human rights and for fundamental freedoms for all without distinction as to race, sex, language or religion" ("Human-rights law," 1998). As part of the charter, participants agreed to establish a Commission on Human Rights. Before the creation of this commission in 1946, the term "human rights," as previously noted, had not been a commonly used expression, although the development of human rights principles had been going on for centuries.

High on the agenda of this new United Nations was the drafting of a universal declaration of rights. However, while acknowledging the importance of general statements about the need to protect the human existence, many governments were reluctant to accept detailed provisions concerning human rights. The Soviet Union had its Gulags, or labor camps, for those who spoke against the government; the United States had its numerous racial problems and a still-segregated South; and the Europeans had their colonial empires (Buergenthal, 1988). All these circumstances could be viewed as contrary to human rights principles. Certainly the Soviets did not want human rights inspectors examining their labor camps and talking with dissidents inhabiting the camps. The United States did not want human rights examiners questioning what could be considered near-apartheid conditions, especially in the South. And European countries had no interest in allowing human rights monitors to look into the exploitative activities surrounding their African and Asian colonies.

Contribution of Non-Western Peoples to Human Rights

While human rights principles might appear to be simply a Western concoction aimed at overcoming guilt from the Holocaust and World War II in general, this is not actually the case. Other regions of the world had developed their own laws, principles, and religions that had much in common with concepts embodied in contemporary human rights. For instance, in China, elements of classical Confucian thought formed a basis for modern human rights doctrines (Gangjian & Gang, 1995, p. 36). In South America, nineteenth-century movements led by Simon Bolivar and others provided later impetus for contributions to human rights principles. In the Soviet Union, the Soviet Constitution of 1936 contained numerous references to civil and political rights and stressed economic and social rights (Wronka, 1998).

Indigenous peoples such as Native Americans also contributed concepts of freedom, peace, and democracy to the development of human rights (Wronka, 1998, p. 70). However, during the nineteenth century, European countries and, to a lesser extent, the United States began massive colonial exploitation of indigenous peoples in Africa and parts of Asia. Depending on the colonizer, the degree of political and civil freedoms varied. The "new" citizens of Australia and the United States instigated a massive decimation of their own respective indigenous populations, the idea being that these populations were inferior and had little to contribute to the needs of a modern country (Alexander, 1996; Brown, 1970; Hughes, 1987). Unfortunately, colonization and expulsion of indigenous peoples did much to silence the voices of these groups.

Although non-Western countries and groups have contributed to human rights principles, these populations often receive little acknowledgment for their role in this development. Human rights exist for everyone, and many groups from all over the world have played a role in pursuit of this goal.

While many governments did not desire a set of detailed and comprehensive human rights provisions, the phenomenon of the nongovernmental organization (NGO) came into its own in elevating the status of human rights (Farer, 1989, p. 195). Without the efforts of delegates and representatives of forty-two private organizations serving as consultants, human rights would have received only a passing reference in the new United Nations. By 1947, with the impetus of the NGOs, an international consensus for human rights became evident.

What Is a Nongovernmental Organization (NGO)?

The term "nongovernmental organization," or simply NGO, appears frequently in the media. But just what is an NGO? In simple words, an NGO is an organization formed by people outside of government. Organizations such as the Red Cross, Amnesty International, the Girl Scouts, and Human Rights Watch are all NGOs. However, not all NGOs have large memberships and notoriety; some may be small and local, like an organization to advocate for people with disabilities in a particular city or a coalition to promote women's rights in a refugee camp. The importance of NGOs has become enormous within the human rights field, with many NGOs advising the United Nations of human rights policies (Human Rights Resource Center, 2005).

The Commission on Human Rights held its first session in early 1947, electing Eleanor Roosevelt as president and Rene Cassin from France as vice president. Members of the commission included countries from all parts of the world. The commission drafted an initial document on human rights containing numerous articles on the rights and duties of individuals. The document covered political, social, and economic rights, with differing viewpoints on how much influence should be extended to each set of rights. In June 1948, the commission completed its draft declaration and the entire General Assembly of the United Nations began debating the draft (Morsink, 1999; Wronka, 1998).

In June 1948, the United Nations was still a work in progress compared to the United Nations today. At that time, it consisted of fifty-six countries, with most of these countries located in North and South America, Europe, and the Soviet Union. A few Arabic countries were members, but Africa and Asia had little representation because of colonization by European countries. Only later, beginning in the late 1950s, did colonized territories begin the path to independence and membership in the United Nations.

In spite of a relatively limited and homogenous community of nations, a spirited debate surrounded the draft declaration on human rights. The U.S. contingent focused on political and civil rights, desiring no guarantee to economic and social rights. This viewpoint simply matched common U.S. strains of thought about government and society. Nobody owes anybody a job, unemployment benefits, or medical care. Why should governments be responsible for those items? Yet government should stay out of religion, refrain from censorship, and ensure numerous other safeguards against governmental interference in the liberty of its citizens. In contrast, the Soviet Union viewed free speech and other political rights, American style, as anathema to their society. Instead, the distribution of economic and social benefits to all citizens was a priority. Other countries, such as Saudi Arabia, objected to provisions on the right to change religions and equal rights concerning marriage, believing this would conflict with marriage laws in most Muslim countries. South Africa objected to provisions that could be used to attack its apartheid system of segregation. Chile believed that economic and social rights had to be assured, thereby making a return to fascism impossible (Morsink, 1999).

Finally, after intense discussions about human rights, on December 10, 1948, the General Assembly of the United Nations adopted the Universal Declaration of

Human Rights. The declaration passed unopposed, but the entire Soviet bloc, Saudi Arabia, and South Africa abstained from voting because of objections to certain provisions in the declaration (Morsink, 1999). Although the declaration was not a legally binding document, a common precedent for universal human rights now existed.

The significance of the Universal Declaration of Human Rights can hardly be overestimated. This document has formed the basis for integrating human rights into the vocabulary of social workers, philosophers, educators, political leaders, lawyers, and many other groups. While not perfect, the declaration formed the basis for all subsequent developments of human rights principles.

Human Rights: An American Tragedy?

In its relations with the rest of the world, America struggles with a profound contradiction. On the one hand, our country has been a pioneer in the human-rights movement, providing much of the language and inspiration for international efforts to win equality for all. On the other, our government has repeatedly blocked attempts to bring these rights home to America's own racial minorities, and that hypocrisy lurks at the core of our moral identity as a nation, undermining our claims to global leadership. (McDougall, 2004, p. A21)

One of the greatest ironies concerning the participation of the United States in drafting the Universal Declaration of Human Rights is that country's insistence on human rights for those enslaved by communism while disregarding rights for its own racial minorities. One of the greatest fears of some U.S. politicians, especially those from the South, was the notion that the UN Charter could one day be used to attack racial segregation in the United States (McDougall, 2004). With the apartheid system of racial separation in South Africa under intense scrutiny by many countries, the United States found itself in a corner. "Under the circumstances, the United States had only two choices: It could declare that the UN Charter prohibited racial discrimination and bring an end to segregation in America, or it could pull down the curtain on further international scrutiny of American practices. The Truman administration took the latter path. The cause of racial justice was sacrificed" (p. A22). Only after decades of civil rights turmoil and supportive decisions by the U.S. Supreme Court has the United States established a legal and moral basis for racial equality. Had the United States taken a different path, one of accepting that the Universal Declaration prohibited racial discrimination, perhaps the country would have experienced considerably less racial conflict.

In any case, a certain outcome of the United States' failure to embrace key provisions of the Universal Declaration of Human Rights has been the suspicion and distaste many U.S. politicians and officials now hold toward human rights documents. By frequently viewing human rights as a negative development, the United States has found itself out of sync with many other countries. The U.S. emphasis on abstract freedoms and selected political human rights (i.e., the American Dream) immediately puts it at odds with most other countries, especially Europe:

> One could point to many reasons why Europeans seem to be leading the way into the new era. But among all the possible explanations, one stands out. It is the cherished American Dream itself, once the ideal and envy of the world, that has led America to its current impasse. That dream emphasizes the unbridled opportunity of each individual to pursue success, which, in the American vernacular, has generally meant financial success. The American Dream is far too centered on personal material advancement and too little concerned with the broader human welfare to be relevant in a world of increasing risk, diversity, and interdependence. . . . While the American Spirit is tiring and languishing in the past, a new European Dream is being born. . . . The European Dream emphasizes community relationships over individual autonomy, cultural diversity over assimilation, quality of life over the accumulation of wealth, sustainable development over unlimited material growth, deep play over unrelenting toil, universal human rights and the rights of nature over property rights, and global cooperation over the unilateral exercise of power. (Rifkin, 2004, p. 3)

The tragedy of human rights in the United States is its reluctance to look beyond the surface and recognize the true concept of human rights. Unquestionably, individuals and governments can misuse human rights and twist them to suit their own selfish purposes, justifying a measure of suspicion toward universal human rights. However, the United States' resistance in joining the rest of the world in at least trying to develop a meaningful human rights agenda that goes beyond a few selected political rights could eventually cost Americans dearly.

Social Workers and Development of Human Rights

Social workers have played a key role in the historical development of human rights through their involvement with various organizations, including the Red Cross, Women's International League for Peace and Freedom, and Save the Children (Ife, 2001). Social workers have been active worldwide in international issues that relate to human rights. For instance, in 1929, social workers formed the International Association of Schools of Social Work, with 46 member schools in 10 countries. Goals of this association included development of an improved approach to humanitarian work and closer international cooperation among social workers.

During the 1930s, social workers became active in economic and social justice issues, with social worker Jane Addams receiving the Nobel Peace Prize in 1931. Unfortunately, with events in the late 1930s leading to international armed conflict, much of the human rights activity of social workers halted. International connections among social workers became increasingly difficult and eventually impossible in the wartime environment.

After World War II, social workers played a large part in creating the foundation for the current human rights movement. Many of the goals of the profession stem from human rights concepts even though, in the United States, the social work profession infrequently refers to the term "human rights" (Reichert, 2003, p. 33).

Exercises

Exercise 1: Connecting Events, Developments, and Individuals to Human Rights

The purpose of this exercise is to connect historical events, developments, and individuals to human rights.

The following descriptions cover historical events, developments, or individuals that are closely connected to human rights principles. Select one of the box items and do further research on this item. Present the research to others, noting specific connections to contemporary human rights principles as examined in the previous chapter. Analyze the importance of the item to human rights, particularly by responding to the following questions:

- What specific human right(s) do(es) the item involve? Within which area or set of human rights does the item relate?
- What is the importance of the item to contemporary human rights principles?
- What segment of a population does the item affect?
- What response did the item elicit at that period in time? Was there great support for the event, development, or individual?

The Code of Hammurabi (around 1750 B.C.)

Hammurabi was a ruler of Babylon—one of several rival Mesopotamian kingdoms—whose reign marked a golden age of Semitic culture. Hammurabi eventually conquered the other Mesopotamian kingdoms and issued a law code to establish justice throughout Mesopotamia.

Clay tablet records show that Hammurabi was a scrupulous, able administrator. His code—one of the earliest legal documents—influenced Near Eastern civilization for centuries. The code consolidated earlier regulations (of the former rival kingdoms Akkad and Sumer) on practical aspects of trade, labor, property, family, slavery, and the "eye for an eye, tooth for a tooth" punishment. The Code of Hammurabi survives in a stone column discovered in Iran in 1901 (now preserved in Paris, France) and in clay tablet versions, probably originally posted to inform literate citizens of their rights.

Old Testament (around 1200–300 B.C.)

Unlike most ancient peoples who worshiped many gods, ancient Israelites worshiped one universal God. They saw history as an interaction between God and humanity, whose course depended on obedience to God's laws. The Hebrew scriptures—39 books by many authors—recorded the law the Israelites believed their God gave them. Christians and Muslims also founded their ethics on the Hebrew scriptures. Christians refer to these books as the Old Testament, and Muslims regard the first five books, the Torah, as divine scripture.

The Torah contains laws God is said to have given to the Hebrew prophets, beginning with the mosaic laws—the Ten Commandments—given to Moses on Mount Sinai. The mosaic laws commanded respect for life and the property of strangers as well as neighbors by establishing rights in terms of duties (the right to life, for example, was expressed in the commandment not to kill). The asylum tradition in churches and synagogues and the principle that one is innocent until proven guilty also originate in Jewish law.

Confucius (around 551–479 B.C.)

Living in politically and socially turbulent times, Confucius was a philosopher who taught government and social reform. His philosophical teachings revolved around "jen" or benevolence, which he expressed in twin sayings: "Do not do to others what you would not like yourself" and "Do unto others what you wish to do unto yourself." Confucius believed that people should practice jen toward those below them in a social or spiritual hierarchy and that government should practice jen rather than use force. Confucius often encountered disagreements with his superiors when working in government.

Confucius' teachings, collected in his Analects and spread by three thousand disciples, became a code of conduct and the basis of a traditional way of life that made him the most influential philosopher in Chinese history. Confucian teachings emphasize the individual's responsibilities to the community. Those teachings remain influential to this day in China and other Asian countries.

New Testament (around 40–100 A.D.)

Jesus' followers, scattered around the Roman Empire, wrote letters and accounts of his life, which were circulated among early Christian churches. These writings became the New Testament, in which Jesus is reported to have quoted the Old Testament: he maintained that the Spirit of the Lord was in him to preach good news to the poor and that God had sent him to proclaim freedom for the prisoners and recovery of sight to the blind, to release the oppressed, and to invite all to God's kingdom.

The New Testament says that Jesus angered religious leaders by denouncing hypocrisy, healing the sick, and treating women, foreigners, and the poor with dignity. The apostle Paul, who wrote some New Testament books in prison, said that among Jesus' followers, there is neither Jew nor Greek, slave nor free, male nor female. The New Testament also says that Jesus taught that rights come with responsibilities. He urged his followers to feed the hungry, clothe the naked, and forgive their enemies.

Magna Carta (1215)

English nobles and clergy rallied against King John I's abuse of power—heavy taxation to finance expensive, unsuccessful wars and his refusal to accept authority of the Catholic pope, which effectively kept churches in England closed for years. The nobles and clergy subjected the king to the rule of law by enacting a great charter of liberties.

Though King John I soon violated it, the Magna Carta eventually came to be cited widely, in defense of many liberties. In the United States, national and state constitutions contain ideas and even phrases directly traceable to the Magna Carta. For example, the concept of no taxation without representation stems from the Magna Carta, as do the rights of habeas corpus and due process of law—no free man shall be arrested or imprisoned except by lawful judgment.

Treaty of Westphalia (1648)

For centuries after Augustine, the Roman Catholic Church was the unique Christian authority in Europe. However, the church became plagued by depravity and an inability to satisfy its followers' spiritual needs. In the 1500s, a reform movement spread. This reformation and a Catholic Counter-Reformation, along with disputes over sovereignty, racked most of Europe for a century.

Parties to these wars finally ended their conflict by the Treaty of Westphalia (named for the region of Germany where it was signed). The treaty led to the modern notion of national sovereignty by freeing state rulers from the jurisdiction of the Catholic Church. The treaty allowed rulers to choose their subjects' religion, but put an end to the Reformation and the Counter-Reformation by specifying that rulers would forfeit their lands if they changed religions. The treaty also took a step toward religious toleration by allowing Catholic or Protestant minorities in some states rights to private worship, liberty of conscience, and emigration.

English Bill of Rights (1689)

James II, like several kings before him, thought the law inconvenient and often dispensed with it. For this his subjects overthrew him in 1688. When Mary II and William III took the English throne in 1689, Parliament passed a bill declaring that it would no longer tolerate royal interference in its affairs. The bill formed the foundation for the contemporary English constitution, an unwritten set of principles. In the century following the Bill of Rights, most English took pride in the provisions of the bill that inhibited an arbitrary government.

The bill prohibited royalty from suspending law without Parliament's consent, specified free elections for members of Parliament, and declared that freedom of speech in Parliament was not to be questioned, in the courts or elsewhere. The bill also prohibited taxation or maintenance of an army in peacetime without Parliament's consent, excessive bail or fines, and cruel and unusual punishment.

U.S. Declaration of Independence (1776)

Calling themselves the Continental Congress, representatives of Britain's thirteen colonies first met in 1774 to protest British policies. When they convened again after the American Revolution had begun, they voted for independence from Britain and adopted the Declaration of Independence. This Continental Congress became the first government of the thirteen U.S. colonies. The Declaration had far-reaching and lasting influence on individual rights in Western civilization, inspiring rebellion against Spanish rule in South America and against the monarchy in France.

Because of his literary skill, the Congress chose Thomas Jefferson to write the Declaration. Based largely on natural rights theories, the Declaration listed the colonists' grievances against the British king, George, accusing him of systematic tyranny. The Declaration also announced the colonies' separation from Britain, proclaimed the creation of the United States, and provided justification for the revolution. The Congress rejected two proposed statements in which Jefferson vehemently denounced the slave trade and strongly criticized the English people.

U.S. Constitution (1787)

After achieving its goal of independence from Britain, delegates from 12 of the U.S. colonies met in 1787 to rethink the first U.S. Constitution, which had become effective six years earlier. In the years that followed, the colonies had encountered severe economic times and occasional armed revolts against governments, partially because the 1781 constitution resulted in a weak federal government. At the 1787 convention, delegates strengthened the federal government but also limited its power sufficiently to guarantee individual liberty.

The 1787 constitution established three branches of federal government and provided for checks and balances among them. From 1787 until today, the constitution has been amended only twenty-seven times. The first ten amendments, known as the U.S. Bill of Rights, limit power of the federal government to encroach upon individual liberties and state government. The U.S. Constitution is now the oldest in operation and one of the most influential documents in Western history.

Declaration of the Rights of Man and the Citizen (1789)

Since the 1730s, economic decline and the ideas of the Enlightenment had been spreading in France, and the success of the American Revolution had infused French reformers with hope. The Estates General (representatives of the clergy, the nobility, and the commoners) wrote the Declaration of the Rights of Man and the Citizen to exemplify thoughts of important thinkers of that time, including Voltaire, Montesquieu, and Rousseau.

Though the reform efforts failed and France tumbled into revolution, a legacy from the Declaration eventually prevailed. The Declaration attacked the political and legal systems of the French monarchy and defined the natural rights of men as liberty, property, security, and the right to resist oppression. The Declaration replaced the system of aristocratic privileges that had existed under the monarch with the principle of equality before the law.

Emancipation Proclamation (1863)

The U.S. Civil War began in 1861 as a northern struggle to keep the United States from breaking apart. Abolitionists (those who opposed slavery) were a minority. Abraham Lincoln did not champion slaves' moral claims to freedom and could never have been elected president of the United States on a platform of abolishing slavery. But once the southern states seceded from the United States, the political purpose of accommodating slavery disappeared. As U.S. deaths mounted in the war and volunteering declined, pressure grew to enlist blacks to fight against the South. In 1863, President Lincoln issued the Emancipation Proclamation, which called for the freeing of the slaves. At that point, Lincoln transformed a war primarily against secession into a war also against slavery in the South.

Because the proclamation applied only to southern states, taking effect only as the North occupied those states, the proclamation at first freed no slaves. Its initial importance lay in opening the door to enlistment in the U.S. army by blacks, which helped lead to a northern victory. In 1865, the year the Civil War ended, passage of the Thirteenth Amendment to the U.S. Constitution outlawed slavery everywhere in the United States and areas under its jurisdiction.

Geneva Conventions (1864, 1949)

Brought into being by the newly created International Red Cross, the Geneva Convention of 1864 was the first international law treaty governing the conduct of nations in wartime. In this important area, the 1864 convention marked the origin of modern humanitarian and human rights law. The convention provided rules of conduct for treatment of sick and wounded soldiers.

In 1949, the initial Geneva Convention expanded into four separate conventions on war issues. The first and second conventions deal with the care of the sick and wounded in wartime; the third deals with treatment of prisoners of war; and the fourth deals with the protection of civilians and noncombatants. Together, the four Geneva Conventions aim to ensure that human dignity is respected even during hostilities. The International Committee of the Red Cross continues to monitor and enforce provisions of the Geneva Conventions.

Mohandas Karamchand Gandhi (1869–1948)

Mohandas Karamchand Gandhi, born in what is now India, began his career in South Africa, where he practiced law and agitated against racism directed at Indians. In South Africa, Gandhi developed tactics of nonviolent confrontation based on the principle of respect for life. Gandhi called this strategy "*satyagraha*" (truth force). After returning to India, Gandhi led a series of *satyagraha* campaigns against Britain, which was the colonial power in charge of India. Gandhi's campaigns consisted of movements against class discrimination and movements for Muslim-Hindu unity, women's rights, and basic education.

Eventually, due in large part to Gandhi's activities, Britain granted India independence. Also called Mahatma (great soul), Gandhi was assassinated in 1948, during a period of conflict over the division of India and Pakistan into two states. Gandhi's influence has been felt around the world, notably in South Africa and the United States. Martin Luther King Jr. based his activities during the civil rights movement on the nonviolent tactics of Gandhi.

Universal Declaration of Human Rights (1948)

Because representatives at the UN conference in 1945 wrestled with reconciliation of their various conceptions of human rights, references to human rights in the UN Charter remained ambiguous. A primary conflict between the United States and the Soviet Union focused on political and civil rights versus social and economic rights, with the United States favoring political and civil rights, and the Soviet Union favoring social and economic rights. Of course, even the United States had skeletons in the political and civil rights closet, as evidenced by segregationist policies in the southern states. While the Soviet Union appeared to favor social and economic rights, actual policies often inhibited those rights. Other nations also had their own human rights agendas, disliking some proposed rights and favoring others.

To help reconcile the hodgepodge of human rights proposals, the United Nations assigned a commission, with Eleanor Roosevelt as chairperson, to clarify references in the charter to human rights. The result was a declaration of universal goals concerning human rights and freedoms, which the UN General Assembly adopted in 1948. This Universal Declaration of Human Rights is not legally binding. However, many countries have incorporated provisions of the declaration into their own constitutions and laws. The declaration has become a standard for measuring human rights.

The UN Charter (1945)

During the post–World War II climate, 51 nations signed the UN Charter. This charter established an international organization dedicated to maintaining peace and security in the world. The organization was also dedicated to cooperation in solving economic, social, cultural, and humanitarian problems. Although the charter affirmed "faith in fundamental human rights," signers of the charter disagreed on the nature of these human rights. Therefore, delegates at the first UN conference rejected a proposal to include protection of human rights as an article of the charter.

The charter gives the UN General Assembly and its Commission on Human Rights primary responsibility for promoting human rights. The commission has been instrumental in creating declarations and covenants on human rights, including civil, political, economic, social, and cultural rights. While these documents are not legally enforceable unless approved by individual UN members and incorporated into their own laws, members often refer to these documents to interpret human rights provisions.

Adapted from Flowers, Nancy (ed.) *Human Rights Here and Now: Celebrating the Universal Declaration of Human Rights*. Human Rights Resource Center (1998). http://www.umn.edu/humanrts/edumat/hreduseries/hereandnow/Default.htm

Exercise 2: The Spanish and the Taino Peoples—A Case Study in Analyzing Human Rights

In this case study, you will examine encounters between the Spanish and the Taino peoples. The following is a brief overview of the circumstances leading to the encounters.

Overview

In 1492, the Spanish were looking for a water route to the riches of China and the east, when they "discovered" the South American continent. The Taino were the first native people the Spanish encountered in the Western hemisphere. The place where the Taino lived is now called Haiti.

Part I—Analysis of Important Rights

From the Taino perspective, there was one overarching right: the right to be well fed. Everyone worked to see that all members of the community had enough food. They also believed that women had the right to power, and they had male as well as female chiefs.

From the Spanish point of view, there were two main rights: (1) the right (and responsibility) to wage war in order to convert the Taino and take their land and resources, which the pope had given to the Spanish crown, and (2) the right to the forced labor of the Taino through the "*encomienda* system." Under this system, the Spanish crown gave or "commended" Taino to Spaniards, who then owned the rights to their labor. In return the Spaniards were to Christianize the Indians and protect them. Many Taino starved to death under this system.

Your analysis should include an examination of rights that the people involved believed were important. Be sure to use the definition of "rights" that was used at this time. Look at all sides of the issue and identify rights from all perspectives. Relevant questions to ask: Were any rights in conflict? What caused these conflicting perspectives?

Part II—Analysis of Actions Taken

The Spanish enslaved the Taino so that they would mine gold for them and do other forms of manual labor. Dominican friars forced the Taino to convert to Christianity or risk torture and death. (The Inquisition was in full force at this time.) Some Spanish protested the treatment of the Taino. In Spain, groups debated whether or not the Taino were humans with certain rights. The king of Spain suspended colonization to wait for the outcome of these debates. However, after two years of debates, the Spanish could not reach a decision.

Not understanding why gold was more important than food, the Taino offered to grow all the food the Spanish wanted in return for their freedom. When that tactic failed, the Taino resisted in various ways, including the dispatch of envoys to the king, insurrections, migration, rebellions, and suicide. The Taino also asked Bartolome de Las Casas, a Dominican friar later called "the Apostle to the Indians," to represent them in Spain.

Your analysis in this part should include actions that people took:

- List some specific actions that affected many people.
- Were some rights being violated to gain others?
- Were people silent who could have helped the situation?
- Did others take risks to protect rights?

Part III: Analysis of Short-Term Outcomes

The Taino lost a great deal. By 1548, there were fewer than 500 Taino left on the island of Hispaniola (out of an estimated 2.5 to 7 million in 1492). The others either were dead or had fled to other islands in the area. The resistance of other native peoples to colonization has continued to this day. The Spanish eventually gained all the Taino traditional land but abolished the *encomienda* system. They turned to enslaving Africans instead. The Spanish definition of rights held for centuries as Spanish culture spread throughout the Americas.

Your analysis in this part should include reference to short-term outcomes:

- Who won? Who lost?
- Whose rights were strengthened? Whose were violated?
- Whose power was strengthened? Whose power was weakened?
- Did resistance continue or was it silenced by those in power?
- Was the overall result positive or negative for people in general?

Part IV: Analysis of Long-Term Outcomes

Some historians argue that the debates in Spain over treatment of the Taino marked the beginning of the end for the medieval worldview and the beginning of the modern era and the Enlightenment. People still debate the ideas of a "just war" and what rights we have by virtue of being human. Others still view some people, including women and indigenous peoples, as inferior humans suited only for manual labor, servitude, or death. It could be argued that this point of view led to genocide and the Holocaust, which eventually led to the adoption of the Universal Declaration of Human Rights in 1948. Rights that have survived to this day are the Taino rights to food and political power for women.

Your analysis in this part should include reference to long-term outcomes:

- What precedents were set in the area of human rights that are still affecting us today (either negatively or positively)?
- Check the "rights" involved in this case study against the rights outlined in the Universal Declaration of Human Rights.
- Which of those considered rights during the time of the case study are still considered rights today? Which are no longer considered rights?
- Do you believe that this event contributed to decisions made by the United Nations in drafting the Universal Declaration of Human Rights, either directly or indirectly?

Adapted from Flowers, Nancy (ed.) *Human Rights Here and Now: Celebrating the Universal Declaration of Human Rights.* Human Rights Resource Center (1998). http://www.umn.edu/humanrts/edumat/hreduseries/hereandnow/Default.htm

Exercise 3: U.S. History Topics for Analysis

1. Select one of the following topics for analysis and use the same four-part analysis used in Exercise 2. For example, you would begin Part I by listing important rights from the different perspectives of the parties.

   Drafting of the Bill of Rights
   Forced removal of the Cherokee Nation

Dred Scott decision
Women workers in the nineteenth-century New England textile industry
Reconstruction in the post–Civil War South
The Pullman strike
Immigration restrictions and quotas
Child labor regulations
The temperance movement
Women's suffrage
Social Security Act
Fair Labor Standards Act
Desegregation of the U.S. military
Japanese internment
House of Un-American Activities Committee
Major League baseball integration
Pentagon Papers and freedom of the press
Student protests against the Vietnam War
Death penalty for juveniles
Americans with Disabilities Act
Sanctuary movement
Welfare reform
Amistad case
Gay and lesbian movement
Iraqi prisoner abuse/Guantanamo
Patriot Act

2. Before you begin this exercise, make sure your resources are a good mix of both primary (eyewitness) and secondary (those removed from the action) sources from all sides of the issue.

   Include those in power and those traditionally marginalized. Your sources will reflect the biases of whoever created them.

   Analyze the sources for their biases and identify any stereotypes; try to see beyond them while analyzing the event/issue. Sometimes the bias holds clues as to what happened—why there was conflict in the first place.

3. Analyze the event/issue for the rights that the people involved believed were important.

   Be sure to use the definition of "rights" that was used at that time. Look at all sides of the issue and identify the rights from all perspectives.

   Were any rights in conflict? In other words, were people fighting for rights that conflicted with each other? What caused these conflicting perspectives?

Adapted from Flowers, Nancy (ed.) *Human Rights Here and Now: Celebrating the Universal Declaration of Human Rights.* Human Rights Resource Center (1998). http://www.umn.edu/humanrts/edumat/hreduseries/hereandnow/Default.htm

Exercise 4: Studying Biographies of Human Rights Activists

This exercise involves learning about human rights through the study of historical figures.

1. Discuss what we mean when we call someone an "activist." Record responses to this question. Create a list of activists with which you are familiar.

2. After discussion of the term *activist*, select one individual from the list below to research. To avoid duplication within a group, it may be necessary to assign each person an individual to research.

Ralph Abernathy	Sojourner Truth
Jane Addams	Emma Goldman
Susan B. Anthony	Samuel Gompers
Clara Barton	Eglantyne Jebb
Ralph Bunche	Helen Keller
Cesar Chavez	Martin Luther King Jr.
Chief Joseph	Winona LaDuke
Chief Sitting Bull	Audre Lourde
Crazy Horse	Wangari Maathai
Dorothy Day	Malcolm X
Merlai Desai	Thurgood Marshall
Dorothea Dix	Mother Jones
Mahatma Gandhi	Alice Salomon
Nawal el Saadawi	Aung San Suu Kyi

Biographies for many of these individuals can be found in W. J. Jacobs, *Human Rights: Great Lives* (New York: Charles Scribner's Sons, 1990).

3. Conduct research on the selected historical figure. In addition to basic biographical information, analyze the following:
   a. Causes for which the individual worked;
   b. Obstacles encountered and to be overcome; and
   c. Accomplishments and influence on others.

4. Within a group, discuss the following questions:
   a. Do these activists seem to have any similar types of experiences or personal qualities?
   b. What are some of the ways they sought to achieve their goals? Who sought to achieve goals by nonviolent means?
   c. How many of the activists focused on social and economic rights? How many on political and civil rights?
   d. What rights would you focus on if you were a human rights activist?

Adapted from Shiman, David. *Economic and Social Justice: A Human Rights Perspective.* Human Rights Resource Center (1999). http://www.umn.edu/humanrts/edumat/hreduseries/tb1b/index.htm

Exercise 5: Studying Biographies of Social Work Activists

Using the same format and questions as in Exercise 4, select a social work activist to research. Indicate the person's cause, the possible organizations involved in this person's work, and the role this person plays within an organization or alone.

Exercise 6: Interviewing a Local Person About Human Rights

Interview a local figure about the concept of human rights, especially someone born before 1948. Discuss the term "human rights" with that person and his or her own experiences with human rights. Ask the person if his or her life is different because of the development of human rights principles after 1948.

CHAPTER 3

Building the Foundation

Universal Declaration of Human Rights

The inevitable starting point for a contemporary study of human rights is the Universal Declaration of Human Rights. The United Nations adopted this extraordinary document in 1948, and every member country of the United Nations agrees to follow provisions contained in the declaration. Of course, whether countries actually follow provisions within the declaration remains a contested issue. No country wants to be accused of human rights abuses, but political, economic, and cultural considerations often interfere with recognition of human rights contained in the declaration.

The Universal Declaration arose out of the ashes of World War II and the horrors perpetrated by Nazi Germany in the name of racial purity and superiority. Laws in Nazi Germany labeled numerous individuals and groups as non-Germans and undeserving of the rights and benefits of citizens. The intent behind these racial purity laws was to exclude from participating in German society those who did not have the "proper" ethnic or religious background. Individuals or groups who spoke out against this discriminatory treatment encountered the wrath of the Nazi government, which tortured and executed many dissidents. Eventually, the Nazi government rounded up Jews and other individuals—including Gypsies, communists, homosexuals, dissidents, and "asoziale" (persons on welfare)—for transport to concentration camps, where many died under German extermination policies. People with mental illnesses or other disabilities were often killed at hospitals (Hansen, 1991; Otto & Sunker, 1991; Reichert, 2003; Schnurr, 1997). The horrors of Nazi Germany were unimaginable. People from all over the world wondered how they could prevent those atrocities from ever occurring again.

While Nazi Germany and its genocidal policies against Jews and other groups provided the most immediate rationale for universal rules to govern the conduct of nations, other factors also played a role. Poverty and unemployment had afflicted many individuals throughout the world during the Great Depression. Should individuals everywhere be entitled to a social security net to help them during hard times? The colonization of African and Asian countries by Europeans also provided fuel for a universal rule against exploitation of peoples by the more powerful. Should not the colonized have a right to self-determination? In truth, the list of issues concerning the human condition after World War II never seemed to end (Reichert, 2003). Discussion about these issues ultimately led to the idea that some underlying document should exist that defines the essence of a human being's existence. Given the vast cultural and other differences among individuals and their societies, what common needs and freedoms should everyone share? The outcome of this intensive soul-searching was the Universal Declaration of Human Rights, a worthy foundation for advancing political and social rights that everyone should enjoy.

The Universal Declaration is not legally binding, although many countries have incorporated principles within the declaration into their domestic laws. The declaration serves mainly as a springboard from which to promote and further develop human rights principles.

Opening Statement

Before listing specific human rights, the Universal Declaration describes general principles for the human existence.

Principle 1

Foundation of freedom, justice, and peace in the world—inherent dignity and equal and inalienable rights of all members of the human family.

The first principle of human rights rests upon the "inherent dignity" and "equal" rights of every person. Without recognizing these building blocks, the world and its various nations cannot establish a peaceful existence.

Principle 2

Highest aspiration of common people—world in which human beings enjoy freedom of speech and belief and freedom from fear and want.

Ordinary people simply want to be able to speak their mind, worship or not worship as they wish, and have social security.

Principle 3

Prevention of tyranny and oppression—protection of human rights by law.

Nations have an obligation to protect human rights through laws. Unless persons have the right to enforce human rights, the possibility of tyranny and oppression will always exist.

Principle 4

Requirement—promote the development of friendly relations between nations.

The basis of this requirement clearly stems from the circumstances in which the drafting of the Universal Declaration occurred. Much of the world lay in ruins because of the failure to develop friendly relations between nations. In the future, the world simply had to do better.

Principle 5

Pledge of UN member states—promotion of universal respect for and observance of human rights and fundamental freedoms.

To help ensure that countries take human rights seriously, every member of the United Nations pledges to promote human rights. Unfortunately, many countries and individuals do not always take this pledge seriously. The significance of this principle lies in the realization that human rights are a two-way street: governments should provide policies that integrate human rights, but individuals should also respect and observe human rights of others.

Principle 6

Full realization of pledge in Principle 4—common understanding of human rights and freedoms.

Part of the difficulty in prompting countries to take seriously the pledge in Principle 5 is in developing a common understanding of human rights and freedoms. Until nations actually integrate human rights into educational routines, promotion of human rights will remain inconsistent.

Clearly, within the preamble of the Universal Declaration, the United Nations has presented lofty goals and aspirations. The overriding focus is to create a better society, one in which repeats of genocide and oppression do not occur. Of course, merely integrating admirable principles into a nonbinding document does not guarantee that countries or individuals will follow those principles. That has certainly been the case with the Universal Declaration. Yet, would the world be better off without the Universal Declaration? At least every member of the United Nations, which includes practically every country in the world, does acknowledge the importance of human rights, undoubtedly thanks to the Universal Declaration and its influence upon member nations. This acknowledgment allows a starting point for realizing these principles.

Specific Human Rights in the Universal Declaration

The six principles of human rights contained in the Universal Declaration form the basis for the 30 articles that define and specify individual human rights. Nations and individuals may disagree on interpretations and importance of the different articles. However, each member of the United Nations does agree to respect and follow the Universal Declaration.

Political and Civil Rights: Articles 1–21

The initial part of the declaration specifies human rights that generally would fall within the definition of political and civil rights.

> **Article 1: All human beings are born free and equal, are endowed with reason and conscience, and should act towards one another in a spirit of brotherhood.**

This article places a responsibility upon individuals to respect others and not commit acts that would depreciate the value of others.

> **Article 2: Everyone is entitled to the enjoyment of human rights without regard to race, color, sex, language, religion, political or other opinion, national or social origin, property, birth or other status. This entitlement applies regardless of where the individual resides.**

This article aims to prevent the exclusion of a human right on the basis of being "different" from others. These differences include property or wealth. In other words, those having little or no property or wealth should not be denied human rights.

> **Article 3: Everyone has the right to life, liberty, and the security of person.**

This human right highlights the sanctity of life and the right to be free in most pursuits and the right to be safe.

> **Article 4: No one shall be held in slavery or servitude. Slavery and the slave trade are prohibited.**

While the prohibition of slavery appears to be an obvious human right, the consequences of slavery remained even after the adoption of the Universal Declaration in 1948. For instance, segregation in southern states of the United States continued to exist for many years after 1948.

> **Article 5: No one shall be subjected to torture or to cruel, inhuman, or degrading treatment or punishment.**

The U.S. "war on terror" has raised the issue of whether torture might be justified in some circumstances. Under the Universal Declaration, no exceptions exist to the use of torture or other cruel and inhuman punishment.

Article 6: Everyone has the right to recognition everywhere as a person before the law.

This means that every individual should enjoy legal status and protections of that status. Once again, the war on terror in the United States has led some to conclude that not everyone should receive legal standing, especially those deemed to be "terrorists."

Article 7: Everyone is equal and entitled to protection against actual discrimination or incitement to discrimination.

Nobody should be subject to discrimination on any basis or subject to calls of discrimination. Groups such as the Ku Klux Klan would typically violate this human right by encouraging members of the Klan to discriminate against others, even if the discrimination does not actually occur.

Article 8: Everyone has the right to an effective remedy in national tribunals for acts that have violated fundamental rights granted by a constitution or law of the relevant nation.

Everyone should be able to use the courts and other legal bodies to contest acts that violate basic constitutional and legal rights.

Article 9: No one shall be subjected to arbitrary arrest, detention, or exile.

No government has the right to arrest or detain someone without cause. In connection with other human rights, anyone arrested or detained should be able to use the local courts to contest the arrest or detention.

Article 10: Everyone is entitled in full equality a fair and public hearing by an independent and impartial tribunal, in the determination of his or her rights and obligations and any criminal charge against him or her.

Under this political human right, even terrorists must receive a fair trial by an independent and impartial court.

Article 11: (1) Everyone charged with a criminal offense has the right to be presumed innocent until proved guilty in a public trial at which he or she has had all the guarantees necessary for a defense of the

charge. (2) No one shall be charged and held guilty of an act or omission that did not constitute a penal offense at the time he or she committed the act or omission. Nor shall a heavier penalty be imposed than the one that was applicable at the time the penal offence was committed.

This article further promotes the concept of a fair trial, with a presumption of innocence until proven guilty. In addition, nobody can be charged with a crime that was not a crime when the alleged offense occurred. This is an important safeguard against the persecution of others because it prevents the creation and enactment of a dubious criminal offense to punish political opponents.

Article 12: No one shall be subjected to arbitrary interference with his or her privacy, family, home or correspondence, or to attacks upon honor and reputation. Everyone has the right to legal protection against this interference or attacks.

Many countries enforce this human right through privacy and defamation laws.

Article 13: (1) Everyone has the right to freedom of movement and residence within the borders of each State. (2) Everyone has the right to leave any country, including his own, and to return to his or her country.

This human right aims to prevent countries from controlling the movement of political dissidents and not allowing individuals back in the countries after leaving.

Article 14: (1) Everyone has the right to seek and to enjoy in other countries asylum from persecution. (2) This right may not be invoked in the case of prosecutions genuinely arising from non-political crimes or from acts contrary to the purposes and principles of the United Nations.

This human right requires every country to allow applications for asylum based on a well-founded fear of persecution. In the United States, the basis of this persecution may arise from race, religion, nationality, political opinion, membership in a particular social group, or torture convention. The well-founded fear must be personal to the asylum applicant and not simply a general fear of persecution. For example, a member of a particular race may believe that his or her race generally is being persecuted. However, without showing that this persecution has been perpetrated directly upon the asylum seeker, most countries will not grant asylum.

Article 15: (1) Everyone has the right to nationality. (2) No one shall be arbitrarily deprived of his nationality nor denied the right to change his nationality.

Nobody should be deprived of his or her national roots. However, a person may change that nationality if he or she wishes.

Article 16: (1) Men and women of full age, without any limitation due to race, nationality, or religion, have the right to marry and to found a family. They are entitled to equal rights as to marriage, during marriage and at its dissolution. (2) Marriage shall be entered into only with the free and full consent of the intending spouses. (3) The family is the natural and fundamental group unit of society and is entitled to protection by society and the State.

Men and women have a human right to marry and form a family. Based on this human right, marriage is between men and women (although a more contemporary view might include same-sex marriages). Families have special status and are entitled to "protection." This provision appears directed toward preventing governments from separating children from parents for purposes of political indoctrination and other inappropriate reasons.

Article 17: (1) Everyone has the right to own property alone as well as in association with others. (2) No one shall be arbitrarily deprived of his property.

This human right clearly speaks to the free enterprise or capitalistic system. Communist countries did not allow individuals to hold property. Obviously, the violation of this human right occurred throughout countries within the Soviet Union. This is a clear example of how a country might agree to respect a particular human right without any intention of promoting that right.

Article 18: Everyone has the right to freedom of thought, conscience, and religion; this right includes freedom to change his religion or belief, and freedom, either alone or in community with others and in public or private, to manifest his religion or belief in teaching, practice, worship, and observance.

This article also contains human rights that are more Western than others. Although most countries usually claim that they respect freedom of thought and religion, the degree of this freedom varies, with Western countries generally being more liberal in their interpretation of these rights.

Article 19: Everyone has the right to freedom of opinion and expression; this right includes freedom to hold opinions without interference and to seek, receive, and impart information and ideas through any media and regardless of matters.

As with Article 18, Western countries generally interpret this human right in a much more expansive manner than other countries.

Article 20: (1) Everyone has the right to freedom of peaceful assembly and association. (2) No one may be compelled to belong to an association.

This civil right allows peaceful demonstrations. The second part of this article relates to forcing individuals to belong to organizations, such as the Hitler Youth during the Nazi period in Germany. Nobody should be required to join a group.

> **Article 21: (1) Everyone has the right to take part in the government of his country, directly or through freely chosen representatives. (2) Everyone has the right of equal access to public service in his country. (3) The will of the people shall be the basis of the authority of government; this will shall be expressed in periodic and genuine elections which shall be by universal and equal suffrage and shall be held by secret vote or by equivalent free voting procedures.**

This human right forms the basis for free elections and democracies based on desires of the population.

Articles 1 through 21 form the political and civil rights portion of the Universal Declaration. Many of these human rights resemble the Bill of Rights of the U.S. Constitution and other laws aimed at prohibiting discrimination. In that respect, the Universal Declaration has much in common with the laws of U.S. society.

Economic, Social, and Cultural Rights: Articles 22–27

If the Universal Declaration simply stopped at Article 21, the United States could legitimately claim that it makes every effort to satisfy human rights. However, after this article, the Universal Declaration develops the concept of economic, social, and cultural rights. By some standards, the United States has made less effort to satisfy these rights than it has the first set of human rights.

> **Article 22: Everyone, as a member of society, has the right to social security and is entitled to realization, through national effort and international co-operation and in accordance with the organization and resources of each State, of the economic, social, and cultural rights indispensable for his dignity and the free development of his personality.**

This human right grants everyone the right to social security in accordance with a state's resources. This right also entitles everyone to economic, social, and cultural rights necessary for human dignity and free development of personality. Perhaps the scope of this human right is so immense that many countries simply give it lip service but make little effort to further define and enforce the right.

> **Article 23: (1) Everyone has the right to work, to free choice of employment, to just and favorable conditions of work and to protection against unemployment. (2) Everyone, without any discrimination, has the right to equal pay for equal work. (3) Everyone who works has the right to just and favorable remuneration ensuring for himself and his family an existence worthy of human dignity, and supplemented, if necessary, by other means of social protection. (4) Everyone has the right to form and to join trade unions for the protection of his interests.**

	Family	Religious/ Media Institutions	Business Interests	Other Community Actors	State Authority	Regional Authority	International Authority	Other
Education								
Policy/Legislative								
Litigation/Legal								
Organizing/Networking								
Service Delivery								
Media								
Protest/Public Action								
NGO Tribunals/Hearings								
Mobilization/Petition Campaigns								

Figure 3.1 Implementing Human Rights

Source: Mertus, J., Flowers, N., Dutt M. (1999). *Local Action–Global Change: Learning About the Human Rights of Women and Girls*. United Nations Development Fund for Women, New York, NY, and the Center for Women's Global Leadership, New Brunswick, NJ.

The right to employment as a human right clearly arises from the Great Depression, which created conditions for dictatorships such as that of Adolf Hitler. Of course, the question of how to guarantee everyone a job has no easy answer. In communist East Germany, before its reunification with West Germany in 1990, the government provided most people with a job, no matter how menial. After the reunification, many individuals in the former East Germany had no work, as Western-oriented economic policies streamlined employment practices and shed unnecessary workers. This unemployment problem in Germany persists today, with some parts of former East Germany experiencing unemployment rates of more than 20 percent ("German unemployment," 2005).

Nobody disagrees that everyone should have work—the problem is how to guarantee that work.

Article 24: Everyone has the right to rest and leisure, including reasonable limitation of working hours and periodic holidays with pay.

In many countries, the idea of a human right to periodic holidays with pay may seem utopian. Perhaps among all of the various human rights contained in the Universal Declaration, this human right appears the most Western.

Article 25: (1) Everyone has the right to a standard of living adequate for the health and wellbeing of himself (or herself) and of his (or her) family, including food, clothing, housing and medical care, and necessary social services, and the right to security in the event of unemployment, sickness, disability, widowhood, old age, or other lack of livelihood in circumstances beyond his control. (2) Motherhood and childhood are entitled to special care and assistance. All children, whether born in or out of wedlock, shall enjoy the same social protection.

Nobody could reasonably object to the goals of Article 25. The dilemma is how to accomplish these goals, especially in countries with great unemployment and governments with limited resources.

Article 26: (1) Everyone has the right to education. Education shall be free, at least in the elementary and fundamental stages. Elementary education shall be compulsory. Technical and professional education shall be made generally available and higher education shall be equally accessible to all on the basis of merit. (2) Education shall be directed to the full development of the human personality and to the strengthening of respect for human rights and fundamental freedoms. It shall promote understanding, tolerance, and friendship among all nations, racial or religious groups, and shall further the activities of the United Nations for the maintenance of peace. (3) Parents have a prior right to choose the kind of education that shall be given to their children.

The human right of education occupies an important role in social human rights. Certainly this human right does not require that everyone be admitted to a university—only that individuals have equal access on the basis of merit. What about affirmative action? Should those who have been discriminated against in the past merit special treatment? While the drafters of the Universal Declaration probably did not foresee affirmative action policies, certainly a case could be made that merit should include considerations of past discrimination. The second part of Article 26 requires the teaching of human rights, which ideally would begin at the elementary level.

> **Article 27: (1) Everyone has the right freely to participate in the cultural life of the community, to enjoy the arts, and to share in scientific advancement and its benefits. (2) Everyone has the right to the protection of the moral and material interests resulting from any scientific, literary, or artistic production of which he or she is the author.**

This human right intends that every member of a community have the right to participate in culture and scientific activities. For those who produce artistic or scientific creations or products, they should be allowed to benefit from those products, with, for example, protection given in the form of patents or copyrights.

Articles 22 through 27 form the economic, social, and cultural rights contained in the Universal Declaration. While not as extensive as the political and civil human rights, these rights are no less important. The concept of indivisibility requires consideration of economic, social, and cultural rights with the same importance as political and civil human rights. After all, what is more important than having adequate food, health care, shelter, and other basic needs? Without having those needs met, human life cannot even exist. Yet, human life could continue to exist with restrictions on free speech and limited elections.

Unfortunately, the focus of some countries has been to elevate political and civil rights over economic, social, and cultural rights. The reality is that both types of human rights have great importance.

Solidarity or International Human Rights

The third category of human rights contained in the Universal Declaration is often referred to as solidarity human rights. The idea behind these rights rests upon the reasonable proposal that no country occupies the world in isolation. People from all over the world should work together for a better world.

> **Article 28: Everyone is entitled to a social and international order in which the rights and freedoms set forth in this Declaration can be fully realized.**

Not only governments but also individuals must work toward a society in which human rights can flourish. This human right imposes responsibility upon individuals to create conditions and institutions that respect the Universal Declaration.

Reference to an international order in which human rights can be fully realized indicates the need for nations and individuals to cooperate in the area of human rights.

> **Article 29: (1) Everyone has duties to the community in which alone the free and full development of his or her personality is possible. (2) In the exercise of rights and freedoms, everyone shall be subject only to those limitations that are necessary to fulfill the rights and freedoms of others and the just requirements of morality, public order, and general welfare in a democratic society. (3) These rights and freedoms may not be exercised contrary to the purposes and principles of the United Nations.**

Without being specific, this article imposes duties to the broader community upon everyone. The implication is that individuals and nations must respect the rights of others within the local and world communities. Without respect for communities, fullest individual development is not possible. However, individuals and nations should have sufficient leeway to go their own way so long as they do not disrupt the rights of others and the general welfare.

> **Article 30: Nothing in this Declaration may be interpreted as implying for any State, group, or person any right to engage in any activity or to perform any act aimed at the destruction of any of the rights and freedoms set forth herein.**

This final article of the declaration prohibits acts that inhibit or harm the human rights and freedoms of others.

Summary of the Universal Declaration of Human Rights

To understand the significance of the Universal Declaration, it helps to view the declaration as a type of conduct code for every nation and individual. The declaration does not replace constitutions and local laws. But everyone, nation and individual, should study the declaration as a tool for helping local and global communities in their activities. While some politicians and individuals complain about the control of the United Nations over the United States, it was the United States that was a driving force behind the Universal Declaration of Human Rights. Simply agreeing to follow that declaration does not mean a country has relinquished control over its affairs to the United Nations.

The Universal Declaration stands on its own as an extraordinary document. While individuals and countries may place different interpretations on various articles or even fail to acknowledge certain articles, nothing detracts from the importance of the declaration as a standard of conduct.

Exercises

Exercise 1: Human Rights and the Media

The purpose of this exercise is to develop an awareness of human rights issues in everyday life and to recognize both enjoyment/protection of human rights and violations/neglect of rights.

1. Participants should divide themselves into small groups of three or four. Each group receives pages from a recent newspaper, along with scissors, tape, and a sheet of chart paper.

2. Each group will construct a poster using items from the newspaper grouped under these categories:
    a. Human rights being practiced or enjoyed
    b. Rights being denied
    c. Rights being protected
    d. Rights in conflict

Groups should look not only for news stories but also for small features such as announcements and advertisements. For instance, the language of the newspaper itself illustrates the right to language and culture, advertisements can illustrate the right to private property, reports of social events (e.g., weddings and births) can illustrate social and cultural rights, and personal columns can reflect many rights in practice (e.g., freedom of speech).

3. After groups have found stories for each of the four categories, they should select one story from each category to analyze, using these standards:
    a. What specific human rights were involved in the story? List them beside the story.
    b. Find the articles of the Universal Declaration of Human Rights that cover each human right and write the article number(s) beside the right.

4. A spokesperson from each group presents his or her group's selections to other groups and summarizes the reasons behind the selections. The spokesperson should discuss the following:
    a. Specific human rights that were involved in the stories
    b. Articles of the Universal Declaration involved in the stories
    c. Whether more stories were concerned with civil/political human rights or social/economic/cultural rights. If one set of rights was more prevalent, the spokesperson should analyze reasons for this prevalence.
    d. Which of the four categories of human rights listed in number 2 were easiest to find, hardest to find, and why?
    e. Whether some articles of the Universal Declaration seemed more applicable than others. Did some articles of the Universal Declaration never appear in the stories? Why or why not?
    f. Whether any stories specifically mentioned the term "human rights." Was the mentioning of human rights common, or did most of the stories not mention this term? If stories did not mention human rights, what reasons might exist for not mentioning the term?

g. Based on the news stories selected, what seems to be the state of human rights in the world today? In the United States? In your community?

h. What are some positive initiatives and actions for the protection and fulfillment of human rights indicated by the stories? Who is taking these actions?

5. Participants can vary this exercise by comparing coverage of the same human rights stories in different newspapers or media, such as magazines and television. What differences do you observe in the importance given to the story? Are there different features of the story within the various accounts? Are there different versions of a single event? Did any version of the story explicitly mention human rights?

Adapted from Flowers, Nancy (ed.) *Human Rights Here and Now: Celebrating the Universal Declaration of Human Rights*. Human Rights Resource Center (1998). http://www.umn.edu/humanrts/edumat/hreduseries/hereandnow/Default.htm

Exercise 2: Defining Human Rights and Needs

The following is a group exercise.

1. In groups of threes or fours, draw a tree on a piece of large chart paper.
   a. Write on the tree, in the form of leaves, fruit, or branches, those human rights that the group believes all people need to live in dignity and justice.
   b. Draw roots onto the bottom of the tree and label the roots with items that make human rights flourish. For example, roots could be labeled with a healthy economy, antidiscrimination laws, universal education, and any other item that contributes to human rights.

2. After the groups have completed their drawings, each group should present its tree and explain reasons for items included on the tree, including the roots.

3. To extend this exercise, groups can match the fruit, leaves, and branches of their trees with specific articles of the Universal Declaration of Human Rights and write the article number next to each item.

4. Groups can display these trees in classrooms or public places.

5. Groups can identify human rights on the tree that are of particular concern to their local communities.

Adapted from Flowers, Nancy (ed.) *Human Rights Here and Now: Celebrating the Universal Declaration of Human Rights*. Human Rights Resource Center (1998). http://www.umn.edu/humanrts/edumat/hreduseries/hereandnow/Default.htm

Exercise 3: Creating a Human Rights Environment

The purpose of this group exercise is to read the following scenario and create a human rights environment based on the scenario.

Part A: Establishing Rights for a New Country

1. A small new planet (or country) has been discovered that has everything needed to sustain human life. No one has ever lived there. There are no laws, no rules,

and no history. You will all be settlers here. In preparation of your settlement, your group has been appointed to draw up the bill of rights for this all-new planet. You do not know what position you will have in this country.
Your group has the following duties:
    a. Give the country a name.
    b. Decide on ten rights that the entire group can agree upon and list them on chart paper.

2. Each group presents its list of ten rights to the other groups. Assign one person from a group to create a "master list" that includes all the rights the groups mention.

3. When all the groups have presented their lists, examine the master list: Do some of the rights overlap? Can they be combined into one right? Is any right listed on only one list? Should it be included or eliminated?

4. After their presentations of the lists and discussion about similar rights, groups can discuss the following questions: Did a group member's ideas about which rights were most important change during the exercise? How would life be in this country if some of the rights were excluded? Are there any rights a group member feels should be included in the master list? Why is making this list useful?

5. To vary the process in creating the master list of rights, some groups can be assigned a particular status or role. For example, one group might be classified as individuals with disabilities, one as ethnic minorities, one as millionaires, and one as HIV-positive. Other groups would have no particular status or role. After creating a master list of rights based on these assigned roles, group members should discuss whether the assigned status within the new country influenced their ideas about necessary rights: for example, did the status of being a person with a disability affect your ideas about necessary rights?

Part B: Linking Rights to the Universal Declaration of Human Rights

1. After completing the master list, participants should return to their original group and try to match rights on the master list with articles of the Universal Declaration of Human Rights. Some rights may include several articles of the Universal Declaration; others may not be in the declaration at all. (If time is short, rights on the master list can be assigned to each group, without having each group analyze every right on the list.)

2. When a group finishes the matching of rights on the master list with those in the Universal Declaration, a member of the group should write down the article numbers next to the matching right on the master list.

3. Together, the groups should review each right on the master list and any matching right contained in the Universal Declaration. Is there agreement that the matches are correct? If disagreements occur, participants should resolve them.

4. Were some of the rights on the master list not contained in the Universal Declaration? How can you explain this omission? Were some rights in the Universal Declaration not contained in the master list? Why not?

Part C: Selecting Personal Preferences

1. Select the three rights from the master list that mean the most to you.

2. One person, a facilitator, can tally the numbers to see how many participants selected a particular right.

3. The entire group should discuss why certain rights were selected more than others. Are there special circumstances within the local community that might make some rights more important than others?

4. Discuss the distinction between the two sets of rights: civil/political rights and social/economic/cultural rights. Did participants favor one set of rights over another in their selections? If so, discuss why.

Adapted from Flowers, Nancy (ed.) *Human Rights Here and Now: Celebrating the Universal Declaration of Human Rights.* Human Rights Resource Center (1998). http://www.umn.edu/humanrts/edumat/hreduseries/hereandnow/Default.htm

1. Before completing the questionnaire, participants should research conditions within their community, using items in the questionnaire. This research will require at least a couple of weeks. Obtaining detailed knowledge about each item may not be possible. However, participants need to acquire some knowledge about each item to avoid unsubstantiated opinions.

2. After researching items on the questionnaire, participants will complete the questionnaire. For each item, participants need to examine the articles of the declaration referred to in parentheses. For example, in answering item 1, participants would read Articles 3 and 5 of the declaration to see the connection between the item and the human rights principles. In some cases, the item in the questionnaire may be broader than the relatively narrow principles stated in the declaration. However, responses to the items should provide a general sense of the community's climate in consideration of principles found in the Universal Declaration of Human Rights.

3. After completion of the questionnaire, participants will hand in the questionnaires to a facilitator, who will then review the various responses. The facilitator will prepare a summary of the results from the questionnaire. Because the maximum number of points for a single item is 4, with 10 participants, the maximum score for that item would be 40. The facilitator will chart the scores for each item and present them to the participants at the next session or meeting.

Taking the Human Rights Temperature of Your Community

Introduction

The following questions are adapted from the United Nations Universal Declaration of Human Rights. The relevant articles are included parenthetically in each statement. Some of these issues correlate more directly to the articles than others. All of these questions are related to the fundamental human right to education found in Article 25 of the Universal Declaration:

Everyone has the right to a standard of living adequate for health and wellbeing of himself (or herself) and of his (or her) family, including food, clothing, housing and medical care, and necessary social services, and the right to security in the event of unemployment, sickness, disability, widowhood, old age, or other lack of livelihood in circumstances beyond his control.

When discrimination is mentioned in the following questionnaire, it refers to a wide range of conditions: race, ethnicity/culture, sex, physical/intellectual capacities, friendship associations, age, culture, disability, social class/financial status, physical appearance, sexual orientation, lifestyle choices, nationality, and living space. Although this is a much more expansive list than that found in the Universal Declaration of Human Rights, it is more helpful in assessing the human rights temperature in your community.

The results should provide a general sense of the community's climate in light of principles found in the Universal Declaration of Human Rights.

Directions

Take the human rights temperature of your community. Read each statement and assess how accurately it describes your community in the blank next to it. Keep in mind all members of your community. At the end, total up your score to determine your overall assessment score for your school.

Rating Scale

1	2	3	4	DN
no/never	rarely	often	yes/always	don't know

Taking the Human Rights Temperature of Your Community

____ 1. My community is a place where residents are safe and secure. (Articles 3, 5)

____ 2. All persons receive equal information and encouragement about academic and career opportunities. (Article 2)

____ 3. Members of the community are not discriminated against because of their lifestyle choices, such as manner of dress and association with certain people. (Articles 2, 16)

____ 4. My community provides equal access, resources, activities, and scheduling accommodations for all individuals. (Articles 2, 7)

____ 5. Members of my community will oppose discriminatory or demeaning actions, materials, or slurs. (Articles 2, 3, 7, 28, 29)

____ 6. When someone demeans or violates the rights of another person, the violator is helped to learn how to change his or her behavior. (Article 26)

____ 7. Members of my community care about my full human as well as academic development and try to help me when I am in need. (Articles 3, 22, 26, 29)

____ 8. When conflicts arise, we try to resolve them through nonviolent ways. (Articles 3, 28)

____ 9. Institutional policies and procedures are implemented when complaints of harassment or discrimination are submitted. (Articles 3, 7)

____ 10. In legal issues, all persons are assured of fair, impartial treatment in the determination of guilt and assignment of punishment. (Articles 6, 7, 8, 9, 10)

____ 11. No one in our community is subjected to degrading treatment or punishment. (Article 5)

____ 12. Someone accused of wrongdoing is presumed innocent until proven guilty. (Article 11)

____ 13. My personal space and possessions are respected. (Articles 12, 17)

____ 14. My community welcomes persons from diverse backgrounds and cultures, including people not born in the United States. (Articles 2, 6, 13, 14, 15)

____ 15. I have the liberty to express my beliefs and ideas (political, religious, cultural, or other) without fear of discrimination. (Article 19)

_____ 16. Members of my community can produce and disseminate publications without fear of censorship or punishment. (Article 19)

_____ 17. Diverse voices and perspectives (e.g., sexual orientation, gender, race/ethnicity, ideological) are represented in courses, textbooks, assemblies, libraries, and classroom instruction. (Articles 2, 19, 27)

_____ 18. I have the opportunity to express my culture through music, art, and writing. (Articles 19, 27, 28)

_____ 19. Members of my community have the opportunity to participate (individually and through associations) in democratic decision-making processes to develop policies and rules. (Articles 20, 21, 23)

_____ 20. Members of my community have the right to form associations within to advocate for their rights or the rights of others. (Articles 19, 20, 23)

_____ 21. Members of my community encourage each other to learn about societal and global problems related to justice, ecology, poverty, and peace. (preamble & Articles 26, 29)

_____ 22. Members of my community encourage each other to organize and take action to address societal and global problems related to justice, ecology, poverty, and peace. (preamble & Articles 20, 29)

_____ 23. Members of my community work reasonable hours under fair work conditions. (Articles 23, 24)

_____ 24. Employees in my community are paid enough to have a standard of living adequate for the health and well-being (including housing, food, necessary social services and security from unemployment, sickness, and old age) of themselves and their families. (Articles 22, 25)

_____ 25. I take responsibility in my community to ensure that other individuals do not discriminate and that they behave in ways that promote the safety and well-being of my community. (Articles 1, 29)

Temperature possible = 100 Human rights degrees

Your community's temperature _____

Adapted from Flowers, Nancy, Marcia Bernbaum, Kristi Rudelius-Palmer, Joel Tolman. _The Human Rights Education Handbook: Effective Practices for Learning, Actions, and Change._ Human Rights Resource Center (2000). http://www.umn.edu/humanrts/edumat/hreduseries/hrhandbook/toc.html

After completion of this exercise, students or other participants in the exercise should have a working knowledge of human rights principles contained in the Universal Declaration, which provides the foundation for further study of human rights. To move from analysis and evaluation to the development of a plan of action, participants can consider the following questions:

a. In which areas does your community appear to be adhering to or promoting human rights principles?

b. In which areas do there seem to be human rights problems? Which of these are of particular concern to you? Elaborate on the areas of concern, providing examples and identifying patterns in human rights violations.

c. How do you explain the existence of the problem conditions? Do they have race/ethnicity, class, gender, disability, age, or sexual orientation dimensions?

d. Are the issues related to participation in the decision making—meaning whether someone is included or not?

e. Who benefits and who loses as a result of the existing human rights violations?

f. Are there other explanations to consider?

g. Have fellow community members or you contributed in any way to the construction and perpetuation of the existing climate? In other words, have you (or others) acted in certain ways or not acted by ignoring abuses or by not reporting incidents?

h. Were participants representative of the population of the community? Would you expect different results from a different group of people? In what ways might another group's responses differ and why? When determining which human rights concerns need to be addressed and how to address them, how can you be certain to take into account the perspectives and experiences of different people?

i. What needs to be done to improve the human rights climate in your community? What action(s) can you and your group take to create a more humane and just environment where human rights values are promoted and human rights behaviors practiced?

CHAPTER 4

Beyond the Universal Declaration of Human Rights

A
s country after country joined the United Nations, the concept of human rights became much more prevalent. Each member nation of the United Nations pledged to abide by the Universal Declaration of Human Rights, although no real oversight of whether countries followed human rights principles in the declaration existed. Without oversight or a legally enforceable commitment to human rights, countries could always say they promote human rights but, in reality, do little to ensure the integration of human rights into their policies.

The United Nations was aware of the nonenforceable nature of the Universal Declaration. Drafters of the declaration had avoided references to any nation or state. Rather, the point of view within the declaration focuses on the individual or group. For instance, articles in the declaration usually begin with this phrase "everyone has the right" or a similar all-inclusive beginning. However, the declaration contained nothing about any nation or country having to enforce the declaration. The obvious hope was that UN members would take the declaration seriously and do their best to meet the human rights challenges within that document.

In the years after adoption of the Universal Declaration, members of the United Nations began work on documents that would require countries to enforce human rights principles. In 1966, after years of labor, members of the United Nations adopted two key documents with which to implement the Universal Declaration: the International Covenant on Civil and Political Rights and the International Covenant on Economic, Social and Cultural Rights. These two documents derive from the declaration and contain standards for judging human rights violations. In contrast to the declaration, countries approving these covenants are required to enforce provisions contained within them. Compared to the declaration, both of these documents are lengthier and more complex.

What is clear from both covenants is the linking of political and civil human rights to economic, social, and cultural human rights. Neither category of human rights should take precedence over the other. This indivisibility of human rights forms the basis for both covenants. Unfortunately, many countries have yet to attribute the same importance to economic, social, and cultural rights as they have to political and civil rights.

International Covenant on Civil and Political Rights

The International Covenant on Civil and Political Rights focuses on the type of human rights that many U.S. politicians appear to view as the entire scope of human rights. Whenever a politician gives a speech about the need for human rights in Africa or some other region outside the United States, most assuredly the politician means human rights contained in this covenant. This document contains an opening mission statement and 53 articles, divided into six parts. The first three parts list specific civil and political rights, while the last three parts address procedure, interpretation, and monitoring issues.

Before any covenant (or treaty) can become law in the United States, the U.S. Constitution requires that at least two-thirds of the Senate approve the document (U.S. Constitution, Article 2). In 1978, President Carter signed the International Covenant on Civil and Political Rights and submitted it for ratification by the Senate. Not until 1992 did the Senate ratify, or approve, the covenant (Newman & Weisbrodt, 1996). However, simply approving the covenant was not enough to enforce it. Because the U.S. Congress must enact specific laws to enforce the covenant, something that Congress has not done, enforcement of the covenant remains in limbo. Fortunately, many of the provisions within the covenant are already part of the U.S. legal framework and are therefore enforceable. Otherwise, because the U.S. government has never passed specific laws to enforce the covenant, provisions of the covenant would not be enforceable.

> **Part I**
>
> The first part of the covenant on civil and political rights emphasizes that all "peoples" within a state have the human right to "self-determination" (Article 1). A state or country may include many different groups or peoples, who should be free to practice their own religion and exercise their own political beliefs. Self-determination of those groups or peoples requires respect of the public order and general welfare (Article 29 of the Universal Declaration). For instance, groups with the same ethnicity or religion have the human right to associate or worship together but do not have the right to attack the public order or general welfare.

Self-determination has limits, whether on a national or individual level. The right to self-determination does not allow others to do harm to the general community. For instance, the right of an individual to drive a car may be restricted until the individual has reached a certain age or if the individual has a physical impairment. The main purpose of this restriction lies in the harm the individual might do to the general community if permitted to drive without restrictions.

A primary difficulty with self-determination arises when a dominant group arbitrarily or unjustly imposes its will on a minority group. In theory, human rights principles would prevent this. However, reality is not always so clean. Palestinians in the Middle East have attempted self-determination for years but often encounter roadblocks, some obviously created by Palestinian violence toward Israelis but also some created by Israeli discrimination against Palestinians. From a historical perspective, the justness of the Palestinian cause for self-determination may appear evident. Yet, to unravel decades of conflict requires extraordinary sensitivity and respect of universal human rights principles.

Relevant questions for self-determination of groups within a broader national entity include the following:

Should all forms of self-determination be endorsed?

Should one first consider cultural autonomy, in hopes of avoiding struggles over vital economic resources and avoiding tempting ever smaller ethnic or religious factions to seek secession?

Should the case for self-determination be judged in terms of the level of oppression suffered by a given nationality?

To what extent should one consider who the primary beneficiaries (and the likely losers) are, both within and outside the group struggling for independence?

Is the political agenda of the national movement framed in terms of universal human rights?

To what extent is the prospective independent state economically viable?

Seeking answers to these questions is an inescapable part of any effort to evaluate demands for independence in terms of the likely consequences for human rights (Ishay, 2004, p. 198). Clearly, governments and institutions like the United Nations must be involved in the self-determination process, providing a fair and equitable forum for claims of self-determination.

Part II

The second part of the covenant requires states to take steps against discrimination on the basis of race, color, sex, language, religion, political, national or social origin, property, birth, or other status (Article 2). States are to provide assistance for those who believe someone has violated their right to a nondiscriminatory environment. If discrimination has occurred, states are to provide remedies to the discrimination.

Many countries have passed laws to prevent discrimination. However, as a practical matter, discrimination can be difficult to prove, because there are all types of "legitimate" reasons for treating members of a particular class differently. The discrimination described in Part II of the covenant lists some categories that the United States generally does not consider a basis for discrimination. Language and property are two major classifications that the covenant prohibits as a basis for discrimination, but U.S. laws typically do not. With respect to language, the prevailing opinion in the United States is that everyone should speak English, while in European or other countries, people often speak many languages, with some languages clearly favored over others. Canada, Switzerland, many African countries, and other nations have encountered fierce battles over the priority of languages even when social or ethnic origins are similar. This discrimination clearly led to the placement of language as a basis for nondiscrimination within the covenant.

Part III

This part of the covenant lists what U.S. citizens typically refer to as human rights, with a few qualifications or "reservations."

- Every human being has the inherent right to life (Article 6). The death penalty is not looked upon with favor, but no ban on capital punishment exists except for crimes committed by persons younger than 18 years of age and pregnant women.
- No one shall be subjected to torture or to cruel, inhuman, or degrading treatment or punishment (Article 7).
- Except for punishment of a crime, slavery and forced labor are abolished (Article 8).
- Nobody may be arrested without information as to the reasons for the arrest, allowing prompt challenges to the lawfulness of the detention (Article 9).
- Within the prison system, accused persons shall be segregated from convicted persons and juveniles separated from adults (Article 10). Rehabilitation shall be the "essential aim" of the prison system, with humane and dignified treatment for all persons deprived of their liberty.
- Nobody shall be imprisoned simply because he or she did not fulfill a contractual obligation (Article 11).
- Individuals lawfully within a country have the right to reside where they want within the country (Article 12).
- An "alien" or foreigner lawfully within a country shall be entitled to legal safeguards before being expelled (Article 13).
- Persons charged with a crime have the right to legal assistance, detailed information about the charge, examination of witnesses, and silence (Article 14).
- Nobody can be prosecuted for an act that was not a crime at the time the act was committed (Article 15).

- Everyone shall be considered a person before the law, thereby preventing a state from singling out individuals as less worthy of legal protection than others (Article 16).
- Nobody shall be subject to arbitrary or unlawful interference with his or her privacy and reputation (Article 17).
- Everyone has the right to freedom of thought, conscience, and religion, with restrictions allowed only to protect public safety and general welfare (Article 18).
- Everyone shall have the right to freedom of expressions, with restrictions allowed only to protect the rights or reputation of others and the general welfare (Article 19).
- War propaganda and any advocacy of national, racial, or religious hatred that constitutes incitement to discrimination, hostility, or violence are prohibited (Article 20).
- The right to peaceful assembly is recognized, with the usual limitations based on public safety and general welfare (Article 21).
- Everyone has the right to associate with whom they please and to form and join trade unions (Article 22).
- The family, as the "natural and fundamental group unit of society" is entitled to protection by society and the state (Article 23).
- Children have the right to protection, immediate registration after birth, a name, and a nationality (Article 24).
- Citizens have the right to participate in public affairs without discrimination (Article 25).
- All persons shall be treated equally before the law (Article 26).
- Ethnic, religious, and linguistic minorities have the right to enjoy their own culture, to practice their own religion, and to use their own language (Article 27).

The list of political and civil rights contained in the covenant clearly resembles what many U.S. citizens would view as similar rights within their society and culture. However, differences do occur. For instance, upon its ratification of the covenant, the United States placed a "reservation" on the enforcement of the provision prohibiting capital punishment for crimes committed by individuals who were younger than 18 years of age at the time of commission. A reservation expresses the intent of a country to modify or use a different standard from a particular provision of a covenant or treaty. A state may place a reservation on a covenant or treaty unless the covenant specifically prohibits reservations (Vienna Convention, 1969, art. 19). Only in 2005, when the U.S. Supreme Court ruled that capital punishment for individuals under 18 years of age was unconstitutional did the United States join the rest of the world in recognizing this human right (*Roper v. Simmons*, 2005). The United States had been one of the few countries in the world that allowed capital punishment for juveniles.

> **Part IV**
>
> The covenant establishes a Human Rights Committee with the purpose of monitoring steps that states party to the covenant have taken in implementing rights guaranteed by the covenant.

Under this part of the covenant, states are to submit reports to the Human Rights Committee as to steps taken to enforce provisions of the covenant and ongoing enforcement. States can also submit human rights complaints against other states, but this remedy appears to be little used—most likely because the accused state could easily come up with an alleged violation against the accusing state.

The European Court of Human Rights has ruled that two low-income defendants in England (the "McLibel Two") should have been given legal assistance against the fast food giant McDonald's in a defamation case brought by McDonald's (Oliver, 2005). The McLibel Two lost a libel case against McDonald's in 1997, in which the relatively penniless environmental activists famously represented themselves against the firm's expensive lawyers. The firm had sued them for libel because of leaflets the two Londoners had distributed, but not written, titled "What's Wrong with McDonald's."

After losing their case in the English courts, the McLibel Two brought a separate case to the European Court of Human Rights against the English government. They argued that English libel law and the lack of legal aid for defendants of defamation cases had forced them to represent themselves. The human rights court upheld their argument, ruling that having to represent themselves denied them the right to free speech and a fair hearing, human rights guaranteed by England. Lawyers for the McLibel Two had argued that the libel case filed by McDonald's was patently unfair, resulting in a stark inequality between the two sides.

> **Part V**
>
> The covenant may not conflict with other provisions of the UN Charter or specialized UN agencies involved with matters contained in the covenant.

This part ensures that provisions in the covenant do not interfere with other work being done by the United Nations or provisions within the UN Charter.

> **Part VI**
>
> The final part of the covenant contains procedural points, including who may sign the covenant and when the covenant becomes effective.

Connection of Covenant on Political and Civil Human Rights to Social Work

At first glance, social workers may feel that the International Covenant on Civil and Political Rights has little to do with social work. However, a deeper look at the covenant reveals that social work and the covenant go hand in hand. Many provisions in the covenant directly relate to ethical standards of social workers (NASW, 1999). Important goals of the covenant are to guarantee that everyone can voice opinions, preserve cultural backgrounds, carry out religious practices, and organize employment unions. The covenant also prohibits torture, slavery, cruel and degrading treatment, discrimination, and other violations of the person. Social workers can easily find common cause with these human rights.

International Covenant on Economic, Social and Cultural Rights

In addition to the covenant on political and civil rights, members of the United Nations drafted a covenant to focus on human rights that social workers might view as "quality of life" issues: the International Covenant on Economic, Social and Cultural Rights (United Nations, 1966b).

Certainly, countries must place importance on free speech, elections, religious tolerance, and many other human rights that affect the governing functions of individuals and nations. But is it enough to promote only the category of human rights referred to as negative rights? What about those human rights that guarantee individuals adequate medical care, food, shelter, education, employment, retirement security, leisure time, and other day-to-day concerns? The Universal Declaration of Human Rights makes no distinction between the two categories of human rights. Yet, favoring political and civil rights over economic, social, and cultural rights has definitely occurred in many countries, especially in the United States.

A tragic irony exists in the favoring of "negative" human rights over "positive" human rights within the United States. Americans justifiably pride themselves on having created an environment where peoples all over the world can exist without great discrimination and government interference. Yet, the reality for many is an environment with little or no medical care, inadequate shelter, deficient educational opportunities, or essentially a subsistence level of existence.

The United States occupied the forefront in promoting the Universal Declaration of Human Rights. Yet, when it came to promoting the category of human rights known as positive rights, the United States has frequently paid little attention. In 1978, when President Carter submitted the International Covenant on Political and Civil Rights to the Senate, he also signed and submitted the International Covenant on Economic, Social and Cultural Rights to the Senate for ratification. While the Senate eventually approved the covenant on political and civil rights, the Senate has yet to approve the covenant on economic, social, and cultural rights and most likely never will. The Senate has obviously tossed the covenant onto the shelves of Capitol Hill to gather dust.

Why the inaction on the covenant of economic, social, and cultural rights? After all, as a member of the United Nations, the United States has promised to follow the Universal Declaration. The covenant on economic, social, and cultural rights generally derives its provisions from the declaration, which has approval by the United States. For historical reasons, the United States has emphasized civil and political rights over economic and social rights (Rifkin, 2004). Still, the U.S. disconnect from the covenant on economic, social, and cultural rights raises disturbing issues. The economic, social, and cultural health of a nation surely depends on political and civil human rights—but is not the opposite also true: without economic, social, and cultural rights, of what use are political and civil rights?

The International Covenant on Economic, Social and Cultural Rights consists of five parts and 31 articles. The opening statement (preamble) of the covenant emphasizes that the "ideal of free human beings enjoying freedom from fear and want can only be achieved if conditions are created whereby everyone may enjoy his economic, social, and cultural rights, as well as his civil and political rights." This placement of economic, social, and cultural rights on the same level as political and civil rights highlights the indivisibility of the two categories of rights.

> **Part I**
>
> This initial part of the covenant states that all peoples have the right to self-determination of their economic, social, and cultural systems.

This human right to self-determination appears to allow different economic systems, such as communism and capitalism. However, indivisibility of human rights also requires that countries adhere to political and civil human rights. Therefore, countries certainly have the right to operate a government-controlled economy as long as they also promote political and civil rights.

> **Part II**
>
> The second part allows countries unable to satisfy economic, social, and cultural rights in the covenant to limit those human rights. However, countries must take steps to progressively realize those rights, in accordance with available resources.

The covenant recognizes that not all countries will be able to fulfill the human rights contained in the covenant. More leeway to limit those rights exists than in the covenant on political and civil rights.

Part III

This part contains the substantive economic, social, and cultural rights:

- Everyone shall have the opportunity to gain his or her living by work freely chosen (Article 6, para. 1). States must take steps to effect this right to work, including the establishment of technical and vocational guidance and training programs. States must also create policies and techniques to achieve steady economic, social, and cultural development and full and productive employment (para. 2).
- States recognize the right of everyone to the enjoyment of just and favorable conditions of work, with women receiving equal pay for equal work and workers entitled to holidays and leisure time (Article 7).
- Workers have the right to form trade unions with the right to strike (Article 8).
- Everyone has the right to social security (Article 9).
- States must protect the family, the natural and fundamental group unit of society (Article 10). Mothers and children receive special protection, and spouses have the right to enter into marriages without prearranged rules.
- Everyone has the right to an adequate standard of living, including adequate food, clothing, and housing (Article 11). States are to take steps both individually and on an international basis toward ensuring an adequate food supply for everyone.
- Everyone has the right to enjoyment of the highest attainable standard of physical and mental health (Article 12). States are to take steps to ensure that everyone receives medical service and attention in the event of sickness.
- Everyone has the right to education, with free primary education (Articles 13, 14).
- Everyone has the right to take part in cultural life and to enjoy the benefits of scientific progress and its applications (Article 15). Everyone also has the right to benefit from the protection of the moral and material interests resulting from any scientific, literary, or artistic production of which a person is the author.

A review of the substantive economic, social, and cultural benefits shows five main areas concerning human rights: employment; protection of the family; social security, including food, housing, and medical care; education; and participation in cultural and scientific pursuits.

Part IV

This part requires States to submit regular reports on measures they have taken to realize human rights in Part III and progress toward meeting those goals.

Monitoring provisions of this covenant appear less stringent than those contained in the International Covenant on Civil and Political Rights. For states that have adopted the covenant on economic, social, and cultural rights, more leeway exists on determining whether a state has fulfilled human rights in the covenant. Also, no country has the right to complain about another country for possible violations of the covenant, as a country does in the covenant on political and civil rights.

> **Part V**
>
> This part provides procedural guidelines for states that wish to adopt the covenant.

As noted previously, although President Carter signed and submitted the International Covenant on Economic, Social and Cultural Rights to Congress for approval, Congress has not acted upon the covenant. For more than 25 years, Congress has had the opportunity to consider and ratify the covenant. Because Congress has taken no steps to support the covenant, ratification or approval of the covenant by Congress at any time appears highly unlikely.

Connection of Covenant on Economic, Social, and Cultural Rights to Social Work

Many of the provisions within the covenant on economic, social, and cultural human rights relate to important social work practices and policies. However, the importance placed upon this set of human rights by the United States simply does not equal the importance placed upon political and civil human rights.

Social workers know firsthand the effects of depreciating economic, social, and cultural human rights. Not having a right to health care can be both physically and financially devastating for many families. Social workers who provide counseling services may be called upon to deal with the stress of those who do not have affordable medical coverage. The high cost of shelter may lead to homelessness, another social problem often encountered by the social work profession. Listing social ills related to the belittling of economic, social, and cultural human rights could easily fill pages.

By learning more about economic, social, and cultural human rights, social workers will develop a more complete understanding of human rights, which occupy a central role in the social work profession. Human rights mean much more than the right to vote, to be free from discrimination, and to enjoy other political freedoms. Without economic human rights, political freedoms also lose importance.

Conclusion

The social work profession has an obligation to advocate for human rights, with the first step being a recognition that human rights play an important role in social

	Human Rights	**Human Responsibilities**
From Above		
From Below		

Figure 4.1   Rights and Responsibilities

Source: Ife, J., & Fiske, L. (2004, October). Human rights and community. Paper presented at Global SocialWork, Reclaiming Civil Society, IFSW, AASW, Adelaide.

work policies and practice. Simply inserting the term "human rights" into broad mission statements without careful study of that term does not help the profession. Social work educators and students should understand the differences between political and economic human rights and recognize that both types of rights are crucial to overall human dignity.

Exercises

Exercise 1: Political/Civil Human Rights

The purpose of this exercise is to help social workers understand the connection between political/civil human rights and the social work profession.

1. Select any three political/civil human rights listed in Part III of the International Covenant on Political and Civil Rights.

2. On separate sheets of paper, write each of the rights on the top left-hand side of the sheet. On the top right-hand side of the sheet, write "Importance to social work." For instance, if you select as one of the three rights the right to be free from torture or cruel punishment, you would prepare one sheet as follows:

   Freedom from torture and cruel punishment   Importance to social work

3. After preparing each of the three sheets as above, list reasons under "Importance to social work" why the selected human right has relevance to social work. Reasons for this example could include prevention of domestic violence, child abuse, and torture to civilians/social workers in war zones.

4. Within a classroom environment, assign one particular human right under Part III of the covenant to each student, using the previously described format. Have each student then present the human right and reasons for its importance to social work. Questions for discussion include the following:
   a. On a scale of 1–5, with 5 being the most important, what level of importance to social work would you assign the right? Why?
   b. What real-life situations within the social work profession can you relate to the human right? Would these situations occur often? Would acknowledgment of the human right be helpful in resolving any problems related to the situation?
   c. Based on your experiences, does any current enforcement of the particular right now exist within the social work profession? If so, how does this enforcement occur? Through general laws, social work policy statements, administrative guidelines?
   d. Overall, do you believe that enforcement of the human right directly benefits or, if not currently enforced, would benefit the social work profession? Why or why not?

Exercise 2: Economic, Social and Cultural Human Rights

The purpose of this exercise is to help social workers understand the connection between economic, social, and cultural human rights and the social work profession.

1. Repeat Exercise 1 but substitute Part III of the International Covenant on Economic, Social and Cultural Rights for political/civil rights.

2. Compare reasons given for the importance to social work with those in Exercise 1. Does there appear to be greater importance to social work when analyzing economic, social, and cultural rights? Were the rankings higher in this exercise than the previous one? If so, why?

3. Further questions for discussion:
   a. Should economic, social, and cultural rights be legally enforceable? For instance, if everyone has the right to adequate health care without a direct payment, should that person have the right to sue the government if he or she does not receive necessary medical treatment? Does this human right go too far? Why or why not?
   b. Is it realistic to expect governments to give more than lip service to most human rights contained in the two covenants described in this chapter? What responsibilities does the individual have with respect to these rights? For instance, if someone smokes cigarettes and suffers lung cancer, should that person receive medical treatment as a right?

4. List human rights contained in the two covenants that you believe should be legally enforceable and those that should not be enforceable. How do the lists compare with the actual covenants? What reasons would you give for not enforcing a right within the covenants?

5. Should the United States approve the International Covenant on Economic, Social and Cultural Rights? Why or why not?

Exercise 3: Creating a Human Rights Commission

The purpose of this exercise is to create a human rights commission that hears human rights complaints. The exercise requires a group/class of at least eight members and will last several meetings. Goals of this exercise are aimed at helping students to develop skills in analyzing fact situations where human rights violations may have occurred.

1. Within the group/class, assign five members to be commissioners on the human rights commission. The role of the commissioners is to hear and decide human rights complaints brought before it. During any proceedings before the commission, commissioners are encouraged to ask questions and make their own findings as to alleged violations of human rights.

2. Assign one of the group/class members to be the complainant. This is the person who is alleging that her or his human rights have been violated.

3. Assign one of the group/class members to be the respondent. This is the person who has allegedly caused the harm leading to the alleged violation.

4. Assign one of the group/class members to be the hearing officer. This is the person who initially hears the complaint and makes a decision. It is this decision that is then appealed to the commission, either by the complainant or by the respondent.

5. For purposes of this exercise, use the following fact situation:

Fact Situation

Respondent/employer (We Care, Inc.) is a private, not-for-profit agency that contracts with the local department of child and family services to provide home studies for placement of foster children. Respondent has employed the complainant (Betty Foster) as a child welfare specialist for ten years. Complainant (Betty) is now 60 years old, and respondent believes that Betty is too old for her present job and costs too much. Respondent can hire a much younger person to fill Betty's position at half the cost of Betty's salary.

Respondent has received a few complaints from foster families that Betty does not understand the needs of contemporary children and families and makes outdated recommendations. For example, in one case, a prospective foster family stated to respondent that Betty allegedly told them that they could not allow any gay individuals into their home in the presence of children placed with them. Respondent never discussed this or other alleged complaints with Betty to verify the facts.

Respondent informs Betty that her employment will be terminated in 30 days. The reasons given to Betty are that she is not following good practices and is not meeting the needs of respondent. Under the terms of her employment with respondent, either Betty or respondent can terminate Betty's employment simply by providing the other party with 30-days' notice.

6. Begin the exercise by having the person assigned to be complainant, Betty Foster, submit a written complaint to the hearing officer. The person assigned to be Betty must state the reason for the complaint. To substantiate the complaint,

Betty should cite every human rights principle found in the two covenants that could support a violation of Betty's human rights.

7. Respondent will then answer that complaint in writing, also citing any human rights provisions supporting its termination of Betty's employment.

8. After reviewing the written complaint and response, the hearing officer will hold an investigative hearing to question both Betty and respondent. Individuals assigned to play Betty and respondent should refer to the facts outlined in paragraph 5 but also have leeway to ignore and add additional facts so long as additional facts do not contradict those stated in paragraph 5.

9. The hearing officer must not refer to the facts stated in paragraph 5 but should ask his or her own questions about the circumstances leading to termination of Betty's employment. The hearing officer should construct questions that focus on the human rights principles relevant to the case. For instance, because Betty is 60 years old, the hearing officer would obviously ask questions relating to Betty's age.

10. After the investigative hearing, the hearing officer will make a decision as to whether a human rights violation occurred or not. The officer must base that decision on facts stated at the hearing and application of relevant human rights principles to those facts. The officer must cite actual provisions of human rights covenants and the Universal Declaration.

11. After the hearing officer issues his or her decision, the losing party will appeal that decision to the human rights commission. The losing party will submit a written appeal, stating why the decision of the hearing officer is incorrect (e.g., facts clearly show that human rights principles were violated).

12. The five-member commission will then hold its own hearing, with Betty and respondent present. The commission will review the officer's written decision and ask Betty and respondent questions about the employment termination. At the end of this hearing, the commission will discuss the matter and issue its own opinion.

13. After the commission issues its opinion, the entire group/class will then discuss the opinion within a human rights context. Specific factors to consider in this discussion follow:
    a. Did either Betty or respondent try to hide facts or avoid explaining certain facts? Did the facts clearly indicate a human rights violation?
    b. Did the hearing officer conduct a fair hearing? Did the officer appear to be biased against either party?
    c. Did the commission adequately review the decision of the hearing officer? Did they discuss relevant parts of the officer's decision that the losing party raised?
    d. Overall, was the procedure fair? Did one party seem to have an advantage over the other? Did the "system" favor either party?

After developing some expertise in this exercise, the group/class can easily substitute different fact situations. The key point is to assist students in developing skills for analyzing fact situations and applying human rights principles to those situations.

Exercise 4: Using Statistics to Measure Human Rights

The purpose of this exercise is to help social workers examine statistics and then analyze human right aspects of those statistics. The exercise can be performed individually or with a group. Consider the following statements:

Statistics indicate the following:

- The United States has the highest economic production in the world. However, in the United States, one out of four children is born into poverty as measured by government guidelines. Those guidelines fall below the actual cost of minimally adequate housing, health care, food, and other necessities.
- The United States is first in the world in defense spending and in military exports, but last among the 26 most industrialized countries in protecting children against violence. The rate of child deaths by gunfire far exceeds rates in comparable countries. Annual reports of child abuse and neglect number total over 3 million.
- African Americans, who make up only 14 percent of the population, vastly exceed this percentage in terms of rates of executions and imprisonment. Yet, on paper, the United States guarantees equality within its legal system.
- Forty percent of Hispanic and African American children officially live in poverty, but only 16 percent of white children fall within this category. In the United States, full-time work at minimum wage pays below the official poverty line for a family of two; two out of three workers who earn the minimum wage are women; and living standards are falling for younger generations.
- The United States has passed laws protecting its children from unfair, inhumane labor practices. However, the U.S. government has done little to block the importation of merchandise produced by child labor. Each year, Americans purchase billions of dollars of foreign products made from that labor.
- The United States grows enough food to feed all its people and millions around the world, but more than 10 percent of the U.S. population does not have enough food itself (Sklar, 1997). After studying the previous information, do the following:

Match the conditions described in each paragraph to relevant provisions in the two covenants discussed in this chapter. Discuss this matching of provisions and statistics. Do the statistics give the full story of whether the United States satisfies human rights provisions? Is it ever possible to fulfill all the human rights listed in the two covenants? If not, should we ignore the covenants?

Examine whether any failure to meet human rights provisions is the fault or responsibility of the U.S. government or individuals. The issue of responsibility plays a large role within the context of human rights.

Try to relate the national statistics cited earlier to local circumstances. Do circumstances within the local communities appear to mirror the national situation? Why or why not?

- After analyzing these points, write either an individual or group letter to local newspapers that examine the position of the United States toward various human rights provisions. This letter may take any position desired by the individual or group: for example, the letter could be either critical or supportive of the United States and its position toward human rights. The key point is to use statistics to support the position. For this exercise, you may refer to additional statistics and human rights documents (e.g., Universal Declaration of Human Rights).

Exercise 5: Analyzing Local Circumstances Within a Human Rights Context

The purpose of this exercise is to develop skills in analyzing local circumstances through a human rights prism. This exercise can also be done individually or within a group.

Select one of the following human rights problems/issues to analyze:

- Child abuse and neglect
- Homelessness
- Lack of adequate health care
- Access to court system
- Inadequate wages and unemployment

After selecting one of these issues, develop a strategy that would examine whether your local community attempts to meet human rights principles related to the issue. For example, you could start by asking the following:

1. Does the problem/issue exist in your community?

2. How severe is the problem?

3. What are, or will be, your sources of information? Which agencies would you interview? Are the sources reliable and complete?

Once you have selected a particular issue and considered the previously mentioned factors, develop a set of questions for interviews or other research that you might conduct. For example, if you have chosen homelessness, the following questions might be relevant to your research:

- Are there homeless people in this community? How many?
- How many are served by shelters? How many are not?
- How accurate are these numbers? How are they determined?
- Have the numbers of homeless been going up or down?
- Are there characteristics that many homeless people have in common? Is there a typical age? Gender? Racial or ethnic group? How do they become homeless?
- Has the composition of the homeless population been changing?
- What effect have government policies had on creating homelessness?
- What's the likelihood that those who are homeless also share other characteristics (e.g., have been deinstitutionalized, have substance abuse problems, have experienced domestic violence, have a mental or physical disability, are unemployed, or are younger than 18 years of age)?
- What permanent housing is available for the homeless? Does anyone help them find housing?
- Is the housing adequate in terms of size and other conditions? Are there people on waiting lists?

- Are conditions in this housing healthy and safe (e.g., free of rats, lead paint, structural damage, environmental pollution, electrical/fire hazards, gang/drug-related violence)?

- Are services provided in a respectful way to those in need?

These are only sample questions, and you should either supplement or revise the questions depending on local circumstances.

After compiling data for your project, prepare a written report that details the local situation concerning the selected human rights problem/issue and results of your research. The primary goals are to determine the extent of the human rights problem/issue, level of current resources being devoted to the problem, and efforts being made to address the problem.

Adapted from Shiman, David. *Economic and Social Justice: A Human Rights Perspective.* Human Rights Resource Center (1999). http://www.umn.edu/humanrts/edumat/hreduseries/tb1b/index .htm

CHAPTER 5

Human Rights and Vulnerable Groups

The initial documents outlining human rights principles do not single out any particular group for special treatment. The Universal Declaration of Human Rights and international covenants on political and economic rights generally do not contain provisions that favor a particular group. Certainly those documents prohibit discrimination on the basis of gender, age, national origin, property, and other classifications. The documents also promote families, motherhood, and children. However, nothing within those documents details special human rights treatment for any particular group. After all, considering the universal nature of human rights, why should a particular group be given additional attention? Would not this defeat the purpose of viewing human rights as something for everyone, and not restricted to a special group?

Within the United States, laws exist to protect women, children, and the elderly; persons with disabilities; cultural, ethnic, and religious minorities; and others against discrimination. In some states, agencies in charge of investigating discrimination have titles that include the term "human rights" (e.g., in Illinois there is a Department of Human Rights). Without considering the competency of those agencies in determining discrimination, the notion that human rights refers only to discrimination is misleading. Human rights cover a vast range of human needs essential for a meaningful existence. Why focus on human rights as something that resembles a crutch for those more susceptible to negative treatment? Unfortunately, this use of human rights in a purely discriminatory context does little to explain the true meaning of human rights. Instead, human rights may even take on an unintended derogatory meaning when viewed only in the context of discrimination.

Yet, despite the importance of viewing human rights within a universal context and not simply as something for the disadvantaged, instances arise when particular groups often require more attention to ensure human rights of those groups. This does not mean that these groups are being elevated above others. The term *vulnerable* refers to the harsh reality that these groups are more likely to encounter discrimination or other human rights violations than others.

What Is a Vulnerable Group?

In a human rights sense, certain population groups often encounter discriminatory treatment or need special attention to avoid potential exploitation. These populations make up what can be referred to as vulnerable groups. For example, consider the following:

> In the United States, only 6 percent of board seats within public companies are held by minorities, with only 13.6 percent held by women ("Who Is Running the Show?" 2004);

> Child abuse by parents and others is a major problem throughout much of the world, with special departments having been created to investigate complaints of child abuse (United Nations, 1989);

> Within the United States, African Americans continue to experience subtle, if not overt, discrimination in the form of inadequate educational facilities, lower incomes than others, disproportionate number of males in prison, and so on;

> Elderly persons frequently find themselves victims of scams and other schemes that cost them dearly financially and otherwise (United Nations, 1999);

> Ethnic cleansing or even genocide continues to occur in some parts of the world, with milder forms of discrimination on the basis of national or ethnic origin occurring elsewhere;

> Persons with disabilities often have no recourse to decent employment or adequate treatment; and

> HIV-AIDS afflicts large numbers of populations in many countries (United Nations, 2004).

Circumstances in which a particular group encounters obstacles or impediments to the enjoyment of human rights could continue indefinitely. The idea that all things are equal within the application or distribution of human rights remains idealistic and outright naïve. For these reasons, human rights advocates have emphasized the significance of vulnerable groups and the need to pay special attention to the human rights of those groups. When people are in unequal situations, treating them in the same manner invariably perpetuates, rather than eradicates, injustices (van Wormer, 2001).

Women as a Vulnerable Group

In societies around the world, female status generally is viewed as inferior and subordinate to male status (Bunch, 1991). Societies have modeled their gender-role expectations on these assumptions of the "natural order" of humankind. Historic social structures reflect a subordination of females to males. This subordination occurs within

the organization and conduct of warfare,

the hierarchical ordering of influential religious institutions,

attribution of political power,

authority of the judiciary, and

influences that shape the content of the law (Bunch, 1991).

The historic subordination, silencing, and imposed inferiority of women are not simply features of society but a condition of society (Cook, 1995). Legal precepts traditionally exclude women from centers of male-gendered power, including legislatures, military institutions, religious orders, universities, medicine, and law.

Women's Rights Are Human Rights

Soon after the adoption of the Universal Declaration of Human Rights in 1948, criticism of its language arose. The declaration refers to "man" and uses the pronoun "he" when discussing individuals. While drafters of the declaration did not appear to intentionally exclude women from human rights, central concerns about the male focus have persisted (Morsink, 1999). Subsequent human rights documents did little to correct the male orientation of human rights until 1980, when delegates from the United Nations endorsed the Convention on the Elimination of All Forms of Discrimination Against Women (United Nations, 1980). Since then, the concept that human rights are for women, as well as men, has gained significant momentum, if not always put into practice.

Convention on the Elimination of All Forms of Discrimination Against Women

The most prominent human rights document concerning the human rights of women is the Convention on the Elimination of All Forms of Discrimination Against Women (CEDAW). This convention became effective in September 1981, and at least 170 countries have approved the convention. The United States is one of the few countries that has not ratified the convention.

Provisions of CEDAW

The focus of CEDAW is elevating the status of women to that of men in the area of human rights. Countries that agree to follow human rights principles contained in CEDAW recognize that the "full and complete development of a country, the welfare of the world, and the cause of peace require the maximum participation of women on equal terms with men in all fields" (United Nations, 1981, preamble). Adherents to CEDAW note "the great contribution of women to the welfare of the family and to the development of society," which so far is not fully recognized.

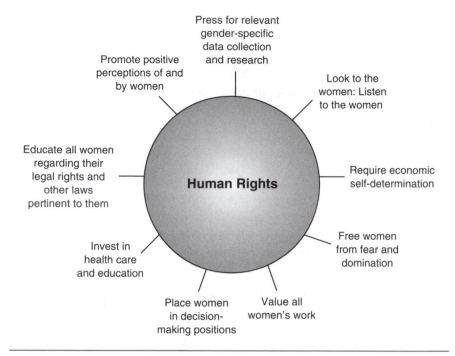

Figure 5.1   Women and Human Rights

Source: Adapted from Wood Wetzel, J. (1996). On the road to Beijing: The evolution of the international women's movement. *Affilia: Journal of Women and Social Work, 11*(22), 221–236.

States "are aware that the role of women in procreation should not be a basis for discrimination but that the upbringing of children requires a sharing of responsibility between men and women and society as a whole." Countries party to CEDAW agree to adopt measures required for elimination of gender discrimination in all its "forms and manifestations."

> **How does CEDAW define gender discrimination?**
>
> Any distinction, exclusion, or restriction made on the basis of sex that has the effect or purpose of impairing or nullifying the recognition, enjoyment, or exercise by women irrespective of their marital status, on a basis of equality of men and women, of human rights and fundamental freedoms in the political, economic, social, cultural, civil, or any other field (Article 1, para. xx).

The definition of gender discrimination contained in CEDAW appears to include more instances of possible discrimination than what U.S. laws interpret as discrimination. By stating that any distinction, exclusion, or restriction has the "effect" as well as "purpose" of discriminating, CEDAW includes unintentional as well as intentional discrimination. Courts in the United States generally have not gone so far in defining discrimination. Some actions having the effect of gender discrimination may be allowable if a legitimate reason exists for the discriminatory treatment.

Other important provisions of CEDAW include

equality of genders within political and public life, including equality in voting (Part II);

equality of men and women in the fields of education, employment, health care, and economic benefits (Part III); and

equality between men and women in civil matters, including the right to conclude contracts and administer property (Part IV).

The underlying purpose of CEDAW is to ensure that women's human rights receive the same attention as those of men. Of course, some may object to special treatment of women as a vulnerable group. The underlying concept of human rights aims to avoid favoring one group over another. However, when one group appears disadvantaged or discriminated against in respect to other groups, human rights principles suggest that assistance be provided to the vulnerable group. To simply say that women enjoy the same human rights as men does not make it so. Consequently, the human rights of women receive additional consideration within a human rights context.

Why no CEDAW in the United States?

Most countries in the world have approved CEDAW and agree to follow provisions contained in the convention. Not the United States, however. Why? Part of the U.S. resistance to approving CEDAW lies within the legal framework for adopting or ratifying international treaties or conventions. In 1980, President Carter signed CEDAW and submitted it for consideration by the U.S. Senate later that year. Ten years later, in 1990, the Senate had only begun to hold hearings on CEDAW. Another ten years passed without action on CEDAW. On International Women's Day in 2000, Jesse Helms (R-NC), the U.S. senator responsible for conducting hearings on CEDAW, vowed never to allow the Senate to vote on CEDAW. Instead, he promised to leave the treaty in the "dustbin" for several more "decades" (Human Rights Watch, 2000, p. 457). Helms even went so far as introducing a Senate resolution rejecting CEDAW (p. 457).

While not all U.S. senators reacted as negatively as Helms to CEDAW, certainly the predominantly white male composition of the Senate plays a role in attitudes toward CEDAW. Even if the Senate were to approve CEDAW, that body has placed four reservations or exceptions to the convention. The United States would not be obligated to

1. assign women to all units of the military;

2. mandate paid maternity leave;

3. legislate equality in the private sector; and

4. ensure comparable worth, or equal pay, for work of equal value.

> The politics of human rights often determines the outcome of whether a particular human right has importance or gathers dust, to paraphrase Senator Helms. The Convention on the Elimination of All Forms of Discrimination Against Women provides an example of how human rights policies within the United States often have little to do with the underlying human rights.

Connection of Women's Rights to the Social Work Profession

A primary mission of the social work profession is to advocate and work on behalf of vulnerable populations. In regard to women, a human rights perspective helps to illuminate the complicated relationship between gender and other aspects of identity such as race, class, religion, age, sexual orientation, disability, culture, and refugee or migrant status (Reichert, 2003). For example, viewing domestic violence against women as a human rights violation cuts through layers of resistance to recognizing that domestic violence has no place anywhere in the world. Culture, religion, class—nothing justifies domestic violence within a human rights context. States and individuals are responsible for this abuse whether committed in public or private.

Women's rights are human rights. By promoting human rights for women, the social work profession can work toward the fulfillment of its primary mission to assist vulnerable populations.

Children as a Vulnerable Group

Perhaps even more than women, children occupy a special role within human rights protections. Children need special protection because of their fragile state of development. Children are readily susceptible to abuse and neglect and often do not have means to defend themselves against these wrongs. In its Convention on the Rights of the Child, the United Nations states that the "child, by reason of his physical and mental maturity, needs special safeguards and care, including appropriate legal protection, before as well as after birth" (United Nations, 1989).

Most, if not all, countries have little difficulty recognizing the vulnerability of children in respect to human rights and other abuses. Throughout the United States, agencies exist with the specific goal of protecting children from abuse and neglect. States have established juvenile courts to hear allegations of abuse and neglect by adults and criminal acts by juveniles. These courts have a primary goal of assisting parents and children and, at least in theory, are not as adversarial as other court proceedings.

Convention on the Rights of the Child

Recognizing that children need special protection, the United Nations adopted the Convention on the Rights of the Child in 1989. This convention specifies basic rights that every child should enjoy. To date, almost every member country of the United Nations has approved this convention—the United States is the exception. President Clinton signed the convention in 1993, but, as with other conventions, the U.S. Senate has failed to approve the convention.

Who Is a Child?

Under the convention, a child "means every human being below the age of eighteen years unless, under the law applicable to the child, majority is attained earlier" (Article 1). This definition of *child* allows states to define a child as having reached adulthood before the age of 18 years if, in a particular instance, the law allows this earlier age of adulthood. In the United States, children are sometimes treated as adults before the age of 18 in the prosecution of serious felony cases.

What Rights Does a Child Have Under the Convention?

The following list summarizes important rights contained in the Convention on the Rights of the Child:

States may not discriminate against a child on the basis of "race, color, sex, language, religion, political or other opinion, national, ethnic, or social origin, property, disability, birth, or other social status" (Article 2, para. 1).

In all actions concerning children, the best interests of the child shall be a primary consideration (Article 3, para. 1). The convention does not expressly define the term "best interest," but leaves the matter open to individual countries. However, states are expected to follow established human rights principles in matters relating to children.

Parents and guardians have primary responsibility for the upbringing of their children but are expected to carry out those responsibilities in a manner consistent with the evolving capacities of the child (Article 5).

A child has the right to a name, nationality, and, as far as possible, to know and be cared for by his or her parents (Article 7, para. 1).

A child has the right to maintain contact with both parents unless that contact is contrary to the child's best interest (Article 10, para. 2).

A child capable of forming his or her own views has the right to express those views with due weight given to the age and maturity of the child (Article 12, para. 1).

A child has the right to "freedom of expression," including the freedom to "seek, receive, and impart information and ideas of all kinds" (Article 13, para. 1). However, a state may restrict this right to protect the reputations of others and the national security, public order, public health, or morals (para. 2).

A child has the right to be free from arbitrary or unlawful interference with his or her privacy, family home, or correspondence (Article 16).

A child has the right to adequate health care (Article 24); treatment for mental health (Article 25); social security (Article 26); adequate standard of living, including nutrition, clothing, and housing (Article 27); and primary education (Article 28).

Education of a child shall include development of the child's personality, talents, and mental and physical abilities to their fullest potential (Article 29, para. 1[a]); respect for human rights (1[b]); development of respect for the child's parents, his or her own cultural identity, language, and values, and his or her own country and other civilizations (1[c]); preparation of the child for responsible life in a free society (1[d]); and development of respect for the natural environment (1[e]).

A child has the right to rest and leisure, recreation, and participation in cultural and artistic life (Article 31).

States must protect the child from hazardous work (Article 32), improper drug use (Article 33), sexual exploitation and abuse (Article 34), and abduction and sale of children (Article 35).

No child shall be subjected to torture or other cruel, inhuman, or degrading treatment or punishment (Article 37[a]).

Neither capital punishment nor life imprisonment without possibility of release shall be imposed for an offense committed by persons younger than 18 years of age (Article 37[a]).

States shall use all feasible measures to prevent children under the age of 15 from participating in hostilities (Article 38, para. 2).

States shall take measures to protect children who are affected by armed conflict (Article 38, para. 4).

A child has the right to be treated with dignity and worth during criminal proceedings against the child (Article 40, para. 1).

The range of rights contained in the convention is broad and far reaching. While almost every country has adopted the convention, respect for all these rights obviously raises issues. Where are the resources to provide every child with adequate health care, including mental health treatment, social security, and an adequate standard of living? Some countries would have difficulties with these rights of the child. Also, does the convention give too much freedom to a child? Under the convention, does a child have the right to tell his or her parents to get lost if he or she gets angry? This interpretation of the convention seems too loose.

Why doesn't the United States adopt the convention, when almost every other country has? Clearly, provisions requiring adequate health care and standard of living run afoul of U.S. policies, as do the restrictions on juvenile executions. Essentially, the failure of the U.S. Senate to adopt the convention illustrates (once again) the reluctance of the Senate to adopt laws that would require a rethinking of the status quo. In the meantime, the United States distances itself ever further from other countries in the area of children and human rights.

Victims of Racism as a Vulnerable Group

No violation of human dignity ranks as destructive as that of racism, which can manifest itself from discrimination at the workplace to outright genocide. In 1978, the United Nations, through its branch known as the UN Educational, Scientific and Cultural Organization (UNESCO), addressed the problems associated with racism:

All human groups, whatever their composition or ethnic origin, contribute according to their own genius to the progress of the civilizations and cultures. However, racism, racial discrimination, colonialism, and apartheid continue to afflict the world in ever-changing forms, a result of government and administrative practices contrary to the principles of human rights. Injustice and contempt for human beings leads to the exclusion, humiliation, and exploitation, or to the forced assimilation, of the members of disadvantaged groups. (United Nations, 1978, preamble).

Specific provisions to fight racism include recognition of the following:

All human beings belong to a single species and are descended from a common stock. They are born equal in dignity and rights and all form an integral part of humanity (United Nations, 1978, Article 1, para. 1).

All individuals and groups have the right to be different, to consider themselves as different, and to be regarded as such. However, the diversity of lifestyles and the right to be different may not, in any circumstances, serve as a pretext for racial prejudice; they may not justify any discriminatory practice, nor provide a ground for the policy of apartheid, which is the extreme form of racism (para. 2).

Differences between achievements of the different peoples are entirely attributable to geographical, historical, political, economic, social, and cultural factors. Such differences can in no case serve as a pretext for any rank-ordered classifications of nations or peoples (para. 5).

The purpose of these provisions is to make the point that no race or group may elevate itself over another. Yet, from birth many people are taught to compare themselves to others from different ethnic groups and countries, with a hidden or even open agenda of highlighting superior traits. This type of education ensures the continuation of discrimination against other people on the basis of being racially different.

The United States: Greatest Country in the World!

Almost from their day of birth, U.S. citizens hear about the greatness of the United States. Politicians and citizens are constantly saying that the United

States is the greatest country on Earth. The implication is that, because Americans are citizens of the United States, they are the greatest people. Considering the UNESCO declaration on race and racial prejudice, should U.S. politicians really go around bragging about the superiority of the United States and, by extension, U.S. citizens? Probably not.

When Americans claim that the United States is the greatest country on Earth, other countries obviously take offense to this claim. Not only does the ranking of the United States as superior simply antagonize others, it does not follow the spirit of the UNESCO declaration.

Even before the 1978 UNESCO declaration, the United Nations had presented a Convention on the Elimination of All Forms of Racial Discrimination (United Nations, 1966a). This convention contains provisions similar to those in the 1978 declaration.

Persons With Disabilities as a Vulnerable Group

Another group receiving special protection within a human rights context is that of persons with disabilities, including mental illness. In 1975, the United Nations adopted a declaration on the rights of persons with disabilities (United Nations, 1975). The declaration defines a person with a disability as

any person unable to ensure by himself or herself, wholly or partly, the necessities of a normal individual and/or social life, as a result of deficiency, either congenital or not, in his or her physical or mental capabilities (para 1).

Persons with disabilities are entitled to

measures designed to enable them to become as self-reliant as possible (para. 5);

medical, psychological, and functional treatment, including prosthetic and orthetic appliances (para. 6);

medical and social rehabilitations, education, vocational training and rehabilitation, counseling, placement services, and other services to assist in social integration (para. 6);

economic and social security and a decent level of living. People with disabilities have the right to secure and retain employment or to engage in a useful, productive, and remunerative occupation and to join trade unions (para. 7);

live with their families and to participate in all social, creative, or recreational activities (para. 9);

protection against exploitation and treatment of a discriminatory, abusive, or degrading nature (para. 10).

In addition to the previously listed human rights principles, in 1991, the United Nations adopted a document listing principles for persons with mental illnesses, which states that mental health care shall be part of the health and social care system (United Nations, 1991). Persons with mental illness shall also receive protection from discrimination and other exploitation (paras. 3 and 4).

As with many human rights documents, the circumstances proposed in the declaration on persons with disabilities resemble an idealistic situation. In many countries, resources simply would not be available to provide all the services required to satisfy the listed human rights. However, in other countries, the powers that be may decide not to allocate sufficient funds for persons with disabilities. Human rights policies can easily fall victim to politics and power structures that social workers inevitably find frustrating.

Persons With HIV-AIDS as a Vulnerable Group

The current prevalence of persons with HIV-AIDS has become a major concern the world over (United Nations, 2004). This disease afflicts all parts of the world, with particular severity in sub-Saharan Africa and regions of Asia. Persons with HIV-AIDS often encounter discrimination, especially because of the association with homophobia and prostitutes.

In 2001, the United Nations adopted a resolution to combat AIDS (Swarns, 2001). The resolution specified goals to be met by various timelines. By 2003, countries proposed to

develop national strategies and financing plans that confront stigma, silence, and denial and eliminate discrimination against people living with HIV-AIDS; and

develop programs to prevent HIV-AIDS and to treat those afflicted with the disease.

By the year 2005, countries proposed to

institute a wide range of prevention programs, aimed at encouraging responsible sexual behavior, including abstinence and fidelity, and expanded access to male and female condoms and sterile injecting equipment;

develop strategies to provide access to affordable medicines to treat the disease;

reach a target of annual expenditures of between $7 billion and $10 billion in low- and middle-income countries for care, treatment, and support for those with the disease (Neuffer, 2001, p. B8).

Despite the proposed goals to be met by 2005, "rates of [HIV/AIDS] infection are still on the rise in many countries in Sub-Saharan Africa. Indeed, in 2003 alone, an estimated 3 million people in the region become newly infected. Most alarmingly, new epidemics appear to be advancing unchecked in other regions, notably Eastern Europe and Asia" (United Nations, 2004, p. 8). Clearly, to ignore the extraordinarily wide reach of the HIV problem would be disastrous.

Older Persons as a Vulnerable Group

Persons aged 60 and older often find themselves in circumstances that render them less active within society. At this time of their lives, many people begin to think about withdrawing from employment and retiring. Income levels may drop off at retirement time and, in many countries, the elderly often become dependent on children or other relatives. Attention to the needs and care of the elderly can easily subside, as their presence becomes diminished within the mainstream of society. In addition, older persons may lose mental and physical capabilities, leaving them vulnerable to financial, physical, and other types of exploitation.

In 1999, the United Nations issued a document known as Principles for the Older Person (United Nations, 1999). The document emphasized that "priority attention" should be given to the "situation of older persons" and referred specifically to five areas:

Independence—Older persons should have access to adequate food, water, shelter, clothing, and health care through the provision of income, family and community support, and self-help. Older persons should have the opportunity to work and to participate in determining when to retire. Older persons should be able to reside at home for as long as possible.

Participation—Older persons should remain integrated in society, participate actively in the formulation and implementation of policies that directly affect their well-being, and share their knowledge and skills with younger generations. Older persons should be able to serve as volunteers in positions appropriate to their interests and capabilities and to form associations.

Care—Older persons should benefit from family and community care and have access to adequate and appropriate health care. Older persons should have access to social and legal services to enhance their autonomy, protection, and care.

Self-fulfillment—Older persons should be able to pursue opportunities for the full development of their potential. Older persons should have access to the educational, cultural, spiritual, and recreational resources of society.

Dignity—Older persons should be able to live in dignity and security and be free of exploitation and physical or mental abuse (United Nations, 1999).

As the population of the world continues to age, voices of the elderly will become ever louder in respect to human rights. Because the vulnerability of old age afflicts every society, recognition of human rights concerning the elderly may be the easiest to accomplish.

Gays and Lesbians as a Vulnerable Group

The United Nations has yet to issue any human rights documents recognizing gays and lesbians as a vulnerable group. Because the United Nations includes many countries that discriminate against gays and lesbians for religious or cultural reasons, finding harmony on this issue has been elusive. Countries may claim that homosexuality is against religion and culture and therefore not entitled to protection under any human rights theory.

Certainly, however, the Universal Declaration of Human Rights contradicts discrimination against gays and lesbians. After all, a major premise of that declaration states: "All people are born free and equal in dignity and rights" (United Nations, 1948). Unfortunately, many countries fail to attribute this premise to gays and lesbians. This issue will undoubtedly be a major concern of human rights advocates in future years.

Conclusion

Some human rights advocates and critics dislike the separation of particular groups for special treatment. This violates the notion that because human rights apply to everyone, no individual or group merits special attention. In theory, that makes sense. In reality, however, without providing additional protection to certain groups, it becomes too easy to discriminate or otherwise exploit those groups. For that reason, human rights principles have created the concept of vulnerable groups.

Exercises

Exercise 1: Examining the Concept of "Vulnerable" Groups

The purpose of this exercise is to examine the concept of vulnerable groups and question the need for such a category within a human rights context. You can do this exercise alone or in a group.

1. List your own definition of the word *vulnerable*. Use a dictionary or similar resource tool to create your definition. Relate that definition to an individual or group. For instance, a dictionary might define *vulnerable* as open to attack or damage. Therefore, if someone is vulnerable, he or she is open to attack or damage.

2. What is your reaction to this definition? How do you feel towards the concept of vulnerable groups or individuals? Do you support the idea of vulnerable individuals or groups within the broader society? Why or why not?

3. Do you feel that you belong to a vulnerable group? Why or why not? If you do feel that you are part of a vulnerable group, do you feel any solidarity with that group? What are your thoughts about the group? Do you wish that you were not part of that group?

4. Do you feel that a vulnerable individual or group should receive special treatment? Why or why not? If you feel that special treatment is acceptable, what type of special treatment would you grant the vulnerable individual or group?

5. Based on the vulnerable groups discussed in this chapter, are there any groups that you feel should not be considered vulnerable? Explain your reasons.

Exercise 2: Women's Rights Are Human Rights

The purpose of this exercise is to examine the statement "Women's rights are human rights" and critically analyze claims that women are not treated equally to men.

1. Discuss the meaning of the sentence "Women's rights are human rights." What do you feel this statement means? Do you believe that women are treated less equally than men? Is there any question that women's rights do not receive the same status as human rights? What rights are meant by this statement?

2. List at least five different situations in which you feel the status or circumstances of women differ from that of men within the broader society. (For instance, most nurses in hospitals are women; women occupy most clerical roles in offices; women tend to be the primary caregivers of young children.) Do these situations necessarily mean that women are discriminated against? Do some of the situations simply reflect the way things are: men are men and women are women?

3. From the list you created, select situations where you definitely believe discrimination against women is the cause of the situation. How would you remedy the situation? What measures would you take to change the situation? Would you pass a law to remedy the situation?

4. Take the position that laws are necessary to protect women from discrimination. How would you write those laws? Would you write a generic law that attempts to cover every possible instance of discrimination? Or would you write laws that deal with specific situations of discrimination?

5. Write a general law against gender discrimination of any type, including discrimination against men.

6. Write specific laws against gender discrimination that you noted in number 3 of this exercise.

7. Do you feel that laws are effective in resolving gender discrimination issues? What other remedies or tools might be as effective as laws in dealing with discrimination?

Exercise 3: Women and HIV-AIDS

The purpose of this exercise is to analyze recent statistics indicating that women are increasingly becoming the majority of HIV-infected people around the world.

1. Consider the following headline from the *Economist,* a weekly newsmagazine: "Women will soon be a majority of those infected with HIV. Male chauvinism is largely to blame" ("New Face of AIDS," 2004, p. 82). Without actually reading the article, what reaction do you have to the headline? Are you curious as to why "male chauvinism" might be the major cause of women becoming the majority of HIV victims? What reasons could you think of that would prompt such a headline?

2. The article in the *Economist* was based on a report by the United Nations (2004). Here are some details within that report:

a. The women's rights movement and the AIDS movement must come together if the world is to win the fight against HIV.

b. Women and girls in all parts of the world are increasingly becoming infected by HIV, especially in less economically developed regions. However, while economic status may play a role in resources devoted to preventing and treating infected persons, many factors determine the infection rate, with gender inequality being a major factor.

c. Current prevention strategy means little to the millions who lack the power to say no to sex or to insist on condom use.

d. The inequality that women face—from poverty and stunted education to rape and denial of women's inheritance and property rights—is a major obstacle to victory over the virus.

3. After examining the details of the report, do you feel that HIV affects you in your environment? Is HIV now something that is more a "poor man's or woman's" disease? Do you feel that discrimination against women is a major cause of the HIV problem? List aspects of this discrimination.

4. What measures would you take to assist women in preventing infection of HIV? Consider existing power structures in your answer.

Exercise 4: Women and the Convention on the Elimination of All Forms of Discrimination Against Women (CEDAW)

The purpose of this exercise is to familiarize you with provisions of CEDAW.

1. Do you feel that the United States should approve CEDAW and follow its provisions? Do you believe that the four "reservations" stated by the U.S. Senate in respect to CEDAW are reasonable?

2. Analyze the following statement: "The United States has its own laws against discrimination and does not need another set of laws such as those contained in CEDAW."

3. On a sheet of paper, write the following:

   Convention on the Elimination of All Forms of Discrimination Against Women

   Advantages   Disadvantages

4. Using the format in number 3, list all the advantages and disadvantages of CEDAW you can think of. Have you listed more advantages than disadvantages, or is it the other way around? If you have listed more advantages, what are the reasons? If disadvantages, why? What do you feel would be the most important advantage of CEDAW? The most important disadvantage? On what facts or statistics do you base these views?

5. Do you believe there would be any benefit to the social work profession if the United States approved CEDAW? Do you feel that much would change, or would situations stay the same?

Exercise 5: The Child and Human Rights

The purpose of this exercise is to link human rights to children. As with many of the exercises in this book, you may do the exercise alone or in a group.
Respond to the following questions:

a. What are human rights?

b. How does having human rights affect family life?

c. What are your feelings about children having rights?

d. What do you know about the UN Convention on the Rights of the Child?

e. What is a basic human right that your (or any) child has?

f. What do you feel is your responsibility in maintaining rights for your (or other) child?

g. Do you feel that your community is "child friendly," meaning it takes into consideration needs of children? For example, are there parks with playground equipment, swimming pools, and organized activities for children?

h. Do you feel that the state and federal governments do enough for children? What about private organizations, such as churches?

i. What would you do to improve the community environment for children? The state and national environment?

Exercise 6: Exploring the UN Convention on the Rights of the Child

The purpose of this exercise is to familiarize you with the UN Convention on the Rights of the Child. Keep in mind that the U.S. government has refused to accept some provisions in this convention and will not approve the convention, whereas almost every other country has.

Part I: Examining the Convention

Respond the best you can to the following questions about the Convention on the Rights of the Child. To answer these questions, you can refer to information provided in this chapter, the actual convention, and other outside resources. If you feel that the convention is not necessary (in your response to Exercise b) then list your reasons for this response.

a. What is the Convention on the Rights of the Child?

b. Why is a document describing children's rights necessary?

c. How does the convention define a child?

d. Will the convention replace the laws in a particular country?

e. Who checks to see if countries are meeting the standards set by the convention?

f. Does the convention take responsibility for children away from their parents and give more authority to governments?

g. Article 12 of the convention says that children have the right to express their views in all matters affecting them. Does this mean that children can now tell their parents what to do?

h. Will the convention affect the way that parents pass on religious and moral teachings to their children?

i. Does the convention encourage respect for others along with children's rights?

j. Can children still be expected to help their parents with chores?

k. What does the convention say about the ways that parents discipline their children?

l. Will the convention affect authority and discipline in schools?

m. Doesn't the convention raise rights issues that children are too young to understand?

After writing your answers to these questions, discuss answers with others if you are doing the exercise in a group. Consider how your answers may differ from those of others.

Part II: Responses to Questions by UNICEF

Here are responses to the above questions provided by the United Nations (UNICEF, 2005). Compare their responses with yours.

a. What is the Convention on the Rights of the Child?

The Convention on the Rights of the Child, adopted by the United Nations in 1989, spells out the basic human rights to which children everywhere are entitled: the right to survival; the right to the development of their full physical and mental potential; the right to protection from influences that are harmful to their development; and the right to participation in family, cultural, and social life.

The convention protects these rights by setting minimum standards that governments must meet in providing health care, education, and legal and social services to children in their countries.

The convention is the result of 10 years of consultations and negotiations between government officials, lawyers, health care professionals, social workers, educators, children's support groups, NGOs, and religious groups from around the world.

More countries have ratified the convention than any other human rights treaty in history—as of November 2005, 192 countries had ratified the convention (UNICEF, 2005).

b. Why is a document describing children's rights necessary?

Although many nations have laws relating to children's welfare and rights, the reality is that too many nations do not live up to their own minimum standards in these areas. Children suffer from poverty, homelessness, abuse, neglect, preventable diseases, and unequal access to education and justice systems that do not recognize their special needs; children of minority groups are often particularly affected. These are problems that occur in both industrialized and developing countries.

The convention, and its acceptance by so many countries, has heightened recognition of the fundamental human dignity of all children and the urgency of ensuring their well-being and development. The convention makes clear the idea that a basic quality of life should be the rights of all children, rather than a privilege enjoyed by a few.

c. How does the convention define a child?

The convention defines a child as a person under the age of 18, unless the laws of a particular country set the legal age for adulthood as younger than 18.

d. Will the convention replace the laws in a particular country?

When countries ratify the convention, they agree to review their laws relating to children. This involves assessing their social services, legal, health, and educational systems, as well as levels of funding for these services. Governments are then required to take all necessary steps to ensure that the minimum standards set by the convention in these areas are being met. In some instances, this may require changing existing laws or creating new ones. Legislative changes to satisfy the convention are not imposed from the outside, but come about through the same process by which any law is created or reformed within a country.

e. Who checks to see if countries are meeting the standards set by the convention?

Countries that ratify the convention must report to a Committee on the Rights of the Child. A country must submit a report to the committee within two years after the country's ratification of the convention and every five years after the initial report. The committee examines how well governments are meeting provisions of the convention and does not monitor behavior of individual parents.

f. Does the convention take responsibility for children away from their parents and give more authority to governments?

No. The convention upholds the primary importance of the parents' role and refers to it repeatedly. The convention says that governments must respect the responsibility of parents for providing appropriate guidance to their children, including guidance as to how children exercise their rights. Governments have an obligation to protect and assist families in fulfilling their essential role as nurturers of children.

g. Article 12 of the convention says that children have the right to express their views in all matters affecting them. Does this mean that children can now tell their parents what to do?

No. The clear intent of this article is to encourage adults to listen to the opinions of children and involve them in decision making, not to give children authority over adults. This article does not interfere with parents' right and responsibility to express their views on matters affecting their children. The convention also recognizes that participation of children in decision making must occur in a manner that is appropriate to the child's level of maturity (e.g., opinions of teenagers would usually be given more weight than preschoolers).

h. Will the convention affect the way that parents pass on religious and moral teachings to their children?

The convention respects the rights and duties of parents in providing religious and moral guidance to their children. Religious groups around the world have expressed support for the convention, which indicates that it in no way prevents parents from bringing their children up within a religious tradition.

At the same time, the convention recognizes that as children mature and are able to form their own views, some may question certain religious practices or cultural traditions. The convention supports children's rights to examine their beliefs, but it also states that their right to express their beliefs implies respect for the rights and freedoms of others.

i. Does the convention encourage respect for others along with children's rights?

Yes, the convention is explicit about the fact that young people have not only rights but also the responsibility to respect the rights of others, especially of their parents. It states that one of the aims of education should be the development of respect for the child's parents and their values and culture. Rather than creating conflict between the rights of parents and the rights of children, the convention encourages an atmosphere conducive to dialogue and mutual respect.

j. Can children still be expected to help their parents with chores?

The convention protects children from economic exploitation and from work that is hazardous to their health or interferes with their education. It was never intended to regulate smaller details of home life, and there is nothing in the convention that prohibits parents from expecting their children to help out at home in ways that are safe and appropriate to their age.

At times, children's help can also be essential in the running of a family farm or business. However, if they involve their children in such work, parents must be aware of the laws that regulate child labor in their countries. If children help out in a family farm or business, the convention requires that the tasks they do be safe and suited to their level of development. Children's work should not jeopardize any of the other rights guaranteed by the convention, including the right to education or the right to rest, leisure, play, and recreation.

k. What does the convention say about the ways that parents discipline their children?

The convention makes it clear that children shall be protected from all forms of mental or physical violence or maltreatment. Thus, any forms of discipline involving such violence are unacceptable. In most countries, laws are already in place that define what sorts of punishment are considered excessive or abusive. It is up to each country to review these laws in light of the convention.

The convention does not specify what discipline techniques parents should use, but it strongly supports parents in providing guidance and direction to their children. There are ways to discipline children that are nonviolent, are appropriate to the child's level of development, and take the best interests of the child into consideration. Such forms of discipline are effective in helping children learn about family and social expectations for their behavior.

l. Will the convention affect authority and discipline in schools?

The convention places a high value on education, devoting two articles to this issue. And common sense would indicate that schools must be run in an orderly way if children are to benefit from them. But order need not be imposed through the use of violence.

The convention specifies that any form of school discipline should take into account the child's human dignity. Therefore, governments must ensure that school administrators review their discipline policies and eliminate any discipline practices involving physical or mental violence, abuse, or neglect.

m. Doesn't the convention raise rights issues that children are too young to understand?

Children's interest in rights issues and the way in which parents handle those issues will vary depending on the age of the child. Helping children to understand those rights does not mean pushing them to make choices with consequences they are too young to handle. The convention encourages parents to deal with rights issues with their children in a manner consistent with the evolving capacities of the child.

Compare your responses from Part I to those from UNICEF in Part II. Do you agree with every response by UNICEF? With which responses do you agree or disagree? Do you feel that their responses give too much "power" to children?

After a careful review of the convention, do you feel that the United States should approve the convention or continue to ignore it? Give reasons for your response.

Exercise 7: Racism and Human Rights

The purpose of this exercise is to examine issues associated with racism. This is a group exercise.

1. The facilitator (professor/teacher/group leader) assigns to each member of the group an ethnic classification that must differ from the actual classification. For instance, an African American would be assigned an Asian American classification, or a white student would be assigned a Hispanic or African American classification.

2. Along with the ethnic classification, the facilitator lists an employment or other economic/social status of the member. For instance, the facilitator might assign a white student to be an African American lawyer. The more members within the group, the more diverse the classifications.

3. After assigning every group member a different ethnic classification/status, the facilitator will allow each member a few minutes to imagine and write down specific details of his or her family life, including working environment, location and type of residence, cultural activities, and hobbies. Of course, these details can only be imagined—however, the group member should draw on everything he or she knows about the new ethnic origin to create these details. In other words, the group member must try to "fill the shoes" of a member of the assigned ethnic classification.

4. After group members have "created" their new existence, the facilitator gives them about 15 minutes to interact with other members, talking about where they live, what they do for a living, and so on. Each member would have a label clearly indicating his or her ethnic classification/status.

5. After 15 minutes of interaction, the facilitator then questions group members on how they felt about their new ethnic classification/status. Specific questions for discussion would include the following:
    a. Did anyone feel inhibited by their classification/status?
    b. How much previous contact had a member had with individuals of the new classification?
    c. What formed the basis for shaping a member's new identity? Previous contact with individuals within the ethnic classification? Television or other media portrayals of those individuals? Stereotypes?
    d. Did anyone feel that others were reluctant to approach him or her because of the classification?
    e. Did anyone feel reluctant to approach another member because of the classification?
    f. What reactions did members experience?
    g. Were members proud of their new ethnic identity?
    h. Did members of the group who actually belong to the ethnic group being portrayed by other members feel that those members portrayed their actual ethnic origins accurately?

6. After the group discussion, each member writes a short two-page essay on how they view their true ethnic classification within broader society. The essay needs to cover aspects of this exercise, with particular attention to these issues: How do you feel about your classification? feel superior, equal, inferior? Do you wish you had a different ethnic origin? If so, why? Do you perceive bias or prejudice from others on the basis of your ethnic origin? (modified from Human Rights Resource Center, 2005)

Adapted from the Human Rights Education Series (1998–2006) published by the University of Minnesota Human Rights Resource Center, http://www1.umn.edu/humanrts/edumat/hreduseries/default.shtm

Exercise 8: Examining Disability Within a Human Rights Context

The purpose of this exercise is to analyze aspects of persons with disabilities within a human rights environment.

*   Refer to the 1975 UN declaration on the rights of persons with disabilities (United Nations, 1975). Within a ranking system of 1 to 10, with 10 being the most important, how do you rank the various human rights for persons with disabilities (paras. 5 through 10)?
*   Within the context of all the "vulnerable" groups discussed in this chapter, how would you rank persons with disabilities? For instance, should as much attention or resources be devoted to persons with disabilities as to children?
*   How many persons do you know (include yourself if relevant) who have disabilities? From your perspective, would you consider those persons disadvantaged in comparison to those without apparent disabilities? Why or why not?

- Do you believe that the government has an obligation to provide benefits to persons with disabilities listed in the 1975 UN Declaration?
- Is it economically realistic to expect every country to take measures specified in the 1975 declaration?

Exercise 9: HIV-AIDS as a Human Rights Issue

This exercise relates to HIV-AIDS as a human rights issue.

- What specific human rights provisions from the Universal Declaration or international covenants relate to HIV-AIDS?
- Has HIV-AIDS become a poor country's problem? Do richer countries, with lower infection rates than poorer countries, have an obligation to assist the poorer countries in fighting HIV? Refer to specific human rights provisions.
- What is your reaction to this statement: "HIV-AIDS is the greatest problem faced by the world today." Do you agree with it? Use factual resource materials to support your position.

Exercise 10: Older Persons and Human Rights

The purpose of this exercise is to examine treatment of older persons as a vulnerable group. The exercise should be completed within a group of at least six persons.

1. A facilitator (e.g., teacher) selects four members of a group to role-play persons older than 60 years of age. The four group members are to put themselves in the positions of one of the following individuals:

Joan, who is 70 years of age, in good health, is employed by a local school as a social worker who counsels students. The school has a policy of allowing any employee to work until age 65, but then can decide whether to terminate that employment if "conditions" justify that termination. Each year, the school has reviewed the employment record of Joan to determine whether to extend her employment. Finally, the school decides to terminate Joan's employment, but Joan objects.

John, who is 67 years of age, is divorced and retired from employment because of a debilitating disease that requires daily assistance in his home. John lives alone and has to rely on others for assistance, which includes doing dishes and help with bathing, cooking, and other daily tasks. John currently receives home care, but occasionally this care is insufficient to provide all of John's needs. John's two adult children want to place John in a nursing home, something to which John vehemently objects.

Beulah and Horace are an elderly married couple in their 80s who are still able to maintain a household without outside assistance. However, maintaining this household does require significant effort by Beulah and Horace. Beulah now wishes to live in assisted living but Horace is against moving.

---

2. The remaining members of the group will serve as a committee of social work-
    ers assigned to help these individuals and other relevant parties to work out
    their differences. This committee must refer to human rights principles in assist-
    ing the individuals. Refer to the 1999 Principles for the Older Person (United
    Nations, 1999).

3. The facilitator will allow each member playing a role to present reasons, relying
    on human rights principles, before the committee as to why he or she took
    the stated position. For instance, Joan would state reasons why she should be
    allowed to keep working.

4. During the presentations, committee members can ask questions of the
    presenter.

5. After each of the three presentations (Horace and Beulah would be one pre-
    sentation, although each would speak), the committee must evaluate the situa-
    tions and provide written recommendations based on human rights principles.

6. The entire group then discusses the written recommendations of the commit-
    tee. Specifically, the group should focus on the following points:
    a. Are there any competing human rights involved in the recommendations? For
        instance, does self-determination conflict with safety concerns?
    b. Should the hiring rights of an employer prevail over the desires of an elderly
        employee?
    c. What issues of human dignity enter into the previously discussed situations?
    d. Within a marriage, should one spouse be allowed to rely on human rights
        principles to support a decision? Does the entity of marriage exclude human
        rights?
    e. What are the interests of the broader society within each of the previously
        discussed situations?
    f. Do the recommendations follow human rights principles?

Exercise 11: Are Gay Rights Special?

The purpose of this exercise is to examine gay, lesbian, bisexual, and transgender
(GLBT) rights as human rights.

Part I: Collecting Articles on GLBT Rights

1. About one or two weeks before beginning Part II of the exercise, collect at least
    five articles from newspapers, news magazines, and Web sites about GLBT rights.
    Articles about these rights might describe how they are denied, demanded, or
    respected. These articles can describe any part of the world, though most will
    probably focus on the United States.

2. Topics of the articles might include the following:
    *   Local or state initiatives for or against gay rights
    *   Child custody or adoption issues
    *   Same-sex marriage
    *   Gay-straight alliances or curricular issues in schools

- Refugee or immigration issues
- Sexual minorities in the military, ministry, or other job
- Out or outed celebrities
- Gay bashing or hate crimes
- Public opinion polls
- Reports on gay pride parades or gay pride month
- Book, television, or movie reviews

Part II: Making a Human Rights Analysis

1. Using the articles you have collected, describe what rights were denied, demanded, or respected. Possible rights might include the following:
   - Right to privacy
   - Right to form a family
   - Right to employment
   - Right to housing
   - Right to an identity
   - Right to be equal before the law
   - Right to medical care and information
   - Right to an education
   - Right to free speech
   - Right to assembly
   - Right to be free of cruel and unusual punishment
   - Right to a fair trial

2. In addition to describing rights denied, demanded, or respected in the articles you collected, describe those rights within the following situations:
   - A mother loses custody of her child in a divorce judgment because she is a lesbian.
   - State legislators discuss amending state law to define marriage as only between a man and a woman.
   - A student is kicked out of the Naval Academy because he admits he is gay.
   - Two male sports celebrities write a book about their relationship.
   - A state review committee demands that health textbook publishers delete any references to homosexuality.
   - A woman kisses another woman on a network television show.
   - A man is "bashed" on a Saturday night by a group of teenagers shouting, "Faggot."
   - A teacher refuses to allow students to use words like *fag* or *homo* in her classroom.
   - The police in an East European nation keep a file of men and women they suspect are gay and lesbian.
   - The military in a Latin American nation torture a man because he is gay.
   - The city grants a permit to hold a GLBT parade.
   - Amnesty International calls for state governments to drop laws that criminalize homosexuality.
   - A lesbian is fired when her boss learns about her sexual orientation.
   - Students at a local high school form a gay-straight alliance.

Part III: Connecting GLBT Rights to Human Rights

After you have completed Part II and described rights denied, demanded, or respected in your articles and situations listed earlier, look for those rights in the Universal Declaration of Human Rights. Then write down whether the Universal Declaration guarantees those rights or whether language exists in the declaration that would preclude sexual minorities from those rights. Write a final report and consider the following questions:

- What GLBT rights respected are guaranteed in the Universal Declaration?
- What GLBT rights demanded are guaranteed in the declaration?
- What GLBT rights denied are guaranteed in the declaration?
- Were any of the demanded, denied, or respected rights *not* mentioned in the declaration?
- Using the Universal Declaration as a reference, how would you respond to someone who says, "Lesbian, gay, bisexual, and transgender people are asking for special rights?" (modified from Human Rights Resource Center, 2005)

Adapted from the Human Rights Education Series (1998–2006) published by the University of Minnesota Human Rights Resource Center, http://www1.umn.edu/humanrts/edumat/hreduseries/default.shtm

CHAPTER 6

Cultural Relativism

Most people simply do not appreciate being told what to do by outsiders. Certainly not U.S. citizens, who stand practically alone in their reluctance to adopt conventions drafted by the United Nations on human rights. In no way is the United Nations going to tell the United States how to run its affairs.

Of course, the United Nations as a group rarely intervenes in the affairs of others. Usually this occurs only in the context of a peacekeeping mission in some military hotspot. What the United Nations does is provide guidance on principles deemed important by its almost universal world membership. The United Nations does not force other countries to follow these principles. Only if a country wishes to adopt or ratify various human rights conventions do those conventions become law within a particular country. In other words, the United Nations does not dictate to others what they should do within the context of human rights or other principles.

Unfortunately, a common U.S. portrait of the United Nations appears to be that of an incompetent, corrupt, and unfriendly group with a primary purpose to counter U.S. policies (Gold, 2004). Considering that the United Nations includes countries from all over the world with diverse interests, it only makes sense that views emanating from the United Nations might, at times, diverge from those of the United States. However, instead of criticizing this situation, U.S. citizens should carefully examine what occurs in the United Nations, especially in regard to human rights. Whenever the United Nations issues a resolution, convention, or other document on human rights, the background leading to completion of the document has included diverse opinions and views. The document does not simply materialize out of thin air and without extensive debate. The underlying goal of the United Nations is to create universal rules that all countries, including the United States, can apply to their particular situations.

The United States is no different from most countries when it comes to outside interference in their affairs—they do not like it. From this perspective, the universal concept of human rights immediately encounters a legitimate obstacle—the local cultural, religious, and legal norms. Why should any country accept rules that have been devised by a world body whose members often appear to have little in common? The response goes back to the background leading to the creation of the United Nations and its Universal Declaration of Human Rights. Genocide, poverty, unemployment, colonization, and other afflictions led to a better form of world government, one that would at least help prevent or ease these afflictions. No single nation could do that. Only by working together and agreeing on a universal set of principles could all nations obtain some success in creating a better world.

Of course, universal principles impose responsibility upon nations of the world to enforce those principles. It is this responsibility that often becomes a sticking point when local cultural norms contradict established human rights principles. Which prevails—local culture or broad statements of human rights? While no simple answer exists to this question, some general rules do apply to the issue of cultural relativism.

Cultural Relativism—What Is It?

The term "cultural relativism" often creates confusion in discussions of human rights. Simply stated, cultural relativism refers to a view that all cultures are equal and universal values become secondary when examining cultural norms. No outside value is superior to that of the local culture. If the local culture allows female genital mutilation, then the human right prohibiting cruel or degrading treatment should not prevent the genital mutilation. If the culture accepts genital mutilation, then no outside principle should overrule the cultural norm.

When an uninsured American fails to obtain adequate medical treatment for an illness because he or she has insufficient income, the local culture and legal system accepts that result—even though the Universal Declaration of Human Rights states that everyone is entitled to adequate medical care. This is another example of cultural relativism. The result seems appalling. How can someone be denied medical care? Imagine, though, if the United Nations tried to intervene by saying this was a human right violation? The United Nations would get nowhere.

The problem with an uncritical acceptance of cultural relativism lies within the failure to examine the societal structure creating the cultural norm. Who determines culture? As with many cases of cultural relativism within a human rights context, the power to define cultural, religious, and legal norms controls the outcome. For that reason, social workers need to avoid an uncritical acceptance of culture over universal human rights principles.

Guidelines for Analyzing Cultural Relativism

In a human rights context, guidelines can help identify and resolve conflicts between local cultural, religious, and legal norms and universal principles of human rights. For purposes of illustrating these guidelines, consider the following example:

> Social policies in the United States do not guarantee economic human rights, including food, shelter, and medical care. While some assistance in these areas may be available through private donors, government, relatives, and other avenues, U.S. cultural and legal standards do not view these circumstances as human rights. Why does this situation exist in the United States, one of the world's richest countries?

The following guidelines will analyze this example of cultural relativism from a human rights viewpoint.

- *Examine closely the history of the cultural practice.* What is the background or history leading to the cultural norm that conflicts with a particular human right? What apparent rationale or reasons have created the cultural norm? A critical analysis of this question would require reference to the ideals behind the founding of this country and their emphasis on the individual's right of freedom. This emphasis on the individual has led to a cultural norm that government does not owe anyone a living. The very idea of "welfare" may antagonize people even if they need economic assistance. However, historical background does not always provide a complete picture of a cultural practice. The original rationale for a cultural practice may no longer have relevance because of historical changes in a society. More and more people in the United States depend on the government for basic services. Where would the elderly be without the government health care program of Medicare? The high cost of health care would prevent many elderly from even

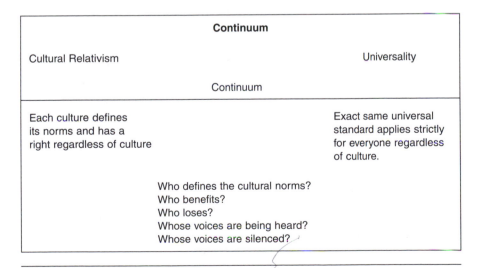

Figure 6.1   Cultural Relativism Continuum

seeking medical care. The famed "rugged individualism" of Americans simply has much less relevance now than it did two hundred years ago. Essentially, the underlying rationale for not providing economic human rights to everyone has been diluted through historical evolution. Americans currently rely on government to provide many services—to ignore the role of government in providing a basic economic existence for everyone seems dated. Yet, the myth of independence persists, with government refusing to update certain social policies to reflect changed social conditions. By contemporary standards, the use of cultural relativism to justify a neglect of economic human rights seems misguided.

• *Examine the power brokers who determine the cultural norm.* Has a democratic process of any kind been instrumental in establishing the cultural norm in question? After analyzing the history and background of a cultural practice, the next step in placing the practice into a human rights context requires analysis of who has actually determined the cultural norm. U.S. social policies generally provide meager assistance to low-income individuals, and social workers need to determine the source of these policies. Do people with minimal resources actually support or tacitly agree with the status quo? Have they been part of the decision-making process in deciding social policies? Certainly within the United States, a democratic process exists where citizens do have some input into policies. In spite of deficiencies within the voting system, the government generally allows people to vote. In other words, participation in a democratic process is available to the poor in the United States, unlike circumstances in dictatorships. Does this mean that the cultural practice of not guaranteeing economic human rights is acceptable because a democratically elected government sanctions this situation? The problem with accepting this position lies in the finer points of U.S. democracy that actually are not so democratic.

Elected officials often construct social policies on the basis of lobby groups, or forces that have special interests to pursue. These groups have little to do with the voting public and often represent a limited viewpoint. Yet, their influence on policies can be much greater than that of the individual voter. In other words, these power brokers often determine social policies. Some of these power brokers may not even be voters, but rather operate under a corporate structure. Governments bestow all types of tax breaks, subsidies, contracts, and other forms of corporate welfare upon these entities. Yet, the individual needing health care, shelter, and a living wage receives little. Despite the democratic process, policymakers have traditionally assisted the wealthy, including large corporations, rather than the lowly individual. Even within a democracy, the occupants of power positions can shape social policies with little regard to the poor, knowing they probably will not vote. This disempowerment of the poor helps perpetuate the cultural norm of ignoring economic human rights.

While those who do not vote should accept some responsibility for existing social policies in the United States, the reality is that most people in the United States are not poor. This demographic consideration may always work against greater integration of economic human rights within the United States. The historical emphasis on individual effort, as recently reinforced by the 1996 federal welfare law (Reichert & McCormick, 1998), and the lack of participation by the poor within the decision-making process can only help perpetuate existing social policies. While the emphasis on work makes sense, efforts should also be made to ensure that the working poor receive health care and other benefits necessary to satisfy human rights principles (Ehrenreich, 2001).

- *Analyze the cultural practice within a contemporary human rights standard.* What are the contemporary human rights standards against which the cultural practice should be compared? Over time, cultural norms that have existed for many years may appear incompatible with contemporary human rights standards. For instance, in the United States, a distinct segregation between whites and blacks had existed in many southern states for years before government enacted civil rights laws. Cultural and legal principles prohibited blacks from going to schools established for whites, drinking from the same water fountains as whites, eating at the same lunch counters as whites, sitting in the front part of buses reserved for whites, and generally mixing with whites. However, after the introduction of the Universal Declaration of Human Rights in 1948, southern segregation policies no longer appeared appropriate for a country that had taken the lead in promoting human rights. Contemporary human rights standards that prohibited discrimination on the basis of color began to prevail against the cultural relativism of segregation.

The evolution of thought within human rights standards has great relevance in viewing any conflict between cultural relativism and human rights. Not too many years ago, many countries, including the United States, accepted domestic violence against women as something that was more a private than a legal affair. Now, however, domestic violence has become much less culturally acceptable, with many countries strictly enforcing laws against that abuse. Clearly, contemporary human rights standards play a role in the weight given to cultural relativism in local policies. If human rights principles become widespread, then the local culture will likely begin to shape policies around human rights.

By analyzing a particular policy or practice by reference to historical background, relevant democratic factors, and contemporary human rights standards, social workers can better understand the role of cultural relativism in human rights. This analysis also enables social workers to determine how cultural relativism plays a role when the policy or practice conflicts with human rights.

Analysis of Example

Referring back to the example of economic human rights within the United States, should cultural relativism prevail by not recognizing food, shelter, and adequate medical care as human rights? While few would question everyone's need for food, shelter, and medical care, the relevant question becomes should everyone be able to claim those items as a human right?

Historical Issue

Certainly an examination of U.S. history supports an individualism that negates a concept of economic rights being elevated to the status of human rights. However, that was back in the days of self-sufficiency, when government barely existed in some areas of the country. The individual and his or her community provided the focus for support. The situation is different today, with government existing on all levels of society. Is there really such a person today as the rugged individual? While history may support that concept, the reality is obviously different.

Democratic Factors

Who has decided that economic human rights are not enforceable in the United States? As a general rule, many individuals probably agree that government should not guarantee economic human rights. However, what happens when one of those individuals finds himself or herself without medical care or shelter? Would the opinion of the individual change? How many elderly individuals would want to be without Medicare, the government program insuring most elderly? It is inconceivable that politicians would ever dismantle Medicare, at least not without replacing that system with some other form of guaranteed health care for the elderly. Why should one segment of society receive guaranteed health care and the other segment not? Most likely, the current policy of not guaranteeing basic economic human rights has more to do with government policies based on special interests rather than individual desires.

Contemporary Human Rights

Many countries have identified economic human rights as being just as important as political human rights and consequently adopted the International Covenant on Economic, Social and Cultural Rights. However, because many countries do not have sufficient resources to guarantee those rights, economic rights often take a backseat to political rights. Yet, governments today at least recognize the importance of economic rights and take steps to ensure broader delivery of economic rights.

The United States can no longer hide behind cultural relativism and ignore what one writer has called the "second bill of rights," a reference to President Franklin Roosevelt's original plan to connect economic rights to political rights (Sunstein, 2004):

> Twenty percent of American children live in poverty—the highest rate of any industrialized nation in the world. Millions of young Americans receive an inadequate education. Millions of Americans are unemployed. Millions experience serious hunger. Millions lack health insurance—and as a result, thousands of Americans die prematurely each year.
>
> The numbers mask larger issues. Too many of the nation's citizens neglect the extent to which their own well-being is a product of a system of government

that benefits them every day. Too many Americans complain about government intervention without understanding that the wealth and opportunities they enjoy exist only because of that intervention—aggressive, pervasive, coercive, and well funded. In a society that purports to provide opportunity for all, too many citizens lack a minimally fair chance. In the past decades, we have disregarded some of our deepest ideals. . . .

Freedom from fear is inextricably linked to freedom from want. Liberty and citizenship are rooted in opportunity and security. In a sense, America lives under the second bill. But in another sense, we have lost sight of it. The second bill of rights should be reclaimed in its nation of origin. (p. 234)

This passage places the cultural relativism versus economic human rights debate in perspective. Only by distorting historical background, democratic participation, and interpretations of contemporary human rights can cultural relativism prevail. This will often be the case when analyzing cultural relativism against human rights, regardless of the particular country or circumstances.

Cultural Relativism—This Era's Fascism?

In a speech given by Maryam Namazie in November 1998, she compared cultural relativism to fascism, or an extremely repressive type of government.

- In Germany, in August 1997, an 18-year-old woman was burnt to death by her father for refusing to marry the man he had chosen. A German court gave him a reduced sentence, saying he was practicing his culture and religion.
- In Iran, women and girls are forcibly veiled under threat of imprisonment and lashes, and cultural relativists say that it is their religion and must be respected.
- In Holland, the Ministry of Foreign Affairs states that Iran's prisons are "satisfactory for third world standards," allowing the forcible return of asylum seekers.

Cultural relativism serves these crimes. It legitimizes and maintains savagery. It says that peoples' rights are dependent on their nationality, religion, and culture. It says that the human rights of someone born in Iran, Iraq, or Afghanistan are different from those of someone born in the United States, Canada, or Sweden." (Namazie, 1998, p. 1)

Cultural relativists say that we must respect people's culture and religion, however despicable. This is absurd and calls for the respect of savagery. Yes, human beings are worthy of respect but not all beliefs must be respected. If culture allows a woman to be mutilated and killed to save the family "honor," it cannot be excused. . . . If religion says that women who disobey should be beaten, that flogging is acceptable, and that women are deficient, it must be condemned and opposed.

Cultural relativists go further to say that universal human rights are a [W]estern concept. How come when it comes to using the telephone or a car, the mullah does not say it is [W]estern and incompatible with an Islamist society? How come when it comes to better exploiting the working class and making profits, technological gains are universal? But when it comes to universal human rights, they become [W]estern. Even if rights are [W]estern, it is absurd to say that others' [*sic*] are not worthy of them. In fact, though[,] rights are gains forcibly taken by the working class and progressive social movements. Therefore, any gain or right obtained anywhere is a gain and a right for all humanity.

Culture for the sake of culture is not sacred. Racism and fascism also have their own cultures. A culture that cannot defend human beings to live a better life is worthless. Struggling for universal human rights means condemning and disrespecting reactionary beliefs. The struggle against dominant reactionary ideas is a struggle against the ideas of the ruling class. After all, the ruling class must justify the barbarism of capitalism. It must make the intolerable seem tolerable and natural. It must create differences to facilitate profit. Cultural relativism serves that purpose. The idea of difference has always been the fundamental principle of a racist agenda. The defeat of Nazism and its biological theory of difference largely discredited racial superiority. The racism behind it, however, found another more acceptable form of expression for this era. Instead of expression in racial terms, difference is now portrayed in cultural terms. Cultural relativism is this era's fascism. Cultural relativists are defenders of this era's holocausts. (Namazie, 1998, p. 2)

The strong and outspoken views of Namazie clearly extend beyond the normal critique of cultural relativism. Recent events in Iraq and elsewhere involving prisoner abuse by U.S. soldiers support the position of Namazie regarding cultural relativism. The extent of the prisoner abuse by U.S. soldiers leads to an unfortunate but inescapable conclusion that an attitude existed among high-level military and government officials that it was all right to abuse the prisoners. Information obtained by human rights groups from government and other sources indicates that high-level officials knew all along about the prisoner abuse but did little or nothing to address the abuse (Brown, 2004). How did this attitude to accept abuse or torture arise? Investigations into the abuse do not specifically answer or even address this question; they simply conclude that the abuse was the work of a few lower-level soldiers. However, to draw upon concepts presented by Namazie, the element of "difference" clearly infiltrated the general attitude of Americans toward Iraqis, from top to bottom. Most likely, U.S. leaders were simply not as concerned about the well-being of Iraqi prisoners as they might have been had those prisoners been Americans. Many U.S. officials appear to view the so-called war on terror as permission to treat prisoners captured in that war differently from others. Torture, an obvious human rights violation, may even be justified if it serves the purpose of extracting important information (Dershowitz, 2002).

The problem, though, with a new cultural and legal acceptance of torture or other human rights violation is that it breeds contempt for established humane rules. Anything goes, which encourages abuse of human rights. To say that it is OK to abuse individuals because circumstances are different violates the core of any human rights system. When governments and individuals begin to tolerate even one human rights abuse on the basis of cultural or legal necessity, all human rights are at risk.

Living With Cultural Relativism

This discussion illustrates how entrenched cultural and legal norms can overpower what seems to be an obvious human right. Cultural relativism often represents a major challenge to the concept of human rights. Arguing against cultural norms may seem like a fool's errand: Doesn't everyone have the human right to participate in "cultural life" (United Nations, 1996, Art. 15[1][a])?

Certainly the human right to take part in a person's culture has the same importance as any other human right. However, the human right of culture does not validate practices that clearly cause physical, severe emotional, or other harm to another. For instance, the right of men to participate in a culturally accepted form of domestic violence should not prevail over the human rights promoting dignity and freedom from cruel treatment. The human right to adequate health care should always prevail over a culturally accepted health care system that excludes the uninsured from appropriate treatment.

Cultural relativism plays an important role in analyzing how we interpret human rights. It does serve as a check on an unrestrained view of human rights, and it requires a consideration of culture in how human rights are applied to daily life. However, cultural relativism should be viewed critically and not be given an illegitimate priority over established principles of human rights.

Exercises

Exercise 1: Defining Cultural Relativism

The purpose of this exercise is to analyze the term "cultural relativism" within a human rights context.

1. Consider this definition of *relativism*: "a view that ethical truths depend on the individuals and groups holding them" (*Merriam Webster's Collegiate Dictionary*, 2001). Does this mean that any definition of ethics or human rights principles is dependent upon the individual or group, and not a broader societal meaning?

2. Assuming that relativism depends upon whatever views are held by an individual or a group, do you see any potential conflicts lurking within this assumption? What about those who do not belong to the group or everyone else who is not the individual? What would relativism mean to those persons?

3. Can relativism be justified by the following statement?

   "Only an individual or group knows what is appropriate to their environment. Outsiders have no knowledge about that environment and therefore have no business interfering." Give reasons for your analysis.

4. Referring to the definition of relativism stated in number 1, how would you define cultural relativism? Would you agree or disagree with the following: "Culture can only be defined by those belonging to that culture."

5. To belong to a particular culture is a human right. Do you agree that limits should be placed on this human right? Why or why not? What limits would you place on practicing culture? Draft a general law to limit what you believe are inappropriate cultural practices without violating human rights principles. Examine competing human rights.

Exercise 2: Cultural Relativism: A Balancing Act

The purpose of this exercise is to help students develop familiarity with the concept of cultural relativism and how to balance human rights principles. The exercise requires a group of several individuals and a facilitator.

1. The facilitator will divide the group into two roughly equal parts. One group will call itself Protectors of Children and the other group Stop Abuse Now.

2. Members of Protectors of Children all belong to a sect that prohibits children from seeking any medical treatment for illnesses. Members of this group are mistrustful of doctors and say that modern medicine has no role in curing illnesses. Only natural healing can cure illnesses. They believe that doctors and modern medicine are nothing more than profit-driven enterprises that care little about the children they treat.

3. Members of Stop Abuse Now come from the general population and consider Protectors of Children individuals who do harm to children. This group wishes to force Protectors of Children to accept the benefits of modern medicine and require medical treatment of their children who become ill.

4. Referring to human rights principles contained in relevant documents, both groups are to write a manifesto stating why their viewpoints should be given priority.

5. After writing the manifestos, the groups must then debate their views.

6. After the debates, the facilitator leads a discussion with both groups, focusing on these points:
   a. Identify any competing human rights, for example, right to practice culture versus right to adequate medical care; self-determination versus protection of public health. Make a list of these competing rights.
   b. Are any vulnerable groups involved that might be entitled to special protection?
   c. Examine methods that might be useful in respecting both sets of competing rights.
   d. Within the given circumstances, should one set of rights be given priority over the other? If so, which?

Exercise 3: Case Studies

The purpose of this exercise is to help you develop greater skill in addressing issues of cultural relativism. Read the case studies and identify issues of cultural relativism within them. Refer to the section in this chapter titled "Guidelines for Analyzing Cultural Relativism" in responding to the case studies.

Case Study 1: The Head Scarf

Fatima is a 15-year-old Muslim student at a public high school in Somewhere, USA. This high school has numerous Muslim students, both boys and girls. Fatima's parents are strict Muslims and require her to wear traditional Islamic dress to school, which includes a head scarf to cover her head. Fatima's teachers have complained to the principal of the school that they find the head scarf distracting. They are not used to seeing a student cover part of her face but also find the head scarf discriminatory, as Muslim boys are not required to wear head scarves. Also, no other Muslim girls at the school wear a head scarf. The principal of the high school discussed the matter with the school board, which then issued a policy against all religious dress and symbols (e.g., head scarves, crosses, pictures of Jesus).

You are a school social worker at the school, and Fatima comes to you for advice. She does not want to violate school policy but insists that she must be allowed to wear traditional dress. She tells you that the head scarf is part of her cultural identity and heritage, not simply a religious symbol. To strip her of this part of her cultural identity would devastate her emotionally. She does not believe she threatens anyone by wearing the head scarf. Fatima gives you permission to discuss this matter with school officials.

Draft a written report to school officials, listing relevant human rights issues, analyzing those issues within a human rights context, and making recommendations on resolving the issue. Freedom of religion clearly enters into your analysis, but consider also the political aspect of this issue.

France has recently banned the wearing of veils or head scarves in public schools. The justification for banning veils or head scarves is based on the need for a neutral place of education. French law states, "In public elementary schools, middle schools, and high schools, it is forbidden to wear symbols of clothes through which students conspicuously display their religious affiliation. Internal rules require that a dialogue with the student precede the enforcement of any disciplinary procedure" (Kramer, 2004). While the law bans all religious oriented clothing, the ban clearly stems from the wearing of veils.

Arguments surrounding the French ban on religious oriented clothing illustrate the complexity of this human rights issue:

- France, with several millions of Muslim residents, encountered concerns by some segments of its population that the wearing of veils contributed to the exclusion of young girls from the broader society. Many see the veil as a symbol of oppression and segregation.
- In favor of the veil, parents and their children argue that the veil serves as a political response to injustices against Islamic people everywhere. The veil also counters loose moral standards that depict naked or scantily clothed women in public.

Examine the French situation as part of your written report.

Case Study 2: Indirect Cultural Relativism

You are a social worker employed by the International Red Cross in Iraq. Your job is to interview Iraqi prisoners to determine whether U.S. soldiers or its allies have used torture on those prisoners to extract information. When asked whether they have been physically or otherwise harmed, prisoners tell you that U.S. soldiers hand them over to Iraqi soldiers who then beat them. The U.S. soldiers know this occurs but do not stop it, saying to you that this is how Iraqis treat prisoners and there is nothing they can do about it.

Draft a written report to your supervisor, listing relevant human rights issues, analyzing those issues within a human rights context, and making recommendations on resolving the issues.

Case Study 3: Health Care

Jackson is a 43-year-old man living in Anywhere, USA. He works for minimum wage at a convenience store. Jackson's employer cannot afford to provide its employees with health insurance. Therefore, Jackson must purchase his own insurance but finds that a one month premium for the lowest cost health plan would cost more than 80 percent of his net income. Jackson asks his state and federal government representatives about help. They both tell him that the law does not require anyone to provide health insurance for someone in his circumstances. The representatives explain to Jackson that this is the good thing about the U.S. health care system: no socialized medicine. They then tell him that, if he has a medical emergency, the law does allow him to seek medical care at the emergency room of a public hospital. However, the hospital can also bill him for those services. Jackson decides that he cannot afford health insurance and does without.

Jackson subsequently contracts a severe case of pneumonia but refuses to go to a doctor because he feels he cannot afford that cost. The pneumonia progresses to a stage where it has become a life or death matter. Jackson still refuses to seek medical treatment, insisting that it would bankrupt him. He dies at home.

You are a social worker investigating Jackson's case for a group called Coalition for Universal Health Care. Draft a written report to the coalition, listing relevant human rights issues, analyzing those issues within a human rights context, and making recommendations on how to prevent future cases where someone fails to seek health care because of costs.

Case Study 4: Cultural Relativism and Gay/Lesbian Culture

Joy is a four-year-old child who lives with her parents, a lesbian couple. Joy's parents know that they cannot marry but have created a loving home for Joy. A neighbor of Joy's has complained to the local department of child and family services that Joy's parents engage in lewd behavior in the presence of Joy. This allegedly lewd behavior consists of Joy's parents openly kissing and hugging each other.

You are a social worker called upon to investigate this matter. Draft a written report to your supervisor, listing relevant human rights issues, analyzing those issues within a human rights context, and making recommendations.

Case Study 5: The Car

You have decided to venture out into the world and take a job as a social worker in Saudi Arabia. You are a licensed clinical social worker (LCSW) and will work in an agency that assists women who are without spouses. Your specific role is to counsel these women with Western counseling techniques, but your employer has specifically warned you not to incorporate Western cultural norms into the counseling process.

One of the women you have been counseling wants to drive a car, but the government prohibits her from doing this solely on the basis of her gender.

Draft a written report as to how you would counsel this woman from a human rights viewpoint. Remember that your employer wants the benefit of Western counseling techniques but not necessarily your culture.

Case Study 6: Death Penalty

You live in Texas, and an acquaintance of yours has been convicted of a crime that could result in a sentence of the death penalty. The criminal court has scheduled a sentencing hearing for your acquaintance to determine whether the death penalty should be imposed. You have decided that you must attend this hearing on behalf of your acquaintance and argue against the death penalty.

Draft a written report that you intend to submit to the court. List relevant human rights issues and arguments that support your view. How does cultural relativism play a role in your report?

Case Study 7: Welfare

You are a case worker for the state, and a client of yours can no longer receive any public assistance because of the five-year limitation of benefits. Without public assistance, the quality of life for your client will greatly diminish. Your client has tried to find work, but no employer has shown any interest in hiring your client. You wish to advocate for your client.

You have learned that an advocacy group for economic human rights has filed a petition with the Inter-American Commission on Human Rights challenging the five-year lifetime limit on receiving benefits. The petition is based on violations of economic human rights.

Draft your own petition (in social work language) in support of your client and her human rights to receive economic benefits. How would you address the issue of cultural relativism, which apparently supports the termination of welfare benefits after five years?

Case Study 8: Infant Mortality

According to the latest CIA World Factbook, Cuba is one of 41 countries that have lower infant mortality rates than the United States (World Factbook, 2004). Singapore has the lowest infant mortality rate in the world: only 2.3 babies die before the age of 1 for every 1,000 live births. In the United States, 7 babies die for every 1,000 live births.

Research the issue of infant mortality and submit a report on the status of infant mortality in the United States and Singapore. How do you account for the difference in infant mortality rates within those two countries? What role does cultural relativism play in the different rates, if any?

Case Study 9: Women

Women perform two-thirds of the world's work but earn only one-tenth of all income and own less than one-tenth of the world's property (Human Rights Watch, 2000, p. 456). Seventy percent of the world's 1.3 billion people living in poverty are women (p. 456). Women remain economically disadvantaged in most countries, which makes them both vulnerable to violence and unable to escape violence.

Examine whether issues of gender inequality or gender abuse belong within the cultural relativism versus human rights debate. As part of this exercise, read the 1995 Beijing Declaration and Platform for Action (PFA) issued during the women's conference in Beijing, China. Using the Platform for Action as a focus point,

- list social work interventions that counter gender inequality;
- discuss how inequality is a human rights issue;
- explain why the PFA emphasizes that human rights override cultural practices, and give specific examples of the need for human rights to override cultural practices; and
- analyze the status of women within U.S. culture by reference to the PFA and the Guidelines for Analyzing Cultural Relativism found in the text portion of this chapter.

As a further part of this exercise, review the 2004 Report on the Global AIDS epidemic issued by UNAIDS. Analyze cultural issues of women's place in society versus the status that has led to higher incidence of HIV infections.

Case Study 10: One-Child Policy in China

China is a heavily populated country. To ensure that everyone has enough food, shelter, and other basic needs, the government adopted a policy that generally restricts families to only one child. For families that continued to have more than one child, strict penalties apply, including fines, forced abortions, and loss of social benefits.

Because Chinese culture favors boys over girls, the one-child policy in China has led to many families handing over baby girls to orphanages or even infanticide of the girls. The United States views the one-child policy in China as a human rights violation. U.S. immigration laws even allow Chinese families to apply for asylum if they have been penalized in China because of the one-child policy. The Chinese government claims that the one-child policy has been necessary for the public good, citing that the restriction on the birth rate has led to increased prosperity for society as a whole. The Chinese government argues that its cultural and social circumstances override any human rights of the individual parents who may want more than one child.

Examine the Chinese one-child policy within the context of the human rights versus cultural relativism debate. How do you reconcile a situation where the local cultural policy may actually benefit the broader society but deprive some individuals of certain human rights?

As a further part of this exercise, consider the following: orphanages in China are home to thousands of girls whose parents chose to relinquish their children rather than violate the one-child policy. Chinese teachers and other workers in the orphanages typically follow Chinese cultural traditions and emphasize that children should be obedient and good listeners. Children need assistance and guidance from adults, who keep order and control the classroom.

Recently, however, a U.S.-based organization called Half the Sky (www.halfthesky.org) has been sending a group of Western trained preschool teachers to Chinese orphanages to introduce a new way of learning. Instead of relying on the Chinese tenets of adult authority and guidance, Half the Sky teachers introduce a curriculum that stresses the need to trust the children and allow the children to develop their own identities and follow their own interests. The underlying philosophy of Half the Sky teachers is that children need adults who respect them, boost their self-confidence, and encourage the children to speak up for themselves.

Analyze the introduction of Half the Sky teachers into the Chinese system from a human rights versus cultural relativism perspective.

- Does not each country have the right to determine its own culture? Does it make sense to teach Chinese children from a Western perspective when that perspective may clash with broader Chinese society?
- Does it make a difference that Half the Sky is not imposing its will on China but merely presenting another viewpoint? What if that viewpoint violates existing cultural norms?
- How does the Half the Sky program differ, if it does, from forcibly removing Native American children from their natural environments and placing those children in white Christian homes to "improve" their education and upbringing?
- How would you determine whether a particular style of education is more effective than another?

CHAPTER 7

Human Rights and Ethics

For the social work profession, a code of ethics seems indispensable. After all, social workers should follow some rules of conduct in relation to clients, coworkers, and others with whom they interact. A code of ethics provides these rules. Without a code of ethics, social workers would find it difficult to consider their work as part of a profession (Congress, 1999). Ethics presents recognized rules of conduct with respect to a particular class of human action or to a particular group. Ethics also helps in determining a proper course of action within a particular situation (Loewenberg & Dolgoff, 1992; Mannig, 1997; Mattison, 2000; Reamer, 1995).

Within the United States, the predominant code of ethics for social workers is issued by the NASW (Congress, 1999; Loewenberg & Dolgoff, 1992; Reamer, 1995, 1998). The NASW Code of Ethics (1999) explains ethics in the context of social work values, principles, and responsibilities. Many of these provisions contain language similar to articles of the Universal Declaration of Human Rights. However, even with these parallels, the term "human rights" does not appear anywhere within the NASW code. However, NASW policy statements do emphasize human rights (NASW, 2003, pp. 209–217).

A second set of ethics relevant to social workers everywhere, not just the United States, is that issued by the International Federation of Social Workers (IFSW). This organization includes social work organizations, including the National Association of Social Workers, from at least 78 countries. The "purpose of the IFSW's work on ethics is to promote ethical debate and reflection in the member associations and among the providers of social work in member countries" (IFSW, 2005). Documents issued by the IFSW on ethics expressly refer to human rights and the requirement that social workers promote human rights.

Viewed from a human rights perspective, both the NASW and IFSW provide clear connections between social work ethics and human rights principles. For that reason alone, social workers should embrace human rights as a core part of their profession. However, within the United States at least, the connection between ethics and human rights remains relatively unexplored.

NASW Code of Ethics

The first NASW Code of Ethics appeared in 1960 and comprised a single page (Congress, 1999). In its beginning stage, that code focused on proclamations about the duties of social workers: priority of professional responsibility over personal interests, respect for privacy of clients, and professional service in public. This initial code of ethics presented a relatively narrow view of the profession in terms of its role in the broader society. Amendments to the code in 1979 addressed responsibility to clients, colleagues, the profession, and society and incorporated procedures to enforce relevant provisions (Congress, 1999; Loewenberg & Dolgoff, 1992). The latest revision of the code in 1999 expanded ethical responsibilities of social workers to the broader society, including a provision that "social workers should promote conditions that encourage respect for cultural and social diversity within the United States and globally" (NASW, 1999, p. 27). With the 1999 revision, the social work profession in the United States actually subscribed to many human rights principles, without referring to human rights within the code.

As with human rights, criticism of the NASW code of ethics raises issues of the underlying power structure behind the code. For example, less powerful nations may complain that human rights benefit the wealthy nations because wealthy countries have more control over interpretations and enforcement of human rights. After all, could small countries such as Costa Rica ever require larger and more powerful countries such as the United States to abide by human rights principles if those countries refuse to recognize those principles? In most cases, the answer would be no. On the other hand, the United States and other wealthy countries have great clout with their military, economic, and other resources. Those countries could pressure smaller nations to abide by their version of human rights principles. A similar criticism has arisen in respect to the notion that those in power have written the code of ethics in order to regulate conduct with clients (Ife, 2001; Witkin, 2000). As with human rights, those in power can dictate enforcement and interpretations of the code, with a possible result that clients do not receive adequate consideration when ethical issues arise. This unequal power structure can actually lead to unethical situations, just as an unequal power structure can lead to abuses of human rights—those with power may abuse that power simply because they can get away with it.

Certainly the NASW Code of Ethics, or any other code of ethics, contains imperfections, both within the code itself and within its interpretation and enforcement. However, a code can still provide a worthy frame of reference, just as the Universal Declaration of Human Rights forms an important foundation for understanding human rights.

IFSW and Ethics

In 1994, the IFSW issued two documents relating to ethics and social work: the International Declaration of Ethical Principles of Social Work and the International

Ethical Standards for Social Workers. These documents provided basic ethical principles for the social work profession throughout the world. Within the document on ethical principles, social workers are to "respect basic human rights of individuals and groups as expressed in the United Nations Universal Declaration of Human Rights and other international conventions derived from that Declaration" (2.2.7). However, the documents contained no further references to human rights, although specific principles and standards did mirror human rights principles (e.g., 2.2.6, regarding discrimination).

At its general meeting in Australia in October 2004, the IFSW adopted a new statement of ethical principles that replaced the 1994 ethical principles and standards. The difference between the 2004 principles and the 1994 documents is significant: The 2004 document focuses on human rights, with several provisions of the document highlighting the ethical connection between human rights and social work.

Definition of Social Work

The social work profession promotes social change, problem solving in human relationships, and the empowerment and liberation of people to enhance their wellbeing. Utilizing theories of human behavior and social systems, social work intervenes at the points where people interact with their environments. Principles of human rights and social justice are fundamental to social work.

Documents Particularly Relevant to Social Work Practice and Action

International human rights declarations and conventions form common standards of achievement and recognize rights that are accepted by the global community, including the Universal Declaration of Human Rights; the international covenants on civil and political rights and economic, social, and cultural rights; the conventions on elimination of racial and gender discrimination; and the conventions on the rights of the child and indigenous and tribal peoples.

Principles

The document again refers to human rights and human dignity, with an introductory statement that social work is "based on respect for the inherent worth and dignity of all people, and the rights that flow from this" (IFSW, 2005, 4.1). Social workers also have a responsibility to promote "social justice, in relation to society generally, and in relation to the people with whom they work" (4.2). Social justice as defined within the document clearly falls under human rights principles:

Challenging negative discrimination

Recognizing diversity

Distributing resources equitably

Challenging unjust policies and practices

Working in solidarity

Members of IFSW "develop and regularly update their own codes of ethics or ethical guidelines, to be consistent with the IFSW statement" (5). While the NASW code has already incorporated many of the provisions contained in the 2004 IFSW document, NASW does not fully comply with IFSW principles. To bring itself into compliance with IFSW, the NASW should make specific references to human rights and their key role within the social work profession. NASW should also refer to important human rights documents, as does the IFSW. References to human rights are not merely advisory. As a member of IFSW, the NASW has an obligation to make clear the role of human rights within the U.S. social work profession.

Human Rights and Ethics

To better understand the importance of social work ethics to human rights, Table 7.1 compares provisions of the NASW Code of Ethics to human rights contained in the Universal Declaration of Human Rights.

The ethical principles contained in the NASW Code of Ethics easily connect to human rights and principles found within the Universal Declaration of Human Rights. Clearly, human rights play a significant role in the social work profession.

Ethical Responsibilities

The NASW Code of Ethics does not stop at simply stating ethical principles but also derives concrete ethical standards. These standards represent *ethical responsibilities* that social workers have to various groups: clients, colleagues, the social work profession, and the broader society (NASW, 1999). Many of the ethical responsibilities are simply advisory or aspirational and are not strictly enforceable. To an extent, this nonenforceable nature of some ethical responsibilities resembles the situation with human rights, many of which rely on the goodwill and knowledge of individuals in order to promote them. Strict legal enforcement of ethics and human rights often encounters numerous obstacles. After all, how do you adequately enforce the right to dignity? The most relevant tool for enforcing an "aspirational" human right or ethical standard relies on a thorough teaching of human rights and ethics. Education and goodwill can go a long way toward instilling values, standards, and responsibilities that reflect human rights and ethical principles.

In respect to ethical responsibilities to the broader society, social workers should do the following:

Promote the general welfare of society and advocate for living conditions conducive to the fulfillment of basic human needs (6.01). This ethical responsibility ties in with the economic and social human rights contained within the Universal Declaration.

Table 7.1   Connection Between Ethical Principles and Human Rights

Ethical Principles	Corresponding Human Rights
Primary goal of social workers Help people in need and address social problems	Right to standard of living adequate for health and well-being of family, including food, clothing, housing, medical care, and necessary social services for health and well-being of family (Art. 25)
	Right to employment and living wage (Art. 23)
	Right to education (Art. 26)
Social justice Social workers should challenge social injustice	Right to social security and economic, social, and cultural rights (Art. 22)
	Right to be treated without discrimination (Art. 7)
	Other rights involving political and civil freedoms, including right to dignity (Arts. 1–21)
Dignity and worth of person: Social workers should treat each person in caring and respectful fashion, with special consideration to cultural and ethnic diversity.	Right to inherent dignity (preamble and Art. 1)
Importance of human relationships Social workers should recognize central importance of meaningful relationships in everyone's life.	Right to free association (Art. 20) Right to marriage and create family (Art. 16) Right to participate in cultural life of community (Art. 27)
Integrity Social workers should act honestly and responsibly and behave in trustworthy manner.	Everyone has duties to community (Art. 29)
Competence Social workers need to develop and enhance professional expertise.	Every individual shall strive by teaching and education to promote respect for human rights and freedoms (preamble)

Facilitate informed participation by the public in shaping social policies and institutions (6.02). Participation in the community and government are important human rights.

Provide appropriate professional services in public emergencies to the greatest extent possible (6.03). Assistance to others in times of need is a basic premise of human rights.

Engage in social and political action that seeks to ensure that all people have equal access to employment and resources (6.04a). Human rights aim to promote equality in employment and other social and political benefits.

Act to expand choice and opportunity for all people, with special regard for vulnerable, disadvantaged, oppressed, and exploited people and groups (6.04b). This ethical responsibility clearly ties in with the overall theme of human rights as expressed in the Universal Declaration.

Promote conditions that encourage respect for cultural and social diversity within the United States and globally (6.04c). Human rights promote cultural and social diversity on an international level.

Act to prevent and eliminate domination of, exploitation of, and discrimination against any person, group, or class (6.04d). An underlying goal of human rights correlates exactly to this ethical responsibility.

Ethical responsibilities of social workers place them at the forefront of advocacy for human rights. The connection of social work ethics to human rights cannot be avoided. The language of social work codes of ethics closely resembles language contained within human rights documents. Consequently, social workers should recognize the strong connection between their codes of ethics and human rights. By recognizing that connection, social workers can then proceed to develop techniques and interventions based on human rights principles.

Universal Declaration of Human Responsibilities

Recognizing that an exclusive insistence on the rights of humans can lead to "endless dispute and conflict," various groups known as the Inter Action Council have drafted a Universal Declaration of Human Responsibilities (Inter Action Council, 1997). The aim of this declaration is to allow the greatest freedom possible, but also to develop the fullest sense of responsibility that will allow that freedom itself to grow. Freedom without acceptance of responsibility can destroy the freedom itself, whereas when rights and responsibilities are balanced, freedom is enhanced and a better world can be created.

Here are some of the articles contained within the proposed Universal Declaration of Human Responsibilities:

Every person, regardless of gender, ethnic origin, social status, political opinion, language, age, nationality, or religion, has a responsibility to treat all people in a humane way.

No person should lend support to any form of inhumane behavior, but all people have a responsibility to strive for the dignity and self-esteem of all others.

No person, no group or organization, no state, no army or police stands above good and evil; all are subject to ethical standards. Everyone has a responsibility to promote good and to avoid evil in all things.

All people endowed with reason and conscience must accept a responsibility to each and all, to families and communities, to races, nations, and religions in a spirit of solidarity: What you do not wish to be done to yourself, do not do to others.

Every person has a responsibility to respect life. No one has the right to injure, to torture, or to kill another human person. This does not exclude the right of justified self-defense of individuals or communities.

Disputes between states, groups, or individuals should be resolved without violence. No government should tolerate or participate in acts of genocide or terrorism, nor should it abuse women, children, or any other civilians as instruments of war.

Every person has a responsibility to behavior with integrity, honesty, and fairness.

All property and wealth must be used responsibly in accordance with justice and for the advancement of the human race. Economic and political power must not be handled as an instrument of domination, but in the service of economic justice and of the social order.

Politicians, public servants, business leaders, scientists, writers, or artists are not exempt from ethical standards. Professional and other codes of ethics should reflect the priority of general standards such as those of truthfulness and fairness.

The freedom of the media to inform the public and to criticize institutions of society and governmental actions must be used with responsibility and discretion. Freedom of the media carries a special responsibility for accurate and truthful reporting.

As these statements make clear, human rights is not simply a concept that bestows benefits or privileges upon human kind. Ethical considerations of human rights mandate responsibilities, as well as rights. Without understanding and acknowledging those responsibilities, pursuit of human rights can easily lead to human rights violations.

Guns and Butter, or Only Guns?

In early 2005, President Bush submitted a proposed federal budget to Congress that contained numerous cuts in social programs but maintained or increased defense and homeland security spending (Allen & Baker, 2005, p. A1). The president did not even bother to include costs of the Iraq war in the proposed budget. Obviously the president fully expected to obtain all the funding he requested for Iraq, arguing that this was a war to protect the homeland.

But couldn't a social worker argue that, by providing more resources for lower income individuals, we are also protecting homeland security? A well-educated, -housed, and -fed population may be one of the best guarantees in support of security. Well-educated individuals may be better able to detect terrorist activities than poorly educated individuals. Well-housed and -fed individuals would have less reason to support an insurrection against government than not-so-well-housed and -fed individuals.

Government funds simply do not exist to support every program. Having to choose between support for a particular group or program presents all types of ethical and moral issues. These choices define the type of world we live in.

Take the case of funding difficulties in the state of Missouri, as presented by editorial writer Eric Mink of the *St. Louis Post-Dispatch* (Mink, 2005, p. B7). Mink describes these issues within the context of morals:

> Who is more deserving of our help, a 70-year-old diabetic man who needs a wheelchair after his second leg is amputated or a 2-year-old girl with multiple birth defects needing intensive therapy to help her learn to walk and talk?
>
> Should we permit a vital 80-year-old woman to receive physical therapy after a fall, a hip fracture and a hip replacement, knowing that therapy will dramatically increase her chances of remaining active and independent? Or is a 35-year-old single mom with three kids more worthy of getting the asthma medicine that will let her keep working at her two minimum-wage jobs?
>
> Is a 63-year-old part-time clerk suffering from terminal bone cancer entitled to hospice care to ease the pain and fear of his passage to death? Or should we, instead, grant a once-homeless 40-year-old woman the privilege of continuing to receive the medication that keeps her schizophrenia in check?

According to Mink, these are the types of moral issues that Missouri politicians, officials, and residents have been wrestling with since Governor Matt Blunt presented his state budget in February 2005, which proposed funding cuts for various social programs.

Parents of infants and kids with severe disabilities argue, persuasively, that the proposed cutbacks could wreck their children's chances for a decent future. Adults caring for ailing senior parents argue, persuasively, that proposed cutbacks could force them to institutionalize the elderly. Advocates for the working poor argue, persuasively, that the governor's proposals would let sick people get sicker, with enormous human and financial consequences. Nonprofit mental health services argue, persuasively, that low-income people already find it almost impossible to find the help they need to get well and become productive, especially in rural areas (Mink, 2005, p. B7).

While social workers in the United States and other parts of the world discuss the types of choices described by Mink, shouldn't the focus be on addressing all the needs of less privileged individuals, within a human rights context? Yes, fraud, abuse, and lack of results may require questioning of some social benefits. But that is also true with military spending and other nonsocial programs.

In response to the usual excuses offered by politicians as to why government and society cannot help everyone, Mink takes a radical but ultimately sane and moral position:

> True leadership would start with a declaration that Missouri will live by the moral values of a caring community, that being poor is not a sin, that the right

to life, liberty and the pursuit of happiness is meaningless if you don't have enough food to eat, clothes to wear, a safe place for your family to live—and health. (Mink, 2005, p. B7)

Finally, Mink questions the mentality that taxes must always be lowered, especially for the wealthy:

Here's a thought: For 2003, individuals filed 2,612,472 state income tax returns in Missouri. If each of those returns brought in an average of just $5 more per week, we would have an additional $680 million to spend on health care. Poorer taxpayers could pay less; rich taxpayers more. How many jobs would that kill? Zero? Is $5 more a week really too high a price to pay for taking care of the poor, the elderly and the disabled? (Mink, 2005, p. B7)

Guns and butter? Which will it be? This type of cost analysis goes to the heart of the social work profession and what it represents. Viewing these types of issues within a moral and human rights perspective is what social work is all about.

Exercises

The following exercises require analysis of various ethical values, standards, and responsibilities, as well as human rights principles.

Exercise 1: To Be or Not to Be: A Code of Ethics?

The purpose of this exercise is to examine the need or importance of a code of ethics within a human rights context.

Respond to the following statements, examining whether any human rights issues come into the picture:

- A code of ethics for social workers is nonsense. Nobody will enforce them anyway.
- Social work ethics are too idealistic. The profession does not pay much attention to most of the ethical standards. Therefore, we should simply eliminate most parts of the various codes of ethics.
- Ethics are OK for social workers in terms of client relationships. However, when ethical standards sound like the profession is out to save the world, I am not sure that's my role.
- We really need a strong code of ethics. Social work is a profession with definite goals. Although we may not meet all those goals, we still need to consider how we could meet those goals.
- Ethics and human rights. Both are merely buzzwords, and social work should beware of these sorts of things.
- Social work ethics have everything to do with human rights. Without one, you cannot have the other.
- Ethics are the backbone of the social work profession.

- Social work claims to be a human rights profession. I know that the international code of ethics refers to human rights. But human rights are an international concept, and ethics are more local.
- Ethics are important. I saw a recent survey where members of the public ranked nurses as the most ethical of professions. Social work was not listed, but it would be nice if the public believed social workers to be as ethical as nurses.

Exercise 2: Ethical Dilemmas

The purpose of this exercise is to examine potential ethical dilemmas and how human rights principles can apply to those situations.

Write a response to each of the following situations, referring to specific ethical and human rights principles. Discuss the action you would take, if any, under the particular circumstances, giving reasons for your action or inaction.

- You are a case worker for the local child protection agency. You overhear your supervisor saying to another supervisor, "I really do not like poor people. They do horrible jobs at parenting. I would just as soon see every child taken away from these types of families."
- You are a student of social work at a university. A group of students dislikes a certain professor because she has given them failing grades. The group feels that the professor was arbitrary and unjust in her grading. The group feels justified in circulating a petition to have the professor reprimanded for inequitable grading. However, nobody from the group has actually discussed the matter with administrators. The group asks you to sign the petition.
- You are a social worker for the United Nations at a refugee camp of Palestinians. Israeli soldiers patrol the camp regularly. One day, you see a young Palestinian boy throw a rock at the Israeli soldiers. The soldiers then beat the boy. The soldiers are aware that you saw the incident and tell you to keep quiet.
- You are a case worker for families and individuals on welfare. One day you visit one of your families, which has a young boy with chronic asthma. You note that the family has purchased a very expensive television set. You ask members of the family where they obtained the income to purchase the television. They tell you that the father of the family works on the side but does not report that income to the welfare agency. If they did, the family would not qualify for any public assistance, including medical care. Without this public assistance, especially the medical care, the family could not receive adequate medical care for the boy with asthma.
- You are a social work counselor at a local prison, which is notorious for ill treatment of prisoners (e.g., shoving by guards, poor food, inadequate medical care). One of your clients is a mistreated prisoner. One day, the prisoner tells you that he would like your help in escaping. He asks you to contact someone for him on the outside who will assist him with his escape plan. The prisoner has a specific message that he wants you to convey to the contact person.
- You work at a local high school as a counselor to help prevent problems among students, especially bullying. One day you see two students fighting and try to break up the fight. The students stop fighting, and you ask them what is going on. One student replies that the other was "picking on me." The other says

nothing. You ask the silent student to come into your office to discuss the matter. He refuses, saying that he did not pick on the other student, and besides, he does not need a "shrink."

- You are a child welfare specialist for a social work agency but also do custody evaluations for custody disputes in courts. The attorneys for two divorcing spouses have requested that you do an evaluation for the couple to determine who should have custody of their 10-year-old daughter. During the course of your evaluation, you discover that the mother is divorcing the father so she can live with her lesbian friend. The results of your evaluation indicate that, without this factor—the lesbian friend—the two parents are equally appropriate as the custodial parent.

Exercise 3: Assess Your Ethical Environment Within a Human Rights Context

The purpose of this exercise is to provide skills in assessing the overall ethical environment of your employment, school, church, family, or other circumstances. To do this exercise, you will need nothing more than pen and paper.

1. Begin this exercise by responding to the following questions. Please use the following ranking scale.

   1 no/never

   2 rarely

   3 often

   4 yes/always

2. Respond to the following questions, using the previous scale and values.
   a. ____ Whenever I participate in decisions, I feel that my opinion counts among others making the decision.
   b. ____ Within my environment, I find other people respectful of my beliefs and concerns.
   c. ____ Those in charge of my agency (or place of employment or other entity) always try to treat everyone fairly.
   d. ____ Other employees (or members of the community) will oppose discriminatory or demeaning treatment or behavior.
   e. ____ When someone demeans or mistreats another person, others within my environment will help the violator to learn how to change behavior.
   f. ____ My environment values a right to be heard before any disciplinary action occurs.
   g. ____ Policies and practices within my environment are responsive to complaints of harassment or discrimination.
   h. ____ Freedom of expression is welcomed within my environment.
   i. ____ I can associate with anyone I want within my environment and not feel uncomfortable because others may not like that person.
   j. ____ Within my environment, leaders make every effort to encourage discussions about social issues as long as those discussions do not interfere with assigned duties.

k. ____ Employees within my environment receive enough pay to enjoy an adequate standard of living.
l. ____ My employer cares about the well-being of its employees.

After completion of the ranking, calculate the average mean of your scores. A mean score of less than three indicates that your environment may need improvement from an ethical and human rights context.

Exercise 4: The Pen Game

The purpose of this exercise is to highlight the need for ethical behavior in decision making that affects lives of social workers and their coworkers and clients. The exercise focuses on how arbitrary decision making when applied to laws often results in unjust and unfair results. The exercise requires a group and a facilitator.

Summary of Exercise. Citizens must participate at all levels of decision making that affect their lives. However, this participation is observed more in rhetoric than in practice. The reality of rhetoric over practice applies to laws, which should be made for and by the people, not just for the few and by elites. By not taking into account all people with an interest in a particular law, outcomes can be arbitrary and unjust. Also, rules that are applied arbitrarily breed cynical attitudes toward rules in general, undermine the consensual basis of good rules, and make coercive enforcement more likely. These are circumstances that erode the legitimacy of the rule makers.

Objectives. By the end of this exercise, participants should be able to

- distinguish between good rules and bad rules on the basis of whether they are fair or arbitrary;
- recognize that rules of a game are very much like laws, which are more just if they come about through the approval of the people;
- appreciate that, because ignorance of the law is no excuse for violating the law, the law must be accessible; and
- identify factors that need to be taken into account in the drafting of laws, such as accommodating felt needs, clarity of language and message, and objectivity.

Materials. A pen or pencil or similar item.

Procedures. Participants should be seated in two rows facing each other. They will only be told that they are going to play the "Pen Game." But the rules of the game will not be explained to them. Step 1 may not need more than 5 minutes; Steps 2 and 3, however, require at least 15 minutes each. Step 4 should be given ample time for full critical discussion and reaction. Step 5 provides for further analysis.

Step 1. The facilitator will divide the group in two groups of equal numbers. The facilitator will then begin to act uncharacteristically arbitrary and dictatorial, even reprimand someone for being in the wrong group, without explaining why it is wrong. After setting this tone, the facilitator will begin the game by passing a pen to one of the participants. By pointing and nodding the head, the facilitator encourages the first person to pass the pen on to another person. At some point, the facilitator suddenly says that the pen recipient has made an error and the pen goes to the other group. The facilitator needs to watch closely how, to whom, and in which direction the first person passed the pen. The facilitator can then identify the mistake as the first person using the left hand instead of the right or passing the pen to the person on his or her right instead of the left or passing the pen with its cap off, or whatever other quirk observed by the facilitator. Again, with no explanation, the facilitator asks the person to whom he or she has given the pen to continue the game. After the second or third passing of the pen, the facilitator will again announce another mistake: any type of "mistake" will do, such as passing the pen to a person of the opposite sex, or a person wearing a ring, or to someone with brown or grey hair. The facilitator will then take the pen and give it to someone else. The facilitator continues the pen game in this manner until the pen has gone through both groups. In the process, the facilitator will have cited many persons for mistakes.

Step 2. The facilitator abruptly announces that the game is over and declares one group to be the winner and the other the loser. The facilitator will then separately ask each group whether they liked the game or not.

Step 3. After the game has been completed, the facilitator should ask

- participants to identify mistakes committed by members of the groups as announced by the facilitator;
- alleged defaulters if they will accept their fault, and why;
- participants to explain whatever they feel is amiss, wrong, strange, and unfair about the game; and
- participants to rule on who is to blame for the alleged faults—the facilitator or the declared defaulters, and why?

Step 4. The facilitator asks the participants what remedial measures should be taken to make the game fair and just.

Step 5. The facilitator reads this selection from Chinua Achebe, a famous African writer who said in his book, *Anthills of the Savannah* (1987, p. 45),

> Worshipping a dictator is such a pain in the ass. It would not be so bad if it was merely a matter of dancing upside down on your head. With practice anyone could learn to do that. The real problem is having no way of knowing from one day to another, from one minute to the next, just what is up and what is down.

Using the "go-around" method, the facilitator asks the participants' opinion of this excerpt by Chinua Achebe. Does it remind them of any of their own experiences? Explain that when a country lives under the rule of law everyone should be able to know or learn what the law says and that it should be enforced without arbitrary action by those who are powerful.

Exercise 5: Human and Ethical Responsibilities

Bob was a member of the armed forces in Iraq. Six months ago, he finished his duty in Iraq but has had great difficulty adjusting to his environment back in the United

States. After leaving the military after his tour of duty, Bob was unable to find other employment and is now homeless. Before his combat mission in Iraq, Bob lived with his spouse and their two children in army housing. Upon leaving the military, he lost this benefit. He relocated to New York but soon realized that he could not afford housing for the family. Bob's spouse found it difficult to cope with Bob and his disorientation in the United States. She left to live with relatives. Before she left Bob, the spouse arranged for Bob to seek medical support at a veterans hospital. Doctors at that facility diagnosed Bob with post-traumatic stress disorder, which has contributed to Bob's difficult readjustment.

1. What are the human rights issues within this fact situation?

2. What would you consider to be the ethical responsibilities of the government toward Bob? Toward the broader society?

3. Referring to the Universal Declaration of Human Responsibilities, what responsibilities does the broader society or government have toward Bob?

4. Does Bob have any human responsibilities toward society? If so, what are they?

5. As a social worker assigned to Bob's case, what ethical responsibilities do you have in respect to Bob? What human responsibilities?

Exercise 6: Culture and Ethics

Selective abortions of girls are occurring in parts of India for cultural reasons (Giris, 2005). Some people emphasize that girls cost dowry money, cannot inherit land and do not take care of their parents like boys. You work at an international aid agency in Calcutta, and a pregnant mother tells you that she wants to abort her baby because an ultrasound examination shows the fetus to be a girl. The mother tells you that her family would be very angry at her for giving birth to another girl and that she might get punished. Also, the girl would most likely have a difficult life because of cultural bias against girls. The mother is asking you for advice.

- What social work ethics are relevant to this situation?
- What responsibility does the Indian government have toward the mother? The fetus?
- What cultural issues are problematic in this situation? What is the connection between the cultural issues and ethical and human responsibilities?
- Would you advise the mother to abort her child? Why or why not?

Exercise 7: Other Case Studies

You are one of two social workers hired by a development agency (relief/disaster) organization in Afghanistan. Your assignment is to provide education for girls and boys and assist teachers with the curriculum development. You have been working for three months with the teachers and the children. You now begin to recognize that the number of girls is dwindling. You talk to community leaders who tell you that from now on you should only teach boys. When asked why, the leaders say that there are pressures from the former government (Taliban) and that the community fears for their safety if this rule is not obeyed.

Some parents contact the other social worker and you, asking if you could teach their girls anyway. Your development organization tells you that you should adhere to wishes of the local community. In other words, if community leaders tell you not to teach girls, don't teach girls even if this is a discriminatory practice.

- Identify ethical issues involved with this case study. Do social work values and ethics conflict with what community leaders are saying? How do you reconcile the apparent reason behind not teaching girls—fear—with human rights provisions requiring education of girls? Identify human rights issues.
- Identify each individual, group, and organization likely to be affected by not teaching girls.
- What is your course of action in this situation? Provide reasons for assisting the Afghan community both without teaching of girls and with teaching of girls.

You are a social worker employed by an international relief agency in Iraq. You work with families who have been dislocated from their homes because of the war. The families have lost their homes in bomb attacks and fires. These experiences have traumatized the families. Your specific job duties include helping to provide food, shelter, and trauma counseling.

One day, a member of one of the families tells you that another member of a family is a suspected insurgent against the Iraqi government. Fearing retaliation, your agency orders you and other agency workers to leave the area immediately. However, you feel that you have been able to establish relationships with the families. You believe that if you left, the families would not receive adequate care and would suffer even more.

- What ethical responsibilities do you have to the families? The agency?
- What human rights considerations are involved with this situation?
- What will be your course of action? Do you stay or leave as requested? Give reasons for your decision.

Stephanie grew up in a rural and economically deprived area of the United States. As a child, Stephanie clearly suffered physical abuse and, the local child and family services suspects, sexual abuse by Stephanie's father. However, because Stephanie insisted that her father never harmed her, the local agency quit pursuing the case. Stephanie had her first child at age 16 and her second child at 18. Stephanie's family gave her no support with the children or for herself.

Stephanie is now 30 years old and single. Occasionally Stephanie has obtained employment in menial positions (e.g., convenience store cashier) but none of the jobs has ever provided medical benefits. Most of her adult life, Stephanie has received some type of public assistance. She now struggles with depression, but she has no health benefits to assist her with this affliction.

After five full years of no employment, the state in which Stephanie resides terminated further public assistance. Stephanie has had great difficulties paying her rent, and she now resides with her children in a homeless shelter.

- What human rights issues are relevant to this case study? Cite specific provisions within human rights instruments, including the Universal Declaration of Human Rights and international conventions.
- What ethical issues are involved? Cite specific provisions within the NASW Code of Ethics.
- Are there connections between the ethical and human rights issues? If so, what are those connections? (For instance, a human right to adequate medical care and shelter exists. Does the NASW code of ethics contain a similar provision or mandate to advocate for these benefits?)
- What controversy or conflict might arise from the human rights and ethical issues relevant to the case study?

Exercise 8: Ethics Documents and Human Rights

Examine the NASW Code of Ethics, the IFSW Code of Ethics, the Universal Declaration of Human Rights, and the Universal Declaration of Human Responsibilities. Create a chart analyzing each of the codes of ethics and identifying whether specific provisions within the codes relate to human rights. If so, note the specific human rights provision.

Exercise 9: Analyzing Ethical Decision Making

Reamer (1999) has listed the following steps as necessary in analyzing the making of ethical decisions:

- Identify the ethical issues, including the social work values and duties that conflict.
- Identify the individuals, groups, and organization likely to be affected by the ethical decision.
- Identify all viable courses of action and the participants involved in each, along with the potential benefits and risks for each.
- Thoroughly examine the reason(s) in favor of and against each course of action, relying upon the following:

  Ethical theories, principles, and guidelines

  Code of ethics and legal principles

  Social work practice theory and principles

  Personal values, (including religious, cultural, and ethnic values and political ideology) particularly those that conflict with one's own

  Consultations with colleagues and appropriate experts (agency staff, supervisors, agency administrators, attorneys, ethics scholars)

- After going through these steps, make the decision and document the decision-making process.
- Monitor, evaluate, and document the decision.

Apply this decision-making process to each of the case studies in Exercise 7.

Exercise 10: Ethical Responsibilities to Society at Large

The social work commitment to social justice is clearly and forcefully reflected in the code's preamble and in the final section of the code's ethical standards. Social justice activities include

- facilitating public discussion of social policy issues;
- providing professional services in public emergencies;
- engaging in social and political action to meet basic human needs;
- promoting conditions that encourage respect for the diversity of cultures and social diversity; and
- acting to prevent and eliminate domination, exploitation, and discrimination against any person, group, or class of people.

Identify human rights issues within the Universal Declaration of Human Rights and other human rights documents that correlate to social justice activities listed earlier. Do any human rights issues conflict with those activities? If so, identify those issues.

CHAPTER 8

Social Work Practice and Human Rights

The importance of human rights to social work is clear. However, even with that recognition, how do social workers actually apply concepts of human rights to social work practice? Human rights principles represent admirable policy statements, but without actual integration of those principles into everyday practices, human rights can only remain incidental to the social work profession. While an important starting point in the integration of human rights into practice involves adherence to social work ethics (see Chapter 7), a second stage is also necessary to more fully adapt human rights to social work practice. Human rights encompass social work ethics but also have relevance beyond ethics; human rights should exist alongside established social work practices. Only by truly incorporating human rights principles into actual interventions and day-to-day practice techniques can human rights occupy the desired place in the social work profession.

Preliminary Foundation for Applying Human Rights

Before social workers can even begin applying human rights to social work practice, they need to have a thorough understanding of human rights principles, because, without a fundamental knowledge of human rights principles, no application of those principles is possible. Too often, politicians and other government officials use the term "human rights" without adequate explanation or insufficient knowledge of relevant human rights. Or, as in the social work profession, reference to human rights appears mandatory but, without adequate discussion of the concept of human rights, little advancement of knowledge occurs.

In policy statements, the NASW mandates the adoption of human rights as a foundation upon which all of social work theory and applied knowledge rests:

In a world where increasingly there is a serious questioning of the responsibility of society to ensure that peoples' civil, political, cultural, social, and economic needs are met, social workers should be absolutely clear about where they stand. . . . [Social workers] must speak out against inhumane treatment of people in whatever form it exists. (NASW, 2003, p. 212)

To back up this broad policy statement, NASW then expressly refers to human rights documents and principles:

• Social workers should promote U.S. ratification of the Universal Declaration of Human Rights as well as critical UN treaties such as the International Covenant on Economic, Social, and Cultural Rights, the Convention on the Elimination of All Forms of Discrimination against Women, and the Convention on the Rights of the Child.

• Social workers must be especially vigilant about human rights violations related to children's rights and exploitation such as child labor, child prostitution, and other crimes of abuse and take leadership in developing public and professional awareness regarding these issues.

• Social workers must advocate for the rights of vulnerable people and must condemn policies, practices, and attitudes of bigotry, intolerance, and hate that put any person's human rights in grave jeopardy. The violation of human rights based on race, ethnicity, gender, sexual orientation, age disability, immigration status, or religion provide a few examples.

• Social workers should publicize opposition to the death penalty and work toward its abolition, recognizing that the death penalty has not been found to be a deterrent to violent crime and that it provides inhumane and degrading punishment.

• When entitlements are nonexistent or inadequately implemented, social workers must work in collaboration with governmental and nongovernmental organizations and other groups of people in the community to become a leading force for the health and welfare of all people, including the world's most vulnerable.

• Social workers must become partners with the United Nations in advancing human development and human rights, including economic human rights, and work toward closing the economic gap.

• In all fields of social work practice, whether with individuals or families, with groups, communities, domestic institutions, or nations, social work must be grounded in human rights.

• Recognizing that social workers who advocate on behalf of human rights can become subject to reprisal, NASW should ensure that social workers who are threatened are given the full support of the profession. (NASW, 2003, pp. 212–213)

NASW also states that the "appalling prevalence of wars, genocide, ethnic cleansing; discrimination and social exclusion, gender inequality, battering, rape, and the sale of women; sweatshops, child labor, and enslavement; and the suppression of human rights, demonstrates that the struggle for human rights remains a high priority for the social work profession in the 21st century" (2003, p. 213). Unquestionably, the social work profession views human rights as a critical part of their practice. However, the reality is that, at least within the United States, human rights have remained on the fringe of social work practice.

A primary challenge confronting social workers is how to integrate human rights into practice. Clearly, knowledge of human rights principles occupies the first step in this direction. Both NASW and the CSWE highlight the importance of understanding human rights. By studying human rights principles, social workers will then be ready to start the work of applying those principles to practice.

Application of Human Rights to Practice

The leap from an academic study of human rights to application to practice should be structured as much as possible on existing social work practices or interventions. Numerous interventions exist, with some viewed as more important than others.

Intervention 1: Challenging Oppression

Within the social work profession, challenging oppression is a primary form of intervention. Oppression refers to an unjust use of authority or power over an individual or group. Oppression can take many forms: racial and ethnic discrimination, policies that favor the wealthy over the poor, gender inequality, belittling of gay and lesbians, and other unjust uses of power. Common to each form of oppression is the affected individual's or group's social reality (Appleby, Colon, & Hamilton, 2001; van Wormer, 2004a). In many cases, oppression promotes notions of rage, anger, or self-effacement within the individual or group. For example, repeated exposure to oppression may cause a person or group to internalize negative self-images projected by the external oppressor. If those in power continually state that poor people are inferior to others, the affected group may begin to internalize these images of inferiority. This internalized oppression may lead to rage and resignation from the broader society. Yet, repression of this rage can lead to self-destructive behavior or destructive behavior toward others (Schulman, 1999).

Social workers have a responsibility to challenge individual and social relations that create and maintain oppression (Pinderhughes, 1989). According to social work ethics, the responsibility to challenge oppression rests upon the social work profession (NASW, 1999, p. 6).

Human rights principles also view oppression as unjust and in direct contradiction to those principles. According to the Universal Declaration of Human Rights (1948), every individual has an equal right to human dignity (Article 1). Everyone is entitled to all the rights and freedoms within the Universal Declaration without distinction as to race, color, sex, language, religion, political or other opinion, national or social origin, property, birth, or other status (Article 2).

Oppression creates an unequal and unjust set of circumstances, which the social work profession should challenge. Social workers learn this as part of their fundamental education and training. Just as important, though, is the role human rights play in challenging oppression. To ignore the significance of human rights in the fight against oppression weakens the social work profession. By drawing upon human rights principles, social workers can much more effectively challenge acts of oppression. After all, if a social worker can point to a human rights violation when challenging oppression, those perpetrating the oppression are much more likely to pay attention to their conduct than if no human rights violation is noted.

Intervention 2: Empowerment

Another important intervention within the social work profession is that of empowerment. Like the intervention of challenging oppression, empowerment aims to reduce inequitable power structures (Gutierrez, 1990; Lee, 1994; Salomon, 1976; Simon, 1994; van Wormer, 2004a). The basis of empowerment rests upon an examination of circumstances that contribute to differential treatment concerning ethnicity, age, class, national origin, religion, and sexual orientation. The social worker then attempts to empower individuals or groups by assisting the affected persons to understand their experiences of oppression and form appropriate responses (Saleebey, 2002).

Whether a person has access to resources and power often determines the level of empowerment that can be employed by the affected person. An individual with resources and an opportunity to play an important role in his or her own environment can more easily shape outcomes (Reichert, 2003). For example, an individual who has influence in the community may advocate for better treatment of prisoners. After a criminal conviction for lying to federal investigators, home- and garden icon Martha Stewart served a six-month sentence in a prison for women. This particular prison was the first federal women's prison in the United States, opening in 1920 as a place where "fallen" women could reclaim dignity as well as learn skills (Marks, 2004). However, this rehabilitative tradition no longer exists and has given way to a punitive model that critics claim allows intimidation, humiliation, and sexual harassment. To some, the prison represents all that is wrong with how the criminal justice system deals with women. Will Martha Stewart, having served her sentence, advocate for better prison conditions? Certainly with her resources, she could exercise a level of empowerment that many others can only imagine. The average female prisoner serving alongside Stewart would have a much more difficult time persuading authorities to improve prison conditions.

Assisting individuals and groups to empower themselves to overcome inequitable treatment forms a key part of the social work profession. Empowerment can raise the consciousness level of all parties about inequitable treatment. By assisting others to empower themselves and leading them to available resources, social workers are also promoting human rights, which center on equitable treatment for all. Empowerment and human rights are intertwined. Yet, without noting this integral connection, social workers miss an important tool in helping others empower themselves.

Intervention 3: Strengths Perspective

Another important social work intervention known as the strengths perspective focuses on an individual's or group's strengths, even though other circumstances may indicate drug addiction, child abuse, or some other obstacle. Rather than highlighting deficiencies within an individual's or group's situation, the strengths perspective aims to assist people in using their own attributes in overcoming or coping with particular obstacles. The strengths perspective helps social workers avoid the trap of viewing an individual or group as inadequate or otherwise incapable of improving their situation. Many individuals and groups may find themselves in social predicaments because of structural injustices, lack of resources, or discriminatory treatment. Strengths perspective focuses on resiliency and coping skills within a less than ideal environment.

The realization that an individual's or group's situation in life may, at least in part, be a result of structural injustices and lack of resources or fair treatment helps create a perspective of human dignity and worth, core human rights principles (United Nations, 1948). By acknowledging the strengths of individuals and groups, social workers are better poised to connect human rights to a particular situation. For example, when confronted with an individual who is HIV-positive and has been injecting heroin with used needles, a social worker using the strengths perspective would focus on other elements of the individual's circumstances. By learning about the individual's background and own personal obstacles, the social worker would inevitably look for strengths exhibited by the individual. Within this framework, the social worker could then address human rights issues related to the individual's circumstances (Reichert, 2003). Does the individual have adequate health care? Shelter? Food? What education level does the individual have? Can the individual find employment? The idea is to list the qualities or strengths of the individual and then assess human rights issues. After evaluating strengths and assessing human rights, the social worker could then assist the individual in obtaining health care, shelter, and other necessities.

Intervention 4: Ethnic-Sensitive Practice

A fundamental concept underlying human rights principles is the importance of not discriminating against others on the basis of race or ethnic origin. The social work intervention of ethnic-sensitive practice takes into account the significance of race and ethnic origin in understanding a particular cultural experience and identity (Devore & Schlesinger, 1996; McGoldrick, Giordano, & Pearce, 1996; Swenson, 1998; van Wormer, 2004a, 2004b). Relevant questions with ethnic-sensitive practice include the following: What impact does an individual's ethnic identity have on how others perceive that individual and existing social conditions? How does an individual's day-to-day objective experience compare to his or her subjective perceptions? For instance, an individual of Hispanic origin may subjectively perceive discriminatory conditions at the workplace while the employer applies those same conditions to everyone. The employer may truly believe that it does not discriminate because it treats everyone the same. However, within an ethnic-sensitive practice situation, the perception of discrimination may indeed be valid to the individual.

Human rights principles value nondiscrimination and encourage cultural diversity. The social work intervention of ethnic-sensitive practice goes hand in hand with human rights.

Intervention 5: Feminist Practice

Within the social work profession, gender issues frequently enter into discussions about discrimination, education, child welfare, and other important topics. The importance of women in societal structures should not be understated:

> Around the world, empowering women is now widely considered essential to expanding economic growth, reducing poverty, improving public health, sustaining the environment, and consolidating transitions from tyranny to democracy. A near-universal consensus is calling for fundamental changes in practices that have denied rights to women for centuries. (Chesler, 2004, p. A27)

Yet, even with a "near-universal consensus," actually developing techniques that more fully empower women can be difficult. The discussion of gender issues frequently takes the form of who has power and who does not. At times, a futile tug-of-war results from this view of gender issues as male versus female.

Feminist practice focuses on a critique of power relations characterized primarily by gender domination and subordination (Reichert, 2003). Feminist practice recognizes that gender issues often become shaped by notions of domination and subordination. However, this intervention provides a more constructive approach to gender issues by promoting collaboration and cooperation rather than competition between males and females (Bricker-Jenkins, Hooeyman, & Gottlieb, 1991; Van Den Bergh & Cooper, 1986). The collaborative approach goes beyond the critique of which gender has power but addresses disempowerment or oppression of anyone, whether on the basis of race, religion, sexual orientation, or other category. The goal of feminist practice as an intervention is to be inclusive to all and not simply focus on a gender war.

In connection with human rights principles, feminist practice emphasizes the inherent value of everyone, with the right to be free from discrimination and oppression. Human dignity and human value are primary within feminist practice, which corresponds to human rights principles.

Intervention 6: Cultural Competence

Human rights recognize the value of culture and diversity within any particular society. Prejudice against a particular culture or cultural trait defies the underlying theme of human rights.

As an intervention, cultural competence acknowledges different cultural prejudices that may exist toward various individuals and groups—ethnocentrism, sexism, classism, heterosexism, and racism. For instance, in Western countries, such as the United States and Germany, with large immigrant populations, ethnocentric views of immigrants by "mainstream" citizens may degrade cultural attributes of the immigrants. Even with its admirable history as a nation of immigrants, the United States has not always been so kind to cultural diversity. Yet, both human rights principles and U.S. laws generally promote equal treatment between citizens and noncitizens:

> The United States, famous as a nation of immigrants, should also be infamous for its bouts of anti-immigrant sentiment. Often our intolerance has been fueled by national-security fears. At other times, Americans have made misguided assumptions about who immigrants are and the rights that protect them.
>
> Foreigners in the United States illegally get a lot of publicity, but a substantial majority of noncitizens in America are here legally. They include permanent residents; people legally admitted for work, education, or tourism; refugees; asylum seekers; and people with temporary protected status. All of these noncitizens—including those here illegally—are guaranteed almost all the same rights as citizens. In fact, only three constitutional rights—voting in elections, holding certain political offices, and the absolute ability to enter and remain in the country—are denied noncitizens outright. (Parker, 2004, p. A11)

On paper, noncitizens will not encounter prejudices by society as a whole. However, the reality can be quite different. After September 11, 2001, even the millions of U.S. citizens with Arab heritages have unquestionably encountered suspicion and resentment by the larger society.

Cultural competence entails an understanding that society as a whole possesses and indeed acts on many of its prejudices toward others. This intervention requires continuous effort on the part of the social worker to increase knowledge about the client's culture, including its norms, vocabulary, symbols, and strengths (van Wormer, 1997, p. 209).

Summary of Interventions and Connection to Human Rights

The following table summarizes important social work interventions and their connection to human rights. The connection to human rights is not simply incidental or insignificant. The roots of social work interventions are entwined with human rights principles.

Social Work Intervention	Human Rights Principles
Challenging oppression	– Human dignity – Freedom from discrimination – Right to life, liberty, and security of person – Due process – Freedom of movement – Right to asylum – Freedom of expression – Health care and economic rights – Right to education – Right to participate in cultural life of community
Empowerment	– Freedom from discrimination – Self-determination – Right to participate in cultural life of community – Right to life, liberty, and security of person – Freedom of expression
Strengths perspective	– Self-determination – Human dignity – Human worth
Ethnic-sensitive practice	– Freedom from discrimination – Right to participate in cultural life of community – Human dignity – Right to life, liberty, and security of person – Right to nationality
Feminist practice	– Human dignity – Freedom from discrimination – Right to life, liberty, and security of person – Due process – Equality
Cultural competence	– Freedom from discrimination – Right to participate in cultural life of community – Human dignity – Right to life, liberty, and security of person – Right to nationality – Self-determination

Exercises

The following case studies provide examples for applying human rights principles to social work practice.

Hannah and Carl

Hannah lives with Carl and their two children in a trailer. At times, they do not have water or heat, and the trailer has never been repaired since a tornado hit the area several months ago. Three years ago, Carl suffered an injury in a car accident and has been unable to work since. The couple's marriage had difficulties before Carl's accident and became worse afterward. His long-term unemployment has aggravated a drinking problem, which makes it difficult for him to be there emotionally for Hannah and the children.

Hannah has developed chronic depression, which makes it difficult to take care of her children. What holds the couple together is their affection for their children: four-year-old Jenny and two-year-old Bill.

The social worker in charge of the case makes arrangements for the children to attend day care and pre-kindergarten to take them out of their slumlike environment and provide them with one regular meal a day. Because the children are found to be consistently listless and withdrawn, the social worker arranges an examination by a pediatrician and a child psychiatrist, who suspects—but who has no direct evidence—sexual abuse by the father.

Fearing that the removal of the children would cause the collapse of the family, the social worker and her agency decide to continue monitoring the family for a few months and to concentrate on helping Carl find employment. Jenny and Bill appear to be fond of their parents, and for the time being, the option of taking them into foster home is delayed.

1. What human rights issues are relevant to this case study? Cite specific provisions within human rights instruments, including the Universal Declaration of Human Rights and the Convention on the Rights of the Child.

2. What interventions are appropriate in this situation? How do they connect to relevant human rights issues?

3. What ethical issues are involved? Cite specific provisions within the NASW Code of Ethics.

4. If you were the social worker assigned to this case, how would you assess the situation? Would you remove the children? Refer to human rights provisions to explain your assessment.

Velma

Mrs. Velma Smith, aged 94, lives in a farmhouse in a rural area. She has lived in the house for many years and has raised her family there. She has been a very independent and capable woman all her life. Her two adult children are deceased as are most of her relatives.

Neighbors called the police after they had not seen Velma for several days. The police referred the matter to a social work agency. A social worker managed to reach Velma by phone and got permission from Velma to open the door to Velma's residence. Velma had been lying in her bed for a week, unable to get up. She had some food beside her and had used the bed as a toilet.

The only thing Velma could talk about was her cat. She was worried that she could not feed the cat. She did not want to go to the hospital.

The social worker assessed that Velma should be given home help for 5 hours a day. Velma did not think that she could afford this. The social worker also proposed that someone else take the cat and care for it. However, Velma said that she would rather die than be separated from her cat.

1. What human rights issues are relevant to this case study? Cite specific provisions within human rights instruments, including the Universal Declaration of Human Rights and the Declaration on the Rights for the Older Persons.

2. What interventions are appropriate in this situation? How do they connect to relevant human rights issues?

3. What ethical issues are involved? Cite specific provisions within the NASW Code of Ethics.

4. If you were a social worker assigned to this case, how would you assess the situation? Refer to human rights provisions to explain your assessment.

Anton and Thelma

You are a social worker for a state agency called the Department of Child and Family Services. The purpose of the agency is to assist families in times of difficulty. You are asked to follow up on a case that had been classified as environmental neglect. You visit the home of Anton and Thelma, who live with their three- and four-year-old children in a trailer. There is no heating, no water, no electricity, and the roof has cracks from a previous storm. The sanitary conditions of the house are atrocious. You have to consider the safety for the children and make recommendations:

1. What human rights issues are relevant to this case study? Cite specific provisions within human rights instruments, including the Universal Declaration of Human Rights.

2. What interventions are appropriate in this situation? How do they connect to relevant human rights issues?

3. What ethical issues are involved? Cite specific provisions within the NASW Code of Ethics.

4. If you were the social worker assigned to this case, how would you assess the situation? Would you remove the children? Refer to human rights provisions to explain your assessment.

Mary

You are a social work counselor, and Mary is one of your clients. About one year ago, Mary was reported to the Department of Child and Family Services for physically abusing her children. Mary works and also attends college. You feel that Mary has made significant progress in treatment. Recently, Mary tells you that someone sexually harassed her at her workplace. When Mary reported the harassment, Mary's supervisor fired her. Also, around this time, Mary's boyfriend left her for someone else. Mary then tells you that she "lost" it with one of her children and beat him severely. You must now decide whether to report this recent incident of abuse.

1. What human rights issues are relevant to this case study? Cite specific provisions within human rights instruments, including the Universal Declaration of Human Rights and the Convention on the Rights of the Child.

2. What interventions are appropriate in this situation? How do they connect to relevant human rights issues?

3. What ethical issues are involved? Cite specific provisions within the NASW Code of Ethics.

4. If you were the social worker assigned to this case, how would you assess the situation? Would you report the abuse? Refer to human rights provisions to explain your assessment.

Reva

You are a school social worker. A high school student named Reva, who is an immigrant, tells you that her parents want to follow the tradition of their country and have a clitoridectomy performed on her. The family will take her back to her home country and have this procedure done. Reva does not want this procedure done at all and is severely distressed about it.

1. What human rights issues are relevant to this case study? Cite specific provisions within human rights instruments, including the Universal Declaration of Human Rights, the Convention on the Rights of the Child, and CEDAW.

2. What dilemmas or conflicts do you see?

3. What interventions are appropriate in this situation? How do they connect to relevant human rights issues?

4. What ethical issues are involved? Cite specific provisions within the NASW Code of Ethics.

5. How would you assess this situation? Refer to human rights provisions to explain your assessment.

Alex

Alex is a 40-year-old lawful immigrant from Mexico. Alex has minor children who reside with him. He has never obtained U.S. citizenship. Alex has worked at various jobs in the United States for 20 years, but often Alex's employers do not withhold Social Security payments. Alex is now without any employment. He applied for temporary assistance for needy families (TANF), because he had no other means of assistance. TANF workers told Alex that, because he was an immigrant and not a citizen, and had insufficient payments to Social Security, he was not entitled to receive any welfare benefits.

1. What human rights issues are relevant to this situation? Cite specific provisions within human rights instruments, including the Universal Declaration of Human Rights.

2. What interventions are appropriate in this situation? How do they connect to relevant human rights issues?

3. What ethical issues are involved? Cite specific provisions within the NASW Code of Ethics.

4. If you were the social worker assigned to this case, how would you assess the situation? Refer to human rights provisions to explain your assessment.

Xena

Xena is a 30-year-old woman. She was a "mail order bride" from the Ukraine and hoped for a better life in the United States. She met her future husband, Joe, a U.S. citizen, in the Ukraine, and three days later followed him to the United States. The marriage was difficult from the start. Xena was not familiar with the language or the culture. Joe lived in a rural area, virtually isolated from others. Xena could not drive and had nobody to talk to. Joe lost his job, and he began drinking heavily. One evening, Joe became violent and abused Xena, who had no idea what to do. Joe continued being abusive, but Xena did eventually learn about shelters for battered women. Xena managed to go to a shelter and receive counseling. Because she was not a citizen of the United States, Xena feared that if she divorced Joe, she could have difficulties with U.S. immigration and would be deported.

1. What human rights issues are relevant to this case study? Cite specific provisions within human rights instruments, including the Universal Declaration of Human Rights.

2. What interventions are appropriate in this situation? How do they connect to relevant human rights issues?

3. What ethical issues are involved? Cite specific provisions within the NASW Code of Ethics.

4. If you were the social worker, how would you assess the situation? Refer to human rights provisions to explain your assessment.

Anna

Anna is a single mother with two girls, ages 8 and 10. They became homeless several years ago after Anna left her abusive husband. They lived in a shelter and transitional housing before they got a house last year. Anna holds down two different jobs; however, neither of them provides health insurance. At one of her jobs, Anna applied to move up to a managerial position, but the job was given to a man with the same qualification and less seniority.

Recently, Anna was diagnosed with ovarian cysts that had to be removed. Because of complications after surgery, she will not be able to go back to work for six to eight weeks. Anna has not been able to pay rent for two months, and she has already received notice from her landlord that she will be evicted if she will not pay her rent.

1. What human rights issues are relevant to this case study? Cite specific provisions within human rights instruments, including the Universal Declaration of Human Rights.

2. What interventions are appropriate in this situation? How do they connect to relevant human rights issues?

3. What ethical issues are involved? Cite specific provisions within the NASW Code of Ethics.

4. If you were the social worker, how would you assess the situation? Refer to human rights provisions to explain your assessment.

Lena

Lena is in the process of divorcing her husband. She wants shared custody of their two children, Ray and Tom. However, the husband claims that Lena is a lesbian and, because of this, has contested any custody arrangement with Lena. Lena's employer has terminated Lena's employment. Lena believes that her employer terminated her employment because of past statements by her employer that gay and lesbian lifestyles are sinful. However, the employer claims that Lena simply failed to do her job, possibly because of the time she had to commit to the legal battle over custody. Lena has no specific evidence to link the employment termination with her being a lesbian.

1. What human rights issues are relevant to this case study? Cite specific provisions within human rights instruments, including the Universal Declaration of Human Rights.

2. What interventions are appropriate in this situation? How do they connect to relevant human rights issues?

3. What ethical issues are involved? Cite specific provisions within the NASW Code of Ethics.

4. If you were the social worker, how would you assess the situation? Refer to human rights provisions to explain your assessment.

Rita

Rita works in a social service agency. She learns that the records of clients are being altered. For instance, clients' hours are being falsified. She tells her supervisor of the issue. Soon afterward she realizes that she is being treated different by the management and by some workers. Her annual evaluation is harsh and soon afterward she receives notice that she is being laid off.

---

1. What human rights issues are relevant to this case study? Cite specific provisions within human rights instruments, including the Universal Declaration of Human Rights.

2. What interventions are appropriate in this situation? How do they connect to relevant human rights issues?

3. What ethical issues are involved? Cite specific provisions within the NASW Code of Ethics.

4. How would you assess the situation? Refer to human rights provisions to explain your assessment.

Rose

Rose is 40 years old, and has two children, ages six and nine. Rose also has a disability. Two years ago, Rose was mandated to come to counseling for the non-offending parents group. Her husband was sexually abusing both of her children, and the abuse was substantiated. Rose had a very difficult time believing this. For two years she attended an educational support group for parents who for whatever reason are not able to protect their children. Initially, Rose did not remember anything about her own childhood. When she did start to remember, she realized that she was abused by her father and his friends, while her own mother sometimes watched. Rose's husband is in prison and will be released in two weeks. Initially, Rose wanted to get back with him, but now she is not so sure. Rose has a high school education and works at low-paying jobs.

---

1. What human rights issues are relevant to this case study? Cite specific provisions within human rights instruments, including the Universal Declaration of Human Rights.

2. What interventions are appropriate in this situation? How do they connect to relevant human rights issues?

3. What ethical issues are involved? Cite specific provisions within the NASW Code of Ethics.

4. If you were the social worker, how would you assess the situation? Refer to human rights provisions to explain your assessment.

Don

Don is a 25-year-old Hispanic male and has two children, ages three and five. The mother of the children died two years ago. He was recently in a motorcycle accident and lost his job. Because of his injuries and the long hospital stay, the children were taken care of by relatives. Don's medical expenses are very high, and he has no insurance; in addition, he is in danger of having his house repossessed.

Now the relatives are stating that he is unfit as a parent, but Don wants to raise his children.

---

1. What human rights issues are relevant to this case study? Cite specific provisions within human rights instruments, including the Universal Declaration of Human Rights and the Convention on the Rights of the Child.

2. What interventions are appropriate in this situation? How do they connect to relevant human rights issues?

3. What ethical issues are involved? Cite specific provisions within the NASW Code of Ethics.

4. If you were the social worker, how would you assess the situation? Refer to human rights provisions to explain your assessment.

John

John is an outspoken employee at a social work agency. He has challenged previous acts in his agency, including an incident where his supervisor forged his name on a report. This incident resulted in the firing of the supervisor, who was very popular with some of John's coworkers and the administration. Many of John's coworkers do not feel comfortable with his outspokenness. They now complain behind his back and, at the urging of John's supervisors, signed a petition to have John removed from his current office and separated from everyone else. The petition stated only that John was unethical and should be physically removed from the department. No specific reasons for John being unethical were stated in the petition. Signers of the petition never went to John directly to discuss their grievances. The administration accepted the petition as an expression of free speech and saw nothing wrong with it. John went to his immediate supervisor and asked for specific information about his "unethical" behavior. The supervisor never gave John any reasons for the petition but only said that the matter was under investigation.

1. What human rights issues are relevant to this case study? Cite specific provisions within human rights instruments, including the Universal Declaration of Human Rights and the Convention on the Rights of the Child.

2. What interventions are appropriate in this situation? How do they connect to relevant human rights issues?

3. What ethical issues are involved? Cite specific provisions within the NASW Code of Ethics.

4. If you were a social worker assigned to resolve this matter, how would you assess the situation? What would you do to protect the rights of John and those of his coworkers?

Developing Policies and Practices

You are assigned to draft a social policy program in regard to children and families. Establish policies and practices that promote the well-being of children and families and use human rights principles.

CHAPTER 9

The International Side of Human Rights and Social Work

S ocial workers in the United States may find it difficult to link what they do with social work in other countries. A social worker employed by a local government organization against child abuse would clearly be more concerned with local situations than exploring how social work connects with circumstances abroad. What relevance do human rights in other countries have to social workers employed within local organizations? A definition of international social work helps to answer this question:

> International social work is defined as international professional action and the capacity for international action by the social work profession and its members. International action has four dimensions: internationally related domestic practice and advocacy, professional exchange, international practice, and international policy development and advocacy. (Healy, 2001, p. 7)

Social work organizations that encourage international connections, such as the IFSW, believe that social work professions all over the world should take positive actions to help everyone attain basic human rights (IFSW, 2005). Because the primary U.S. association of social workers, the NASW, is a member of the IFSW, social workers in the United States should familiarize themselves with international human rights issues. Under the NASW Code of Ethics (1999), social workers have an ethical responsibility to promote conditions that encourage respect for cultural and social diversity within the United States and globally (6.04c). The Universal Declaration of Human Rights (United Nations, 1948) also places responsibility upon members of the United Nations to work toward a social and international order in which human rights can be fully realized (Article 28). Certainly the education of social workers in the United States or any other country needs to include the study of social conditions and human rights issues in other countries.

Of course, simply relying on statements contained in documents such as the NASW Code of Ethics or the Universal Declaration of Human Rights can be insufficient to promote interest in social work and its international dimensions. The reality, though, is that international events often influence the involvement of social workers in human rights issues occurring even within their local environments. Consider the following: "International social forces and events—most dramatically, the movement of populations—have changed the makeup of social agency caseloads and affected domestic practice in many countries, including the United States" (Healy, 2001, p. 2).

The reality is that social workers in any country no longer have the option of avoiding international human rights issues. Consider the issue of HIV-AIDS, which affects the entire world. Can social workers localize this issue and not take into account the devastation of HIV-AIDS in other countries? It would be unimaginable to view HIV-AIDS as simply a U.S. problem. Social workers everywhere have an obligation to become part of the solution to this affliction. Of course, HIV-AIDS is only one example of an international social force that begs for international attention. Immigration, asylum, and other movements of populations all raise human rights issues that impact local policies and practices. Should Mexicans who illegally immigrate to the United States be entitled to public health care and other social services? Human rights principles generally make no distinction between legal classifications when it comes to basic social services. What should be the position of social workers in these situations? Social workers should be at the forefront of developing policies for these issues, taking into account human rights principles.

Both more and less economically developed countries now share social problems far more often than in previous decades, making mutual work and exchange increasingly desirable (Healy, 2001, p. 3).

As discussed earlier, HIV-AIDS has become a major social problem all over the world. Sharing of information and international exchanges can only help in understanding the global nature of social work and its role in confronting social challenges. Social workers have an ethical obligation to recognize the global nature of many social problems and provide input into resolution of those problems. This can only be accomplished through international cooperation and understanding.

Unemployment, corporate downsizing, and unequal distribution of resources raise many issues throughout the world, and consequences from these developments often require interventions by social workers. While the fallout from unemployment may appear local, causes of unemployment in a country often relate to developments in other countries. The high cost of manufacturing many items in Western countries has led to massive production in less economically developed countries. Moving production of goods to other countries clearly creates local unemployment in the transported industries. While recipient countries of transported industries may welcome the additional employment, unemployment often exists in those countries too. Unemployment is a worldwide social concern, and social workers could benefit from sharing knowledge about coping with this problem.

The actions of one country—politically, economically, and socially—now affect other countries' social and economic well-being, as well as the overall social health of the planet (Healy, 2001, p. 3).

Actions taken by the United States are prime examples of how those actions can affect other countries' social and economic well-being. For example, the U.S. actions that resulted in the war in Iraq have affected the social and economic well-being of Iraq and even the rest of the world. Clearly the rule of Saddam Hussein violated many human rights of Iraqi citizens who had no freedom of speech, had no right to choose a different leader, and suffered other restrictions on basic human rights. The Iraqis have now had a democratic election and are no longer under the thumb of a dictator. Certainly, within this limited context, the intervention in Iraq by the United States has led to positive results.

However, the action of the United States in removing Hussein from power has also led to various types of negative consequences. According to the Iraq Body Count Web site (www.iraqbodycount.net), as of November 2005, between 26,982 and 30,380 Iraqi civilians had died as a consequence of the war, either through U.S. bombings or attacks by other Iraqis. More than 1,700 U.S. soldiers have died, with many thousands of soldiers wounded. Destruction of buildings, utilities, and other infrastructure has clearly had an impact on residents of Iraq. In addition to the destruction within Iraq itself, the financial costs of that war have been enormous for the United States. Referring again to the Iraq Body Count Web site, a continuously updating chart gives the dollar cost of that war to the second. The Web site also analyzes what the cost of that war would have obtained within a human rights context: for example, education, health, and world hunger.

Social workers could play a large role in Iraq by assisting in the distribution of food and other assistance to civilians. Unfortunately, conditions in Iraq have not been secure enough to allow social workers to adequately perform necessary social assistance. Nonetheless, this example of how the actions of one country—the United States—can have profound effects on another country—Iraq—is instructive in illustrating the global nature of social work. By intervening militarily in Iraq, the United States has created a vast area of need for the social work profession. The unanswered question is whether the profession can help Iraqi society meet its needs, considering the current difficulties within Iraq.

Rapidly advancing technological developments in areas such as communications provide enhanced opportunities for the international sharing and exchanging of information and experiences (Healy, 2001, p. 3). The social worker today in the United States has no excuse for not learning about the social work profession in other countries. The Internet in particular has the potential to distribute knowledge about social workers in almost any country. Sharing information and experiences by e-mail and telephone provides opportunities to exchange views on social work issues. By this exchange of information, social workers will undoubtedly begin to see global connections to their profession.

International Human Rights Issues

An essential premise of human rights is that those rights transcend borders and apply to all countries. While culture, morals, and traditions may alter the interpretation of human rights, the basic premise remains that everyone should enjoy certain aspects of the human existence. Everyone should have the right to free speech;

A human right	Country where human rights are violated	Document that proclaims human rights	Group in your country that wants to deny rights to others	Country where people are denied rights because of their race or ethnicity
Organization that fights for human rights	Film/Video that is about rights	Singer who sings about rights	Right your parents have/had that you do not	Country where human rights situation has improved recently
Type of human rights violation that most disturbs you	Book about rights	Right sometimes denied to women	Right all children should have	Country where people are denied rights because of their religion
Human right not yet achieved by everyone in this country	People denied right to establish their own nation or homeland	Human right being achieved around the world	Right of yours that is respected	Someone who is a defender of human rights

Figure 9.1   Human Rights Squares Handout

Source: Adapted from Shiman, D. (1993). *Teaching human rights*. Denver, CO: Center for Teaching International Relations Publications, University of Denver, pp. 2–3. Retrieved from Human Rights Resource Center, 2005.

everyone should be free from discrimination; everyone should have adequate health care; everyone should have employment; everyone should have an education. Even after allowing for differences of opinion, most countries do not dispute the importance of basic human rights.

The question then arises as to what role countries play in promoting human rights outside their borders. Should countries actively pursue human rights in other countries? "Everyone is entitled to a social and international order in which the rights and freedoms set forth in this Declaration can be fully realized" (United Nations, 1948, Article 28).

Indirectly, this article within the Universal Declaration of Human Rights imposes obligations on each country to help realize human rights contained in the declaration. Countries have an obligation to create an environment where human rights can flourish. Disagreements over the nature or definition of human rights should not prevent attempts to resolve these issues. Despite lengthy theoretical discussions about human rights, basic principles of human rights do apply to each country. While the study of various theories and the morality underlying human rights can be important in their overall understanding of human rights, social workers should first comprehend the universal concepts underpinning human rights. By establishing that framework, social workers can then appreciate the international aspect of human rights and work toward better understanding of human rights issues. The interconnectedness of countries in the approach to human rights is essential for improving the human rights environment.

> Everyone, as a member of society, has the right to social security and is entitled to realization, through national effort and international co-operation and in accordance with the organization and resources of each State, of the economic, social, and cultural rights indispensable for his [or her] dignity and the free development of his [or her] personality. (United Nations, 1948, Article 22)

From an international viewpoint, this statement contained in the Universal Declaration of Human Rights could encounter great skepticism. How realistic is it to expect international cooperation in meeting economic, social, and cultural rights? Most of the wealthier Western countries do provide small amounts of economic and technical assistance to less developed countries. But beyond this welfare-type assistance, countries are on their own to develop social development policies that raise income levels of all residents. Some countries may attempt to increase their wealth by encouraging foreign manufacturers to produce goods in their countries. Certainly, foreign investment can generate income. But how is this income distributed? Who receives the income and in what proportion?

To promote the development of a fair and equitable global system, in 1986, the United Nations adopted a Declaration on the Right to Development (United Nations, 1986). The introduction of that declaration cites Article 28 of the Universal Declaration of Human Rights as its general focus—to create a worldwide environment where everyone can realize basic human rights.

Specific principles contained in the declaration include the following:

- The right to development is an inalienable right (Article 1, para. 1).

- The right to development implies the full realization of peoples to self-determination, including the right to full sovereignty over natural wealth and resources (para. 2).

- The human person is the central subject of development and should be the active participant and beneficiary of the right to development (Article 2, para. 1).

- All human beings have a responsibility for development, and they should promote and protect an appropriate political, social, and economic order for development (para. 2).

- States have the primary responsibility for the creation of national and international conditions favorable to the right to development (Article 3, para. 1).

- States have a duty to cooperate with each other in ensuring development and obstacles to development. States should promote a new international order based on sovereign equality, interdependence, mutual interest, and cooperation. States should encourage the observance and realization of human rights (para. 3).

- States have a duty to take steps to formulate international development policies that facilitate the right to development (Article 4, para. 1).

- States shall take steps to eliminate massive and flagrant violations of human rights resulting from apartheid, racism, racial discrimination, colonialism, foreign domination and occupation, and aggression (Article 5).

- All human rights are indivisible and interdependent; states should give equal attention and urgent consideration to promotion of civil, political, economic, social, and cultural rights (Article 6, para. 2).

- States shall ensure equality of opportunity for all concerning access to basic resources, education, health services, food, housing, employment, and the fair distribution of income. Effective measures should be undertaken to ensure that women have an active role in the development process (Article 8, para. 1).

A close reading of these principles makes it clear that the "state," or government, has the primary obligation to create conditions for development. This imposed obligation on government to promote development seems unrealistic in many cases. The initial obstacle relates to the definition of development itself. What exactly is development? Construction of skyscrapers, airports, education, running water and electricity in all homes, four-lane highways to all major cities, self-sufficiency in food? Obviously, development can be difficult to measure. Consider circumstances within the United States. Some areas of the country appear well developed, with reputable schools, nice homes, well-maintained roads, adequate employment, excellent health care—all the attributes associated with development. However, other areas of the United States are not so fortunate—does this mean they are not developed? Under the Declaration on the Right to Development, even within the United States, regions fail to meet the definition of development. Does the state (or federal, state, and local governments) acknowledge this lack of development? Even if it does, will government do something about these social deficiencies? In many cases, the answer will be no, simply because resources will be insufficient to address the problems.

Clearly, a primary difficulty in promoting international development lies in the lack of guidelines to define development and often a lack of commitment by the state to even address local deficiencies. If a country cannot address its own gaps in development, how can that country benefit from development in other countries? Fortunately, the reality is not so stark. Most economically developed countries of the world do attempt to assist less economically developed countries by transferring resources to those countries. Questions can easily arise as to the effectiveness of this transnational assistance in terms of promoting development in the host countries. Yet, with careful planning and an approach that welcomes input by local residents, cross-country assistance can succeed in addressing social problems.

The U.S. Peace Corps: Grassroots Social Development—But Does It Work?

No organization within the world of foreign development has as much mystical and mythical appeal as the U.S. Peace Corps. Created in 1961, the Peace Corps has now sent more than 182,000 volunteers to 137 countries all over the world (U.S. Peace Corps, 2005).

Much of the impetus and purpose behind the Peace Corps stemmed from the book *The Ugly American* (Lederer & Burdick, 1958). (The movie *The Ugly American* with Marlon Brando appeared a few years after the book was published.) *The Ugly American* described U.S. failings in foreign development, highlighting how aloof and distant many U.S. diplomats had become to local populations of developing nations. U.S. foreign policies often reflected this lack of knowledge about local populations. To remedy these U.S. diplomatic shortcomings, the idea of a grassroots development agency gathered force.

In theory, the Peace Corps has three main goals: (1) to render technical and other assistance to economically developing countries; (2) to acquaint residents of the host countries with down-to-earth Americans; and (3) to acquaint the American volunteers with local residents at a community level, rather than the typical business or diplomatic hierarchy. Has the Peace Corps achieved its goals? Certainly the Peace Corps has achieved partial success with goals 2 and 3. However, measuring the attainment of goal 1 requires a more cautious approach.

During the early 1980s, I served as a Peace Corps volunteer in Cameroon, Africa. At that time, I was amazed at how many other development agencies from numerous countries existed, making the Peace Corps only one of many. When asked about the Peace Corps, many local residents responded with little actual knowledge of that organization. They simply meshed it together with any number of similar agencies. In fact, the Peace Corps often operated at a disadvantage to other agencies because of its minimal level of funding. Other, better-endowed organizations, such as U.S. AID and various European entities, had the funds—in the world of foreign aid, money talks.

My job description was lumped into the area of community development, a dubious program that sought to motivate local residents to make decisions and community improvements on their own. Of course, the textbook variety of CD (as community development was affectionately called) sounded great. But the Peace Corps version inevitably required a value judgment as to whose culture was better: ours or theirs? The reality of CD as practiced by Western groups such as the Peace Corps rested upon Western techniques to solve local problems. Let local residents tell the Peace Corps volunteer what ails the community, and the volunteer will work out the solution. But without a deep understanding of the local community, language, and culture, how could the volunteer do anything else but rely on his or her own cultural and technical experience to provide a remedy?

Some of the most successful Peace Corps programs have centered on education, with volunteers filling roles of teachers in schools. The teaching of science, mathematics, English, and other topics relevant to the local community generally has significant value, with aspects of cultural superiority not so prevalent.

To put the Peace Corps and other development groups into a proper perspective, consider the following example. Suppose that the Cameroonian government offered the U.S. government the services of volunteers from Cameroon to develop programs to improve family relations in the United States. After all, there is much we could learn from Cameroonians in this area—respect for parents, care of siblings, and generally viewing family relations as those to be nurtured. The Cameroonian volunteers would be assigned to U.S. government departments and given status and positions over many local Americans.

Would we accept those Cameroonians telling us how they did things and trying to persuade us that their way was better? Would we start feeling inferior, or would we simply snicker at these intruders? We might find the Cameroonians a marvelous group. But most of us probably would not pay much attention to them.

Some Peace Corps officials and volunteers would object to my sentiments. But even they would struggle to explain why the Peace Corps tends to be a one-way street, with no reciprocal group from host countries coming to the United States. Like many development organizations, the Peace Corps rests on the premise of cultural superiority, a major obstacle to improved international relations and development.

I'm not saying that the Peace Corps has been all in vain. We desperately need organizations that promote international understanding and development. However, I am saying that the Peace Corps has a questionable track record when evaluating its overall achievements.

The people who benefit the most from the Peace Corps are usually the volunteers themselves. To expect host residents to view the Peace Corps with more than bemused notions is wishful thinking.

Robert J. McCormick

Regardless of the difficulty in promoting social development, social workers should direct attention to human rights issues in other countries. The danger of not addressing human development issues lies in the consequences of this neglect: famine, disease, violence, civil war, terrorism, and many other social ills.

To promote understanding of social development and human rights issues within an international context, the following guidelines can be important, even without traveling to a particular country or region:

Never assume that your way of doing things is better than the ways of local populations.

Learn all you can about the local culture, history, and language.

Analyze your own government policies toward a particular country or region.

Choose a social work issue, such as child poverty, and research policies and traditions of that issue within a particular country.

Study conditions relating to human rights by reviewing annual reports by Human Rights Watch, UNICEF, Amnesty International, and similar organizations concerned with human rights.

Familiarize yourself with local social work groups by referring to the Web site of the IFSW. Refer to social work journals.

Analyze your own country's attitudes and policies about your chosen topic.

By following these guidelines, a social worker can gain invaluable knowledge about social work and human rights issues within an international context. By understanding the commonality of the human rights struggle, social workers can better fulfill the mission of their profession.

Andrew Moravcsik (2005) presents some sobering thoughts for Americans.

Not long ago, the American dream was a global fantasy. Not only Americans saw themselves as a beacon unto nations. So did much of the rest of the world. East Europeans tuned into Radio Free Europe. Chinese students erected a replica of the Statue of Liberty in Tiananmen Square. But, as Moravcsik says, the American knee-jerk belief of living in the greatest country, and their belief of how the rest of the world views their country, has hit a divide.

According to a poll by the British Broadcasting Corporation (BBC),

71 percent of Americans see the United States as a source of good in the world. More than half view Bush's election as positive for global security. Other studies report that 70 percent have faith in their domestic institutions and nearly 80 percent believe American ideas and customs should spread globally. Foreigners take an entirely different view: 58 percent of foreigners in the BBC poll see Bush's re-election as a threat to world peace. Among America's traditional allies, the figure is strikingly higher: 77 percent in Germany, 64 percent in Britain and 82 percent in Turkey. Among the 1.3 billion members of the Islamic world, public support for the United States is measured in single digits. Only Poland, the Philippines and India viewed Bush's second inaugural positively. (Moravcsik, 2005)

Perhaps much of this negative feedback about the United States stems from the Iraq war, which had little support by the populations of any country outside the United States and England. But there appears to be much more at stake here:

The truth is Americans are living in a dream world. Not only do others not share America's self-regard, they no longer aspire to emulate the country's social and economic achievements. The loss of faith in the American Dream goes beyond [Bush's] swaggering administration and its war in Iraq. A President Kerry would have had to confront a similar disaffection, for it grows from the success of something America holds dear: the spread of democracy, free markets and international institutions—globalization, in a word.

Countries today have dozens of political, economic and social models to choose from. Anti-Americanism is especially virulent in Europe and Latin America, where countries have established their own distinctive ways—none made in America. . . . Blinded by its own myth, America has grown incapable of recognizing its flaws. For there is much about the American Dream to fault. If the rest of the world has lost faith in the American model—political, economic, diplomatic—it's partly for the very good reason that it doesn't work as well anymore. (Moravcsik, 2005)

The remainder of Moravcsik's lengthy article details specific deficiencies within the American model. One target of disdain is the U.S. health care system, which President Bush declared the best in the world in his 2005 inaugural address. As noted by Moravcsik, the

United States is the only developed democracy without a universal guarantee of health care, leaving about 45 million Americans uninsured. Nor do Americans receive higher-quality health care in exchange. Whether it is measured by questioning public-health experts, polling citizen satisfaction or survival rates, the health care offered by other countries increasingly ranks above America's. U.S. infant mortality rates are among the highest for developed democracies. The average Frenchman, like most Europeans, lives nearly four years longer than the average American. Small wonder that the World Health Organization rates the U.S. healthcare system only 37th best in the world, behind Columbia (22nd) and Saudi Arabia (26th), and on a par with Cuba. (Moravcsik, 2005)

Moravcsik has raised important issues for the U.S. social work profession when establishing connections outside the United States. While U.S. social workers may believe that their own policies and practices are better than those of any other country, the reality is not so clear-cut. If U.S. social workers want to develop a more global outlook, they will have to accept that other countries may actually have more effective policies and practices than those at home.

Exercises

Exercise 1: Developing Skills in Understanding International Social Work Issues

The purpose of this exercise is to promote understanding of international social work issues and connections to human rights. The exercise can be done within a group or individually.

Go to the Web site of one of the following organizations:

UNICEF

Amnesty International

Human Rights Watch

Save the Children

Oxfam

UNIFEM

Global Fund

Select an issue of concern to the organization, such as poverty, torture, sexual slavery, hunger, street children, child soldiers, orphans, child labor, or education. Connect your issue to human rights principles within specific documents. List specific sections or articles of those documents that relate to your issue.

Are there any social work policy statements on those issues? For instance, has NASW or IFSW issued a policy statement on the issue? What position do the statements take?

What is the position of the U.S. government toward the issue? You find this by doing Internet word searches or referring to the Web site for the U.S. Department of State and related country reports.

Do you believe that social work organizations or the U.S. government is doing enough to deal with the issue? Why or why not?

How would you bring this issue to the attention of your community? For example, writing letters to newspapers, addressing professional organizations, holding meetings, and writing legislators are possible ways of raising awareness of the issue.

Exercise 2: Finding a Social Work Counterpart

The purpose of this exercise is to find a counterpart in another country with whom you can communicate about social work issues in that country. This is an exercise for individuals, who can then share their findings with a group.

Go the Web site of the IFSW and examine the list of member countries—there are currently more than 80 member countries.

After examining the list of member countries, write to one of the member organizations. Introduce yourself and state that you would like to converse with a social worker about his or her work and issues. Be patient—it could take a couple of attempts to establish a contact.

Once you have established a contact person with whom you can correspond, state that you would like to find out about his or her country regarding social work policies and practices and how those relate to human rights issues. Be sure that the contact person agrees to this discussion. You should let the contact person know that you are also willing to discuss local social work issues with him or her. You should also inquire as to whether certain topics may be sensitive to discuss.

Possible questions for discussion include:

What are human rights issues in your country?

How does the social work profession in your country view human rights?

What policies/practices enhance/hinder the development of human rights?

What are your personal experiences with human rights?

How difficult is it in your country to talk about human rights?

How does your country view the United States in regard to human rights?

How would you imagine a more just world? What would it look like?

How do you integrate human rights principles into social work action?

What controversies do you see with human rights?

Exercise 3: Creating a Social Workers Without Borders Organization

The purpose of this exercise is to create an imaginary organization known as Social Workers Without Borders. This organization would be similar in structure to the actual organization called Doctors Without Borders. This exercise should be done as a group exercise but could also be done individually.

Research the Doctors Without Borders Web site (www.doctorswithoutborders .org/). This organization involves medical doctors from all over the world who travel to areas where they are very much needed. For instance, a doctor from Spain might travel to Sudan to work in a refugee camp to provide much needed medical attention. Make sure you are familiar with the structure and goals of Doctors Without Borders.

Now imagine an organization called Social Workers Without Borders, in which social workers from all over the world would travel to other countries to assist with social work issues, which could include physical disasters, refugees, famine, and child abuse.

Define the mission of this organization.

What organizational structure would the organization have?

What would be the goals of Social Workers Without Borders?

What similarities would this organization have with Doctors Without Borders?

What differences would there be, particularly in regard to the issues being dealt with by the respective organizations?

How would you propose funding the organization?

How could you get the international social work community involved with this organization?

How important would human rights principles be within the organization?

Exercise 4: Human Rights Charters and Courts

The purpose of this exercise is to learn about the different human rights charters and courts that exist worldwide. The exercise may be done either as a group or individually.

Using the Internet, go to the Web sites for the following:

European Court of Human Rights (www.echr.coe.int/)

African Charter (www1.umn.edu/humanrts/instree/z1afchar.htm)

Inter American Human Rights System (www1.umn.edu/humanrts/inter-american system.htm)

Asian Charter of Human Rights (www.ahrchk.net/charter/mainfile.php/ eng_charter)

Read the descriptions of the various organizations and how they are used. Can individuals file complaints or solicit action by any of the organizations? Is the procedure clearly explained?

Exercise 5: Code of Ethics for IFSW

Research the Web site of the IFSW (www.ifsw.org/) and examine the Code of Ethics and the Policy Statement. How does the IFSW code differ from the NASW Code of Ethics? In making the comparison, examine statements about human rights within the two codes. Also examine the mission statements from different countries.

Exercise 6: Case Studies

The Immigrant

A church group recruits a group of young boys to come to the United States from an African country. The church promises to provide the boys with an education and to allow them to sing in the church choir. The church also promises the boys that their home communities would receive money to build schools. After the boys arrived in the United States, the church provided little or no education. However, the boys had to sing continuously. They were taken from singing appointment to appointment without a break. The church told families hosting the boys not to talk to the boys. Eventually, the boys meet someone who helps them tell their story to legal authorities, who then remove the boys from their "hostage" situation.

Identify human rights principles within the above case study.

Describe any violations and give reasons why they are violations.

Customs

Seva is a 10-year-old girl. In Seva's society, girls her age customarily receive a clitoridectomy. For many generations, this procedure has been the custom for young girls. Seva experiences severe bleeding due to the procedure and goes into shock. The family takes her to a hospital, which is 100 miles away. Because the hospital was overcrowded and understaffed, the workers told her to come back the next morning. Seva died during the night.

Did the above scenario present any violations of human rights? If so, which violations of which rights occurred?

Were any violations personal to Seva? If so, which ones?

What about violations affecting the broader society? What are they?

Imagine yourself as a social worker in a government office responsible for health care. Write a report to your supervisor on Seva's death, listing the facts, how you perceive the human rights situation, and proposals for correcting any violations.

The Child Soldier

Ramu, age 13, lives in a war-torn area of Sierra Leone, an African country. Militants have recruited Ramu as a soldier. He has been actively fighting and has killed others, including civilians. Eventually, the war ends, and a truce now exists. The government sends all child soldiers to a rehabilitation camp where the children can "learn to be children again."

Have any human rights been violated? If so, detail those violations, citing specific sections of human rights documents.

What are the responsibilities of Sierra Leone in this case? Of the United States? Of the broader international community?

You are a social worker at the rehabilitation camp. Write a plan of action for assisting Ramu and others like him. Include proposals that would address any human rights violations.

Child Prostitution

Thai is a nine-year-old girl living in Thailand. Her parents live in a rural impoverished area. One day, a stranger approaches Thai's parents and tells them that he would like to give Thai a job with a wealthy family. The parents agree, and the stranger gives the parents money. Thai goes with the stranger who then takes her to a brothel to work as a prostitute. Western men frequent the brothels and spend considerable money, most of which goes into the pocket of the stranger.

What human rights have been violated in this case? Refer to as many documents as you can find, including the Convention on the Rights of the Child.

As a social worker, what action can you take to prevent child prostitution?

What action can be taken by a social worker to prevent child prostitution? Try to find at least one country that has passed a law making it a crime for its citizens to participate in child prostitution even though this occurs outside the home country.

In this situation, what are the responsibilities of the government? Of individuals?

Sexual Slavery

Irena, a young woman from the Ukraine, corresponds with a person from a Western country who promises her a better life in the West. She is told that she could get a job as a secretary making 10 times what she earns in the Ukraine. Irena agrees to meet the Westerner and soon realizes that she will be forced to work in a brothel. She resists, but after repeated physical abuse sees no way out. It turns out that the brothel is in Croatia, and her "customers" are peacekeeping soldiers from the United Nations. Irena tells the soldiers that she is being held at the brothel by force and cannot leave. She has no passport and no visa. The soldiers tell others about Irena, and the story becomes widely known. Amnesty International also investigates the situation and exposes what has happened. After critical publicity, the Croatian government releases Irena and other "sex prisoners." Irena applies for asylum in Germany and receives temporary residence there, pending a complete review of her application.

Cite the human rights violations in this case.

What are the responsibilities of the government to remedy the situation? Of individuals?

As a social work counselor working for the United Nations, write a report on the situation, noting human rights violations and listing proposals to prevent further violations. On a personal level, how would you help Irena?

HIV-AIDS

Rachel, a married woman, lives in Zaire and has HIV-AIDS. Rachel's two children also have HIV-AIDS. Rachel's husband died a year ago from the disease. For several years, Rachel has been trying to get medication from the local hospital to keep the virus in check. However, the hospital always tells her that brand name medicine is available but too expensive. They are waiting for cheaper, generic drugs to arrive.

What human rights, if any, are violated in this case?

What are the responsibilities of the government in this situation? The international community?

As a social worker assigned to Rachel's case, what steps would you take to assist Rachel?

Exercise 7: Human Rights and Catastrophes

Read the following statement issued by Amnesty International, then discuss these issues:

Identify the human rights noted by Amnesty International, citing provisions of human rights documents.

What obligations do countries not affected by this catastrophe have to assist the affected areas? Refer to human rights documents.

Should some countries provide more than others in terms of assistance?

Indian Ocean Earthquake & Tsunami: Human Rights at Risk in the Aftermath (Amnesty International, 2005)

In the aftermath of the tsunami disaster in the Indian Ocean, Amnesty International (AI) is monitoring the relief effort to ensure that fundamental human rights are respected. These include the principle of non-discrimination in aid provision, principles guiding protection of human rights in situations of internal displacement and the right to protection from physical or mental abuse, including violence against women.

AI is calling on all those involved in the relief effort to respect international human rights and humanitarian norms. Assistance should be provided on the basis of need, without discrimination based on the race, colour, sex, language, religion, political or other opinion, national or social origin, property, birth or other status of recipients.

AI is looking into reports of adverse discrimination, with a focus on groups with particular protection needs, such as indigenous and disadvantaged communities, children, migrant workers and women in vulnerable situations. The organization is also concerned that relief should not be used as cover to forcefully relocate populations, in order to clamp down on or undermine support for opposition groups. Any relocation of internally displaced persons from camps or other accommodation must be voluntary, and should not be coerced in any way, including through the suspension of assistance to those persons.

Human rights are most in jeopardy in situations of crisis and emergency. It is therefore critical that governments and other actors recognize and support the central role of human rights defenders, including those engaged in humanitarian work and those monitoring violations, in the relief and reconstruction process.

Specific areas of concern:

Aceh

Even before the earthquake/tsunami, the Indonesian province of Aceh had been seriously affected by a conflict between the armed group Free Aceh Movement (Gerakan Aceh Merdeka, GAM) and the Indonesian military. At least 3000 people have been killed in this conflict since the declaration of a military emergency in May 2003. Access for international humanitarian and human rights agencies was also severely restricted throughout that period. It will be important to ensure that the situation is not exploited by either party to perpetrate further human rights abuses.

AI is monitoring the Indonesian response to the current crisis, including the leading role played in relief efforts by the Indonesian military. AI is closely monitoring any alleged human rights abuses associated with the continuing conflict in Aceh.

Sri Lanka

Of particular concern are the emerging reports of sexual violence against women in camps for the displaced. AI's ongoing campaign to Stop Violence against Women has highlighted the specific risks faced by internally displaced women and the need for concrete measures to prevent sexual violence and investigate such complaints immediately, thoroughly and independently.

AI is also concerned by reports from Sri Lanka that orphaned children may be recruited as soldiers by the Liberation Tigers of Tamil Eelam (LTTE), in the north and east of the country and is monitoring this closely. Recruitment of children by the LTTE has been a longstanding concern. The organization is continuing to appeal for an immediate halt to this practice and is urging that those children recruited to date are returned to their families or communities.

There were initially some positive signs of co-operation between the LTTE and the government; however there appears to be increasing disagreement between the two parties over the distribution of aid. AI is concerned that these disagreements should not delay or obstruct delivery of essential aid and continues to monitor developments.

Thailand

AI is investigating reports of harassment by the Thai police of Burmese migrants who have lost their identity cards.

Conclusion

This book serves only as a brief introduction to human rights within a social work context. For a deeper understanding of many human rights concepts and theories, the social work student or professional will need to refer to other sources, some of which are cited in the reference section of this book. By itself, though, this book provides the social worker with a sufficient basis to understand and analyze the role of human rights in social work policies and practices. In particular, use of the exercises can help the student comprehend the crucial link between human rights and social work. The exercises require the student to critically think about how human rights fit in the contemporary world of social work issues.

As this book makes clear, human rights present many dilemmas and conflicts within and among societies. Cultural relativism remains one of the most difficult hurdles in promoting a universal view of human rights. Even within human rights principles, everyone has the right to his or her own culture. Where, then, is the line drawn between cultural practices that seem archaic or adverse to social work ethics and principles, and universal human rights? To create a working model for wrestling with these types of issues, the social work student needs to learn how to critically analyze human rights issues. This book provides an initial step toward this goal. Of course, further reading in this area can only enhance understanding of complexities and controversies surrounding human rights.

In addition to providing a working overview of human rights for the social worker, this book illustrates the grassroots nature of human rights. Many important developments within the area of human rights originate from the lower levels of society. However, it is one thing for governments to pass laws mandating human rights policies; it is another to enforce those policies. Without effective monitoring and promotion at the lower levels, government policies can often turn into empty promises. Certainly the role of government in promoting human rights is important, but without local insistence on the exercise of human rights, scant attention to human rights may result.

Exercises in this book view human rights on a basic level and emphasize small steps toward the goal of understanding and instilling human rights. Human rights form a continuing network of obligations and responsibilities, with community being a key part of that network. Reliance upon legislators, government officials, and other "leaders" to actually promote human rights will often lead to disappointment.

A final aim of this book is to highlight the fragile nature of human rights. Erosion of human rights can easily occur without constant diligence. Cultural relativism can easily justify a need to limit human rights, whether for national security or some other plausible reason. Human rights cannot be taken for granted. To ensure that this does not occur, education about human rights needs to be the norm and not the exception, especially within social work, a profession closely linked to human rights.

Appendix A

Universal Declaration of Human Rights

Adopted and proclaimed by General Assembly resolution 217 A (III) of 10 December 1948

On December 10, 1948 the General Assembly of the United Nations adopted and proclaimed the Universal Declaration of Human Rights the full text of which appears in the following pages.

Preamble

Whereas recognition of the inherent dignity and of the equal and inalienable rights of all members of the human family is the foundation of freedom, justice and peace in the world,

Whereas disregard and contempt for human rights have resulted in barbarous acts which have outraged the conscience of mankind, and the advent of a world in which human beings shall enjoy freedom of speech and belief and freedom from fear and want has been proclaimed as the highest aspiration of the common people,

Whereas it is essential, if man is not to be compelled to have recourse, as a last resort, to rebellion against tyranny and oppression, that human rights should be protected by the rule of law,

Whereas it is essential to promote the development of friendly relations between nations,

Whereas the peoples of the United Nations have in the Charter reaffirmed their faith in fundamental human rights, in the dignity and worth of the human person and in the equal rights of men and women and have determined to promote social progress and better standards of life in larger freedom,

Whereas Member States have pledged themselves to achieve, in co-operation with the United Nations, the promotion of universal respect for and observance of human rights and fundamental freedoms,

Whereas a common understanding of these rights and freedoms is of the greatest importance for the full realization of this pledge,

Now, Therefore THE GENERAL ASSEMBLY proclaims THIS UNIVERSAL DECLARATION OF HUMAN RIGHTS as a common standard of achievement for all peoples and all nations, to the end that every individual and every organ of society, keeping this Declaration constantly in mind, shall strive by teaching and education to promote respect for these rights and freedoms and by progressive measures, national and international, to secure their universal and effective recognition and observance, both among the peoples of Member States themselves and among the peoples of territories under their jurisdiction.

Article 1

All human beings are born free and equal in dignity and rights. They are endowed with reason and conscience and should act towards one another in a spirit of brotherhood.

Article 2

Everyone is entitled to all the rights and freedoms set forth in this Declaration, without distinction of any kind, such as race, colour, sex, language, religion, political or other opinion, national or social origin, property, birth or other status. Furthermore, no distinction shall be made on the basis of the political, jurisdictional or international status of the country or territory to which a person belongs, whether it be independent, trust, non-self-governing or under any other limitation of sovereignty.

Article 3

Everyone has the right to life, liberty and security of person.

Article 4

No one shall be held in slavery or servitude; slavery and the slave trade shall be prohibited in all their forms.

Article 5

No one shall be subjected to torture or to cruel, inhuman or degrading treatment or punishment.

Article 6

Everyone has the right to recognition everywhere as a person before the law.

Article 7

All are equal before the law and are entitled without any discrimination to equal protection of the law. All are entitled to equal protection against any discrimination in violation of this Declaration and against any incitement to such discrimination.

Article 8

Everyone has the right to an effective remedy by the competent national tribunals for acts violating the fundamental rights granted him by the constitution or by law.

Article 9

No one shall be subjected to arbitrary arrest, detention or exile.

Article 10

Everyone is entitled in full equality to a fair and public hearing by an independent and impartial tribunal, in the determination of his rights and obligations and of any criminal charge against him.

Article 11

(1) Everyone charged with a penal offence has the right to be presumed innocent until proved guilty according to law in a public trial at which he has had all the guarantees necessary for his defence.

(2) No one shall be held guilty of any penal offence on account of any act or omission which did not constitute a penal offence, under national or international law, at the time when it was committed. Nor shall a heavier penalty be imposed than the one that was applicable at the time the penal offence was committed.

Article 12

No one shall be subjected to arbitrary interference with his privacy, family, home or correspondence, nor to attacks upon his honour and reputation. Everyone has the right to the protection of the law against such interference or attacks.

Article 13

(1) Everyone has the right to freedom of movement and residence within the borders of each state.

(2) Everyone has the right to leave any country, including his own, and to return to his country.

Article 14

(1) Everyone has the right to seek and to enjoy in other countries asylum from persecution.

(2) This right may not be invoked in the case of prosecutions genuinely arising from non-political crimes or from acts contrary to the purposes and principles of the United Nations.

Article 15

(1) Everyone has the right to a nationality.

(2) No one shall be arbitrarily deprived of his nationality nor denied the right to change his nationality.

Article 16

(1) Men and women of full age, without any limitation due to race, nationality or religion, have the right to marry and to found a family. They are entitled to equal rights as to marriage, during marriage and at its dissolution.

(2) Marriage shall be entered into only with the free and full consent of the intending spouses.

(3) The family is the natural and fundamental group unit of society and is entitled to protection by society and the State.

Article 17

(1) Everyone has the right to own property alone as well as in association with others.

(2) No one shall be arbitrarily deprived of his property.

Article 18

Everyone has the right to freedom of thought, conscience and religion; this right includes freedom to change his religion or belief, and freedom, either alone or in community with others and in public or private, to manifest his religion or belief in teaching, practice, worship and observance.

Article 19

Everyone has the right to freedom of opinion and expression; this right includes freedom to hold opinions without interference and to seek, receive and impart information and ideas through any media and regardless of frontiers.

Article 20

(1) Everyone has the right to freedom of peaceful assembly and association.

(2) No one may be compelled to belong to an association.

Article 21

(1) Everyone has the right to take part in the government of his country, directly or through freely chosen representatives.

(2) Everyone has the right of equal access to public service in his country.

(3) The will of the people shall be the basis of the authority of government; this will shall be expressed in periodic and genuine elections which shall be by universal and equal suffrage and shall be held by secret vote or by equivalent free voting procedures.

Article 22

Everyone, as a member of society, has the right to social security and is entitled to realization, through national effort and international co-operation and in accordance with the organization and resources of each State, of the economic, social and cultural rights indispensable for his dignity and the free development of his personality.

Article 23

(1) Everyone has the right to work, to free choice of employment, to just and favourable conditions of work and to protection against unemployment.

(2) Everyone, without any discrimination, has the right to equal pay for equal work.

(3) Everyone who works has the right to just and favourable remuneration ensuring for himself and his family an existence worthy of human dignity, and supplemented, if necessary, by other means of social protection.

(4) Everyone has the right to form and to join trade unions for the protection of his interests.

Article 24

Everyone has the right to rest and leisure, including reasonable limitation of working hours and periodic holidays with pay.

Article 25

(1) Everyone has the right to a standard of living adequate for the health and well-being of himself and of his family, including food, clothing, housing and medical care and necessary social services, and the right to security in the event of unemployment, sickness, disability, widowhood, old age or other lack of livelihood in circumstances beyond his control.

(2) Motherhood and childhood are entitled to special care and assistance. All children, whether born in or out of wedlock, shall enjoy the same social protection.

Article 26

(1) Everyone has the right to education. Education shall be free, at least in the elementary and fundamental stages. Elementary education shall be compulsory.

Technical and professional education shall be made generally available and higher education shall be equally accessible to all on the basis of merit.

(2) Education shall be directed to the full development of the human personality and to the strengthening of respect for human rights and fundamental freedoms. It shall promote understanding, tolerance and friendship among all nations, racial or religious groups, and shall further the activities of the United Nations for the maintenance of peace.

(3) Parents have a prior right to choose the kind of education that shall be given to their children.

Article 27

(1) Everyone has the right freely to participate in the cultural life of the community, to enjoy the arts and to share in scientific advancement and its benefits.

(2) Everyone has the right to the protection of the moral and material interests resulting from any scientific, literary or artistic production of which he is the author.

Article 28

Everyone is entitled to a social and international order in which the rights and freedoms set forth in this Declaration can be fully realized.

Article 29

(1) Everyone has duties to the community in which alone the free and full development of his personality is possible.

(2) In the exercise of his rights and freedoms, everyone shall be subject only to such limitations as are determined by law solely for the purpose of securing due recognition and respect for the rights and freedoms of others and of meeting the just requirements of morality, public order and the general welfare in a democratic society.

(3) These rights and freedoms may in no case be exercised contrary to the purposes and principles of the United Nations.

Article 30

Nothing in this Declaration may be interpreted as implying for any State, group or person any right to engage in any activity or to perform any act aimed at the destruction of any of the rights and freedoms set forth herein.

Appendix B

IFSW General Meeting 2004
Proposal for a New Ethical Document

Agenda Item 11.1

Introduction

This document is the proposal from the Permanent Committee on Ethical Issues to be presented at the IFSW General Meeting in Adelaide in September 2004. It will replace the Ethical Principles and Standards adopted in Sri Lanka in 1994. The document is designed to be shorter than the 1994 version, and remains largely at the level of general principles. It is not the role of IFSW to prescribe more detailed rules of conduct for social workers in the many different countries in membership of IFSW. Rather, it is expected that member organisations will develop their own ethical guidance and codes with reference to this document, along with their own procedures for disciplining those who violate the ethical guidance and mechanisms for promoting education, debate and discussion on ethical issues in social work.

The process to develop a new ethical document has been going on for several years with discussions, consultations and hearings in several IFSW bodies. The first draft document was presented in Geneva in June 2002. The second draft was presented for the IFSW Executive Committee in Copenhagen May 2003. All the member organisations of the IFSW have been asked to comment on the first draft. The IASSW has been informed of the process of the development of the new document, and has had the opportunity to comment as well. Altogether we have got more than 30 comments on the two drafts from organisations and individuals. The responses are quite different in form, but there seems to be a general agreement of support for the draft documents among most of the responding organisations. One comment seems to be directly questioning the content of the document. It questions the inclusion of "sexual orientation" in the anti-discrimination paragraph, and suggests an additional paragraph on "Acceptance." In addition one organisation wants a more developed universal code of conduct. The other comments can be regarded as suggestions for improvements within the line of the drafts. Some organisations have commented on the definition of social work. The Ethical Committee has not seen it as its task to work on changes of the definition, and will therefore forward these comments to the secretariats of IFSW/IASSW.

Final Proposal: Ethics in Social Work, Statement of Principles

1. Preface

Ethical awareness is a necessary part of the professional practice of social workers. Their ability and commitment to act ethically is an essential aspect of the quality of the service offered to those who use social work services.

The purpose of IASSW and IFSW's work on ethics is to promote ethical debate and reflection in the member organisations, among the providers of social work in member countries, as well as in the schools of social work and among social work students. Some ethical challenges and problems facing social workers are specific to particular countries; others are common. By staying at the level of general principles, the IFSW statement aims to encourage social workers across the world to reflect on the challenges and dilemmas that face them and make ethically informed decisions about how to act in each particular case. Some of these problem areas include:

- The fact that the loyalty of social workers is often in the middle of conflicting interests
- The fact that social workers function as both helpers and controllers
- The conflicts between the duty of social workers to protect the interests of the people with whom they work and societal demands for efficiency and utility
- The fact that resources in society are limited

This document takes as its starting point the definition of social work adopted by the IFSW at the General Meeting in Montreal, Canada in July 2000 and then jointly with IASSW in Copenhagen in May 2001 (section 2). This definition stresses principles of human rights and social justice. The next section (3) makes reference to the various declarations and conventions on human rights that are relevant to social work, followed by a statement of general ethical principles under the two broad headings of human rights and dignity and social justice (section 4). The final section introduces some basic guidance on ethical conduct in social work, which it is expected would be elaborated by the ethical guidance and in various codes and guidelines of the member organisations of IFSW.

2. Definition of Social Work

The social work profession promotes social change, problem solving in human relationships and the empowerment and liberation of people to enhance well-being. Utilising theories of human behaviour and social systems, social work intervenes at the points where people interact with their environments. Principles of human rights and social justice are fundamental to social work.

3. International Conventions

International human rights declarations and conventions form common standards of achievement, and recognise rights that are accepted by the global community. Documents particularly relevant to social work practice and action are:

- Universal Declaration of Human Rights
- The International Covenant on Civil and Political Rights
- The International Covenant on Economic[,] Social and Cultural Rights
- The Convention on the Elimination of [A]ll Forms of Racial Discrimination
- The Convention on the Elimination of All Forms of Discrimination against Women
- The Convention on the Rights of the Child
- Indigenous and Tribal Peoples Convention (ILO convention 169)

4. Principles

4.1 Human Rights and Human Dignity

Social work is based on respect for the inherent worth and dignity of all people, and the rights that follow from this. Social workers should uphold and defend each person's physical, psychological, emotional and spiritual integrity and well-being. This means:

1. Respecting the right to self-determination—Social workers should respect and promote people's rights to make their own choices and decisions, irrespective of their values and life choices, provided this does not threaten the rights and legitimate interests of others.

2. Promoting the right to participation—Social workers should promote the full involvement and participation of people using their services in ways that enable them to be empowered in all aspects of decisions and actions affecting their lives.

3. Treating each person as a whole—Social workers should be concerned with the whole person, within the family, community and societal and natural environments, and should seek to recognise all aspects of a person's life.

4. Identifying and developing strengths—Social workers should focus on the strengths of all individuals, groups and communities and thus promote their empowerment.

4.2 Social Justice

Social workers have a responsibility to promote social justice, in relation to society generally, and in relation to the people with whom they work. This means:

1. Challenging negative discrimination—Social workers have a responsibility to challenge negative discrimination on the basis of characteristics such as ability, age, culture, gender or sex, marital status, socio-economic status, political opinions, skin colour or other physical characteristics, sexual orientation, or spiritual beliefs.

2. Recognising diversity—Social workers should recognise and respect the ethnic and cultural diversity of societies in which they practice, taking account of individual, family, group and community differences.

3. Distributing resources equitably—Social workers should ensure that resources at their disposal are distributed fairly, according to need.

4. Challenging unjust policies and practices—Social workers have a duty to bring to the attention of their employers, policy makers, politicians and the general public situations where people are living in poverty, where resources are inadequate or where distribution of resources, policies and practices are oppressive, unfair or harmful.

5. Working in solidarity—Social workers have an obligation to challenge social conditions that contribute to social exclusion, stigmatisation or subjugation, and to work towards an inclusive society.

5. Professional Conduct

It is the responsibility of the national organisations in membership of IFSW to develop and regularly update their own codes of ethics or ethical guidelines, to be consistent with the IFSW statement. It is also the national organisation's responsibility to inform social workers and schools of social work about these codes or guidelines.

Social workers should act in accordance with the ethical code or guidelines current in their country. These will generally include more detailed guidance in ethical practice specific to the national context. The following general guidelines on professional conduct apply:

1. Social workers are expected to develop and maintain the required skills and competence to do their job.

2. Social workers should not allow their skills to be used for inhumane purposes, such as torture or terrorism.

3. Social workers should act with integrity. This includes not abusing the relationship of trust with the people using their services, recognising the boundaries between personal and professional life, and not abusing their position for personal benefit or gain.

4. Social workers should act in relation to the people using their services with compassion, empathy and care.

5. Social workers should not subordinate the needs or interests of people who use their services to their own needs or interests.

6. Social workers have a duty to take necessary steps to care for themselves professionally and personally in the workplace and in society, in order to ensure that they are able to provide appropriate services.

7. Social workers should maintain confidentiality regarding information about people who use their services. Exceptions to this may only be justified on the basis of a greater ethical requirement (such as the preservation of life).

8. Social workers need to acknowledge that they are accountable for their actions to their clients, the people they work with, their colleagues, their employers, the professional association and to the law, and that these accountabilities may conflict.

9. Social workers have a duty to collaborate with the schools of social work in order to support social work students to get practical training of good quality and up to date practical knowledge.

10. Social workers should foster and engage in ethical debate with their colleagues and employers and take responsibility for making ethically informed decisions.

11. Social workers should be prepared to state the reasons for their decisions based on ethical considerations, and be accountable for their choices and actions.

12. Social workers should work to create conditions in employing agencies and in their countries where the principles of this statement and those of their own national code (if applicable) are discussed, evaluated and upheld.

Appendix C

International Covenant on Civil and Political Rights

dopted and opened for signature, ratification and accession by General Assembly resolution 2200A (XXI) of 16 December 1966 entry into force 23 March 1976, in accordance with Article 49

Preamble

The States Parties to the present Covenant,

Considering that, in accordance with the principles proclaimed in the Charter of the United Nations, recognition of the inherent dignity and of the equal and inalienable rights of all members of the human family is the foundation of freedom, justice and peace in the world,

Recognizing that these rights derive from the inherent dignity of the human person,

Recognizing that, in accordance with the Universal Declaration of Human Rights, the ideal of free human beings enjoying civil and political freedom and freedom from fear and want can only be achieved if conditions are created whereby everyone may enjoy his civil and political rights, as well as his economic, social and cultural rights,

Considering the obligation of States under the Charter of the United Nations to promote universal respect for, and observance of, human rights and freedoms,

Realizing that the individual, having duties to other individuals and to the community to which he belongs, is under a responsibility to strive for the promotion and observance of the rights recognized in the present Covenant,

Agree upon the following articles:

Part I

Article 1

1. All peoples have the right of self-determination. By virtue of that right they freely determine their political status and freely pursue their economic, social and cultural development.

2. All peoples may, for their own ends, freely dispose of their natural wealth and resources without prejudice to any obligations arising out of international economic co-operation, based upon the principle of mutual benefit, and international law. In no case may a people be deprived of its own means of subsistence.

3. The States Parties to the present Covenant, including those having responsibility for the administration of Non-Self-Governing and Trust Territories, shall promote the realization of the right of self-determination, and shall respect that right, in conformity with the provisions of the Charter of the United Nations.

Part II

Article 2

1. Each State Party to the present Covenant undertakes to respect and to ensure to all individuals within its territory and subject to its jurisdiction the rights recognized in the present Covenant, without distinction of any kind, such as race, colour, sex, language, religion, political or other opinion, national or social origin, property, birth or other status.

2. Where not already provided for by existing legislative or other measures, each State Party to the present Covenant undertakes to take the necessary steps, in accordance with its constitutional processes and with the provisions of the present Covenant, to adopt such laws or other measures as may be necessary to give effect to the rights recognized in the present Covenant.

3. Each State Party to the present Covenant undertakes:
    (a) To ensure that any person whose rights or freedoms as herein recognized are violated shall have an effective remedy, notwithstanding that the violation has been committed by persons acting in an official capacity;
    (b) To ensure that any person claiming such a remedy shall have his right thereto determined by competent judicial, administrative or legislative authorities, or by any other competent authority provided for by the legal system of the State, and to develop the possibilities of judicial remedy;
    (c) To ensure that the competent authorities shall enforce such remedies when granted.

Article 3

The States Parties to the present Covenant undertake to ensure the equal right of men and women to the enjoyment of all civil and political rights set forth in the present Covenant.

Article 4

1. In time of public emergency which threatens the life of the nation and the existence of which is officially proclaimed, the States Parties to the present Covenant may take measures derogating from their obligations under the present Covenant to the extent strictly required by the exigencies of the situation, provided that such measures are not inconsistent with their other obligations under international law and do not involve discrimination solely on the ground of race, colour, sex, language, religion or social origin.

2. No derogation from articles 6, 7, 8 (paragraphs 1 and 2), 11, 15, 16 and 18 may be made under this provision.

3. Any State Party to the present Covenant availing itself of the right of derogation shall immediately inform the other States Parties to the present Covenant, through the intermediary of the Secretary-General of the United Nations, of the provisions from which it has derogated and of the reasons by which it was actuated. A further communication shall be made, through the same intermediary, on the date on which it terminates such derogation. General comment on its implementation.

Article 5

1. Nothing in the present Covenant may be interpreted as implying for any State, group or person any right to engage in any activity or perform any act aimed at the destruction of any of the rights and freedoms recognized herein or at their limitation to a greater extent than is provided for in the present Covenant.

2. There shall be no restriction upon or derogation from any of the fundamental human rights recognized or existing in any State Party to the present Covenant pursuant to law, conventions, regulations or custom on the pretext that the present Covenant does not recognize such rights or that it recognizes them to a lesser extent.

Part III

Article 6

1. Every human being has the inherent right to life. This right shall be protected by law. No one shall be arbitrarily deprived of his life.

2. In countries which have not abolished the death penalty, sentence of death may be imposed only for the most serious crimes in accordance with the law in force at the time of the commission of the crime and not contrary to the provisions of the present Covenant and to the Convention on the Prevention and Punishment of the Crime of Genocide. This penalty can only be carried out pursuant to a final judgement rendered by a competent court.

3. When deprivation of life constitutes the crime of genocide, it is understood that nothing in this article shall authorize any State Party to the present Covenant to derogate in any way from any obligation assumed under the provisions of the Convention on the Prevention and Punishment of the Crime of Genocide.

4. Anyone sentenced to death shall have the right to seek pardon or commutation of the sentence. Amnesty, pardon or commutation of the sentence of death may be granted in all cases.

5. Sentence of death shall not be imposed for crimes committed by persons below eighteen years of age and shall not be carried out on pregnant women.

6. Nothing in this article shall be invoked to delay or to prevent the abolition of capital punishment by any State Party to the present Covenant.

Article 7

No one shall be subjected to torture or to cruel, inhuman or degrading treatment or punishment. In particular, no one shall be subjected without his free consent to medical or scientific experimentation.

Article 8

1. No one shall be held in slavery; slavery and the slave-trade in all their forms shall be prohibited.

2. No one shall be held in servitude.

3. (a) No one shall be required to perform forced or compulsory labour;
    (b) Paragraph 3 (a) shall not be held to preclude, in countries where imprisonment with hard labour may be imposed as a punishment for a crime, the performance of hard labour in pursuance of a sentence to such punishment by a competent court;
    (c) For the purpose of this paragraph the term "forced or compulsory labour" shall not include:
        (i) Any work or service, not referred to in subparagraph (b), normally required of a person who is under detention in consequence of a lawful order of a court, or of a person during conditional release from such detention;
        (ii) Any service of a military character and, in countries where conscientious objection is recognized, any national service required by law of conscientious objectors;

(iii)   Any service exacted in cases of emergency or calamity threatening the life or well-being of the community;

(iv)   Any work or service which forms part of normal civil obligations.

Article 9

1.   Everyone has the right to liberty and security of person. No one shall be subjected to arbitrary arrest or detention. No one shall be deprived of his liberty except on such grounds and in accordance with such procedure as are established by law.

2.   Anyone who is arrested shall be informed, at the time of arrest, of the reasons for his arrest and shall be promptly informed of any charges against him.

3.   Anyone arrested or detained on a criminal charge shall be brought promptly before a judge or other officer authorized by law to exercise judicial power and shall be entitled to trial within a reasonable time or to release. It shall not be the general rule that persons awaiting trial shall be detained in custody, but release may be subject to guarantees to appear for trial, at any other stage of the judicial proceedings, and, should occasion arise, for execution of the judgement.

4.   Anyone who is deprived of his liberty by arrest or detention shall be entitled to take proceedings before a court, in order that court may decide without delay on the lawfulness of his detention and order his release if the detention is not lawful.

5.   Anyone who has been the victim of unlawful arrest or detention shall have an enforceable right to compensation.

Article 10

1.   All persons deprived of their liberty shall be treated with humanity and with respect for the inherent dignity of the human person.

2.   (a)   Accused persons shall, save in exceptional circumstances, be segregated from convicted persons and shall be subject to separate treatment appropriate to their status as unconvicted persons;

(b)   Accused juvenile persons shall be separated from adults and brought as speedily as possible for adjudication.

3.   The penitentiary system shall comprise treatment of prisoners the essential aim of which shall be their reformation and social rehabilitation. Juvenile offenders shall be segregated from adults and be accorded treatment appropriate to their age and legal status.

Article 11

No one shall be imprisoned merely on the ground of inability to fulfill a contractual obligation.

Article 12

1. Everyone lawfully within the territory of a State shall, within that territory, have the right to liberty of movement and freedom to choose his residence.

2. Everyone shall be free to leave any country, including his own.

3. The above-mentioned rights shall not be subject to any restrictions except those which are provided by law, are necessary to protect national security, public order (*ordre public*), public health or morals or the rights and freedoms of others, and are consistent with the other rights recognized in the present Covenant.

4. No one shall be arbitrarily deprived of the right to enter his own country.

Article 13

An alien lawfully in the territory of a State Party to the present Covenant may be expelled therefrom only in pursuance of a decision reached in accordance with law and shall, except where compelling reasons of national security otherwise require, be allowed to submit the reasons against his expulsion and to have his case reviewed by, and be represented for the purpose before, the competent authority or a person or persons especially designated by the competent authority.

Article 14

1. All persons shall be equal before the courts and tribunals. In the determination of any criminal charge against him, or of his rights and obligations in a suit at law, everyone shall be entitled to a fair and public hearing by a competent, independent and impartial tribunal established by law. The press and the public may be excluded from all or part of a trial for reasons of morals, public order (*ordre public*) or national security in a democratic society, or when the interest of the private lives of the parties so requires, or to the extent strictly necessary in the opinion of the court in special circumstances where publicity would prejudice the interests of justice; but any judgement rendered in a criminal case or in a suit at law shall be made public except where the interest of juvenile persons otherwise requires or the proceedings concern matrimonial disputes or the guardianship of children.

2. Everyone charged with a criminal offence shall have the right to be presumed innocent until proved guilty according to law.

3. In the determination of any criminal charge against him, everyone shall be entitled to the following minimum guarantees, in full equality:
    (a) To be informed promptly and in detail in a language which he understands of the nature and cause of the charge against him;
    (b) To have adequate time and facilities for the preparation of his defence and to communicate with counsel of his own choosing;
    (c) To be tried without undue delay;

(d) To be tried in his presence, and to defend himself in person or through legal assistance of his own choosing; to be informed, if he does not have legal assistance, of this right; and to have legal assistance assigned to him, in any case where the interests of justice so require, and without payment by him in any such case if he does not have sufficient means to pay for it;

(e) To examine, or have examined, the witnesses against him and to obtain the attendance and examination of witnesses on his behalf under the same conditions as witnesses against him;

(f) To have the free assistance of an interpreter if he cannot understand or speak the language used in court;

(g) Not to be compelled to testify against himself or to confess guilt.

4. In the case of juvenile persons, the procedure shall be such as will take account of their age and the desirability of promoting their rehabilitation.

5. Everyone convicted of a crime shall have the right to his conviction and sentence being reviewed by a higher tribunal according to law.

6. When a person has by a final decision been convicted of a criminal offence and when subsequently his conviction has been reversed or he has been pardoned on the ground that a new or newly discovered fact shows conclusively that there has been a miscarriage of justice, the person who has suffered punishment as a result of such conviction shall be compensated according to law, unless it is proved that the non-disclosure of the unknown fact in time is wholly or partly attributable to him.

7. No one shall be liable to be tried or punished again for an offence for which he has already been finally convicted or acquitted in accordance with the law and penal procedure of each country.

Article 15

1. No one shall be held guilty of any criminal offence on account of any act or omission which did not constitute a criminal offence, under national or international law, at the time when it was committed. Nor shall a heavier penalty be imposed than the one that was applicable at the time when the criminal offence was committed. If, subsequent to the commission of the offence, provision is made by law for the imposition of the lighter penalty, the offender shall benefit thereby.

2. Nothing in this article shall prejudice the trial and punishment of any person for any act or omission which, at the time when it was committed, was criminal according to the general principles of law recognized by the community of nations.

Article 16

Everyone shall have the right to recognition everywhere as a person before the law.

Article 17

1. No one shall be subjected to arbitrary or unlawful interference with his privacy, family, home or correspondence, nor to unlawful attacks on his honour and reputation.

2. Everyone has the right to the protection of the law against such interference or attacks.

Article 18

1. Everyone shall have the right to freedom of thought, conscience and religion. This right shall include freedom to have or to adopt a religion or belief of his choice, and freedom, either individually or in community with others and in public or private, to manifest his religion or belief in worship, observance, practice and teaching.

2. No one shall be subject to coercion which would impair his freedom to have or to adopt a religion or belief of his choice.

3. Freedom to manifest one's religion or beliefs may be subject only to such limitations as are prescribed by law and are necessary to protect public safety, order, health, or morals or the fundamental rights and freedoms of others.

4. The States Parties to the present Covenant undertake to have respect for the liberty of parents and, when applicable, legal guardians to ensure the religious and moral education of their children in conformity with their own convictions.

Article 19

1. Everyone shall have the right to hold opinions without interference.

2. Everyone shall have the right to freedom of expression; this right shall include freedom to seek, receive and impart information and ideas of all kinds, regardless of frontiers, either orally, in writing or in print, in the form of art, or through any other media of his choice.

3. The exercise of the rights provided for in paragraph 2 of this article carries with it special duties and responsibilities. It may therefore be subject to certain restrictions, but these shall only be such as are provided by law and are necessary:
    (a) For respect of the rights or reputations of others;
    (b) For the protection of national security or of public order (*ordre public*), or of public health or morals.

Article 20

1. Any propaganda for war shall be prohibited by law.

2. Any advocacy of national, racial or religious hatred that constitutes incitement to discrimination, hostility or violence shall be prohibited by law.

Article 21

The right of peaceful assembly shall be recognized. No restrictions may be placed on the exercise of this right other than those imposed in conformity with the law and which are necessary in a democratic society in the interests of national security or public safety, public order (*ordre public*), the protection of public health or morals or the protection of the rights and freedoms of others.

Article 22

1. Everyone shall have the right to freedom of association with others, including the right to form and join trade unions for the protection of his interests.

2. No restrictions may be placed on the exercise of this right other than those which are prescribed by law and which are necessary in a democratic society in the interests of national security or public safety, public order (*ordre public*), the protection of public health or morals or the protection of the rights and freedoms of others. This article shall not prevent the imposition of lawful restrictions on members of the armed forces and of the police in their exercise of this right.

3. Nothing in this article shall authorize States Parties to the International Labour Organisation Convention of 1948 concerning Freedom of Association and Protection of the Right to Organize to take legislative measures which would prejudice, or to apply the law in such a manner as to prejudice, the guarantees provided for in that Convention.

Article 23

1. The family is the natural and fundamental group unit of society and is entitled to protection by society and the State.

2. The right of men and women of marriageable age to marry and to found a family shall be recognized.

3. No marriage shall be entered into without the free and full consent of the intending spouses.

4. States Parties to the present Covenant shall take appropriate steps to ensure equality of rights and responsibilities of spouses as to marriage, during marriage and at its dissolution. In the case of dissolution, provision shall be made for the necessary protection of any children.

Article 24

1. Every child shall have, without any discrimination as to race, colour, sex, language, religion, national or social origin, property or birth, the right to such measures of protection as are required by his status as a minor, on the part of his family, society and the State.

2. Every child shall be registered immediately after birth and shall have a name.

3. Every child has the right to acquire a nationality.

Article 25

Every citizen shall have the right and the opportunity, without any of the distinctions mentioned in article 2 and without unreasonable restrictions:

(a) To take part in the conduct of public affairs, directly or through freely chosen representatives;

(b) To vote and to be elected at genuine periodic elections which shall be by universal and equal suffrage and shall be held by secret ballot, guaranteeing the free expression of the will of the electors;

(c) To have access, on general terms of equality, to public service in his country.

Article 26

All persons are equal before the law and are entitled without any discrimination to the equal protection of the law. In this respect, the law shall prohibit any discrimination and guarantee to all persons equal and effective protection against discrimination on any ground such as race, colour, sex, language, religion, political or other opinion, national or social origin, property, birth or other status.

Article 27

In those States in which ethnic, religious or linguistic minorities exist, persons belonging to such minorities shall not be denied the right, in community with the other members of their group, to enjoy their own culture, to profess and practise their own religion, or to use their own language.

Part IV

Article 28

1. There shall be established a Human Rights Committee (hereafter referred to in the present Covenant as the Committee). It shall consist of eighteen members and shall carry out the functions hereinafter provided.

2. The Committee shall be composed of nationals of the States Parties to the present Covenant who shall be persons of high moral character and recognized competence in the field of human rights, consideration being given to the usefulness of the participation of some persons having legal experience.

3. The members of the Committee shall be elected and shall serve in their personal capacity.

Article 29

1. The members of the Committee shall be elected by secret ballot from a list of persons possessing the qualifications prescribed in article 28 and nominated for the purpose by the States Parties to the present Covenant.

2. Each State Party to the present Covenant may nominate not more than two persons. These persons shall be nationals of the nominating State.

3. A person shall be eligible for renomination.

Article 30

1. The initial election shall be held no later than six months after the date of the entry into force of the present Covenant.

2. At least four months before the date of each election to the Committee, other than an election to fill a vacancy declared in accordance with article 34, the Secretary-General of the United Nations shall address a written invitation to the States Parties to the present Covenant to submit their nominations for membership of the Committee within three months.

3. The Secretary-General of the United Nations shall prepare a list in alphabetical order of all the persons thus nominated, with an indication of the States Parties which have nominated them, and shall submit it to the States Parties to the present Covenant no later than one month before the date of each election.

4. Elections of the members of the Committee shall be held at a meeting of the States Parties to the present Covenant convened by the Secretary General of the United Nations at the Headquarters of the United Nations. At that meeting, for which two thirds of the States Parties to the present Covenant shall constitute a quorum, the persons elected to the Committee shall be those nominees who obtain the largest number of votes and an absolute majority of the votes of the representatives of States Parties present and voting.

Article 31

1. The Committee may not include more than one national of the same State.

2. In the election of the Committee, consideration shall be given to equitable geographical distribution of membership and to the representation of the different forms of civilization and of the principal legal systems.

Article 32

1. The members of the Committee shall be elected for a term of four years. They shall be eligible for re-election if renominated. However, the terms of nine of the

members elected at the first election shall expire at the end of two years; immediately after the first election, the names of these nine members shall be chosen by lot by the Chairman of the meeting referred to in article 30, paragraph 4.

2. Elections at the expiry of office shall be held in accordance with the preceding articles of this part of the present Covenant.

Article 33

1. If, in the unanimous opinion of the other members, a member of the Committee has ceased to carry out his functions for any cause other than absence of a temporary character, the Chairman of the Committee shall notify the Secretary-General of the United Nations, who shall then declare the seat of that member to be vacant.

2. In the event of the death or the resignation of a member of the Committee, the Chairman shall immediately notify the Secretary-General of the United Nations, who shall declare the seat vacant from the date of death or the date on which the resignation takes effect.

Article 34

1. When a vacancy is declared in accordance with article 33 and if the term of office of the member to be replaced does not expire within six months of the declaration of the vacancy, the Secretary-General of the United Nations shall notify each of the States Parties to the present Covenant, which may within two months submit nominations in accordance with article 29 for the purpose of filling the vacancy.

2. The Secretary-General of the United Nations shall prepare a list in alphabetical order of the persons thus nominated and shall submit it to the States Parties to the present Covenant. The election to fill the vacancy shall then take place in accordance with the relevant provisions of this part of the present Covenant.

3. A member of the Committee elected to fill a vacancy declared in accordance with article 33 shall hold office for the remainder of the term of the member who vacated the seat on the Committee under the provisions of that article.

Article 35

The members of the Committee shall, with the approval of the General Assembly of the United Nations, receive emoluments from United Nations resources on such terms and conditions as the General Assembly may decide, having regard to the importance of the Committee's responsibilities.

Article 36

The Secretary-General of the United Nations shall provide the necessary staff and facilities for the effective performance of the functions of the Committee under the present Covenant.

Article 37

1. The Secretary-General of the United Nations shall convene the initial meeting of the Committee at the Headquarters of the United Nations.

2. After its initial meeting, the Committee shall meet at such times as shall be provided in its rules of procedure.

3. The Committee shall normally meet at the Headquarters of the United Nations or at the United Nations Office at Geneva.

Article 38

Every member of the Committee shall, before taking up his duties, make a solemn declaration in open committee that he will perform his functions impartially and conscientiously.

Article 39

1. The Committee shall elect its officers for a term of two years. They may be re-elected.

2. The Committee shall establish its own rules of procedure, but these rules shall provide, inter alia, that:
    (a) Twelve members shall constitute a quorum;
    (b) Decisions of the Committee shall be made by a majority vote of the members present.

Article 40

1. The States Parties to the present Covenant undertake to submit reports on the measures they have adopted which give effect to the rights recognized herein and on the progress made in the enjoyment of those rights:
    (a) Within one year of the entry into force of the present Covenant for the States Parties concerned;
    (b) Thereafter whenever the Committee so requests.

2. All reports shall be submitted to the Secretary-General of the United Nations, who shall transmit them to the Committee for consideration. Reports shall indicate the factors and difficulties, if any, affecting the implementation of the present Covenant.

3. The Secretary-General of the United Nations may, after consultation with the Committee, transmit to the specialized agencies concerned copies of such parts of the reports as may fall within their field of competence.

4. The Committee shall study the reports submitted by the States Parties to the present Covenant. It shall transmit its reports, and such general comments as it may

consider appropriate, to the States Parties. The Committee may also transmit to the Economic and Social Council these comments along with the copies of the reports it has received from States Parties to the present Covenant.

5. The States Parties to the present Covenant may submit to the Committee observations on any comments that may be made in accordance with paragraph 4 of this article.

Article 41

1. A State Party to the present Covenant may at any time declare under this article that it recognizes the competence of the Committee to receive and consider communications to the effect that a State Party claims that another State Party is not fulfilling its obligations under the present Covenant. Communications under this article may be received and considered only if submitted by a State Party which has made a declaration recognizing in regard to itself the competence of the Committee. No communication shall be received by the Committee if it concerns a State Party which has not made such a declaration. Communications received under this article shall be dealt with in accordance with the following procedure:

(a) If a State Party to the present Covenant considers that another State Party is not giving effect to the provisions of the present Covenant, it may, by written communication, bring the matter to the attention of that State Party. Within three months after the receipt of the communication the receiving State shall afford the State which sent the communication an explanation, or any other statement in writing clarifying the matter which should include, to the extent possible and pertinent, reference to domestic procedures and remedies taken, pending, or available in the matter;

(b) If the matter is not adjusted to the satisfaction of both States Parties concerned within six months after the receipt by the receiving State of the initial communication, either State shall have the right to refer the matter to the Committee, by notice given to the Committee and to the other State;

(c) The Committee shall deal with a matter referred to it only after it has ascertained that all available domestic remedies have been invoked and exhausted in the matter, in conformity with the generally recognized principles of international law. This shall not be the rule where the application of the remedies is unreasonably prolonged;

(d) The Committee shall hold closed meetings when examining communications under this article;

(e) Subject to the provisions of subparagraph (c), the Committee shall make available its good offices to the States Parties concerned with a view to a friendly solution of the matter on the basis of respect for human rights and fundamental freedoms as recognized in the present Covenant;

(f) In any matter referred to it, the Committee may call upon the States Parties concerned, referred to in subparagraph (b), to supply any relevant information;

(g) The States Parties concerned, referred to in subparagraph (b), shall have the right to be represented when the matter is being considered in the Committee and to make submissions orally and/or in writing;

(h) The Committee shall, within twelve months after the date of receipt of notice under subparagraph (b), submit a report:

  (i)   If a solution within the terms of subparagraph (e) is reached, the Committee shall confine its report to a brief statement of the facts and of the solution reached;

  (ii) If a solution within the terms of subparagraph (e) is not reached, the Committee shall confine its report to a brief statement of the facts; the written submissions and record of the oral submissions made by the States Parties concerned shall be attached to the report. In every matter, the report shall be communicated to the States Parties concerned.

2. The provisions of this article shall come into force when ten States Parties to the present Covenant have made declarations under paragraph 1 of this article. Such declarations shall be deposited by the States Parties with the Secretary-General of the United Nations, who shall transmit copies thereof to the other States Parties. A declaration may be withdrawn at any time by notification to the Secretary-General. Such a withdrawal shall not prejudice the consideration of any matter which is the subject of a communication already transmitted under this article; no further communication by any State Party shall be received after the notification of withdrawal of the declaration has been received by the Secretary-General, unless the State Party concerned has made a new declaration.

Article 42

1. (a) If a matter referred to the Committee in accordance with article 41 is not resolved to the satisfaction of the States Parties concerned, the Committee may, with the prior consent of the States Parties concerned, appoint an ad hoc Conciliation Commission (hereinafter referred to as the Commission). The good offices of the Commission shall be made available to the States Parties concerned with a view to an amicable solution of the matter on the basis of respect for the present Covenant;

   (b) The Commission shall consist of five persons acceptable to the States Parties concerned. If the States Parties concerned fail to reach agreement within three months on all or part of the composition of the Commission, the members of the Commission concerning whom no agreement has been reached shall be elected by secret ballot by a two-thirds majority vote of the Committee from among its members.

2. The members of the Commission shall serve in their personal capacity. They shall not be nationals of the States Parties concerned, or of a State not Party to the

present Covenant, or of a State Party which has not made a declaration under article 41.

3. The Commission shall elect its own Chairman and adopt its own rules of procedure.

4. The meetings of the Commission shall normally be held at the Headquarters of the United Nations or at the United Nations Office at Geneva. However, they may be held at such other convenient places as the Commission may determine in consultation with the Secretary-General of the United Nations and the States Parties concerned.

5. The secretariat provided in accordance with article 36 shall also service the commissions appointed under this article.

6. The information received and collated by the Committee shall be made available to the Commission and the Commission may call upon the States Parties concerned to supply any other relevant information.

7. When the Commission has fully considered the matter, but in any event not later than twelve months after having been seized of the matter, it shall submit to the Chairman of the Committee a report for communication to the States Parties concerned:

(a) If the Commission is unable to complete its consideration of the matter within twelve months, it shall confine its report to a brief statement of the status of its consideration of the matter;

(b) If an amicable solution to the matter on the basis of respect for human rights as recognized in the present Covenant is reached, the Commission shall confine its report to a brief statement of the facts and of the solution reached;

(c) If a solution within the terms of subparagraph (b) is not reached, the Commission's report shall embody its findings on all questions of fact relevant to the issues between the States Parties concerned, and its views on the possibilities of an amicable solution of the matter. This report shall also contain the written submissions and a record of the oral submissions made by the States Parties concerned;

(d) If the Commission's report is submitted under subparagraph (c), the States Parties concerned shall, within three months of the receipt of the report, notify the Chairman of the Committee whether or not they accept the contents of the report of the Commission.

8. The provisions of this article are without prejudice to the responsibilities of the Committee under article 41.

9. The States Parties concerned shall share equally all the expenses of the members of the Commission in accordance with estimates to be provided by the Secretary-General of the United Nations.

10. The Secretary-General of the United Nations shall be empowered to pay the expenses of the members of the Commission, if necessary, before reimbursement by the States Parties concerned, in accordance with paragraph 9 of this article.

Article 43

The members of the Committee, and of the ad hoc conciliation commissions which may be appointed under article 42, shall be entitled to the facilities, privileges and immunities of experts on mission for the United Nations as laid down in the relevant sections of the Convention on the Privileges and Immunities of the United Nations.

Article 44

The provisions for the implementation of the present Covenant shall apply without prejudice to the procedures prescribed in the field of human rights by or under the constituent instruments and the conventions of the United Nations and of the specialized agencies and shall not prevent the States Parties to the present Covenant from having recourse to other procedures for settling a dispute in accordance with general or special international agreements in force between them.

Article 45

The Committee shall submit to the General Assembly of the United Nations, through the Economic and Social Council, an annual report on its activities.

Part V

Article 46

Nothing in the present Covenant shall be interpreted as impairing the provisions of the Charter of the United Nations and of the constitutions of the specialized agencies which define the respective responsibilities of the various organs of the United Nations and of the specialized agencies in regard to the matters dealt with in the present Covenant.

Article 47

Nothing in the present Covenant shall be interpreted as impairing the inherent right of all peoples to enjoy and utilize fully and freely their natural wealth and resources.

Part VI

Article 48

1. The present Covenant is open for signature by any State Member of the United Nations or member of any of its specialized agencies, by any State Party to the Statute of the International Court of Justice, and by any other State which has been invited by the General Assembly of the United Nations to become a Party to the present Covenant.

2. The present Covenant is subject to ratification. Instruments of ratification shall be deposited with the Secretary-General of the United Nations.

3. The present Covenant shall be open to accession by any State referred to in paragraph 1 of this article.

4. Accession shall be effected by the deposit of an instrument of accession with the Secretary-General of the United Nations.

5. The Secretary-General of the United Nations shall inform all States which have signed this Covenant or acceded to it of the deposit of each instrument of ratification or accession.

Article 49

1. The present Covenant shall enter into force three months after the date of the deposit with the Secretary-General of the United Nations of the thirty-fifth instrument of ratification or instrument of accession.

2. For each State ratifying the present Covenant or acceding to it after the deposit of the thirty-fifth instrument of ratification or instrument of accession, the present Covenant shall enter into force three months after the date of the deposit of its own instrument of ratification or instrument of accession.

Article 50

The provisions of the present Covenant shall extend to all parts of federal States without any limitations or exceptions.

Article 51

1. Any State Party to the present Covenant may propose an amendment and file it with the Secretary-General of the United Nations. The Secretary-General of the United Nations shall thereupon communicate any proposed amendments to the States Parties to the present Covenant with a request that they notify him whether they favour a conference of States Parties for the purpose of considering and voting upon the proposals. In the event that at least one third of the States Parties favours

such a conference, the Secretary-General shall convene the conference under the auspices of the United Nations. Any amendment adopted by a majority of the States Parties present and voting at the conference shall be submitted to the General Assembly of the United Nations for approval.

2. Amendments shall come into force when they have been approved by the General Assembly of the United Nations and accepted by a two-thirds majority of the States Parties to the present Covenant in accordance with their respective constitutional processes.

3. When amendments come into force, they shall be binding on those States Parties which have accepted them, other States Parties still being bound by the provisions of the present Covenant and any earlier amendment which they have accepted.

Article 52

Irrespective of the notifications made under article 48, paragraph 5, the Secretary-General of the United Nations shall inform all States referred to in paragraph 1 of the same article of the following particulars:

(a) Signatures, ratifications and accessions under article 48;

(b) The date of the entry into force of the present Covenant under article 49 and the date of the entry into force of any amendments under article 51.

Article 53

1. The present Covenant, of which the Chinese, English, French, Russian and Spanish texts are equally authentic, shall be deposited in the archives of the United Nations.

2. The Secretary-General of the United Nations shall transmit certified copies of the present Covenant to all States referred to in article 48.

Appendix D

Optional Protocol to the International Covenant on Civil and Political Rights

Adopted and opened for signature, ratification and accession by General Assembly resolution 2200A (XXI) of 16 December 1966 entry into force 23 March 1976, in accordance with Article 9

The States Parties to the present Protocol,

Considering that in order further to achieve the purposes of the International Covenant on Civil and Political Rights (hereinafter referred to as the Covenant) and the implementation of its provisions it would be appropriate to enable the Human Rights Committee set up in part IV of the Covenant (hereinafter referred to as the Committee) to receive and consider, as provided in the present Protocol, communications from individuals claiming to be victims of violations of any of the rights set forth in the Covenant.

Have agreed as follows:

Article 1

A State Party to the Covenant that becomes a Party to the present Protocol recognizes the competence of the Committee to receive and consider communications from individuals subject to its jurisdiction who claim to be victims of a violation by that State Party of any of the rights set forth in the Covenant. No communication shall be received by the Committee if it concerns a State Party to the Covenant which is not a Party to the present Protocol.

Article 2

Subject to the provisions of article 1, individuals who claim that any of their rights enumerated in the Covenant have been violated and who have exhausted all available domestic remedies may submit a written communication to the Committee for consideration.

Article 3

The Committee shall consider inadmissible any communication under the present Protocol which is anonymous, or which it considers to be an abuse of the right of submission of such communications or to be incompatible with the provisions of the Covenant.

Article 4

1. Subject to the provisions of article 3, the Committee shall bring any communications submitted to it under the present Protocol to the attention of the State Party to the present Protocol alleged to be violating any provision of the Covenant.

2. Within six months, the receiving State shall submit to the Committee written explanations or statements clarifying the matter and the remedy, if any, that may have been taken by that State.

Article 5

1. The Committee shall consider communications received under the present Protocol in the light of all written information made available to it by the individual and by the State Party concerned.

2. The Committee shall not consider any communication from an individual unless it has ascertained that:
    (a) The same matter is not being examined under another procedure of international investigation or settlement;
    (b) The individual has exhausted all available domestic remedies. This shall not be the rule where the application of the remedies is unreasonably prolonged.

3. The Committee shall hold closed meetings when examining communications under the present Protocol.

4. The Committee shall forward its views to the State Party concerned and to the individual.

Article 6

The Committee shall include in its annual report under article 45 of the Covenant a summary of its activities under the present Protocol.

Article 7

Pending the achievement of the objectives of resolution 1514(XV) adopted by the General Assembly of the United Nations on 14 December 1960 concerning the Declaration on the Granting of Independence to Colonial Countries and Peoples, the provisions of the present Protocol shall in no way limit the right of petition granted to these peoples by the Charter of the United Nations and other international conventions and instruments under the United Nations and its specialized agencies.

Article 8

1. The present Protocol is open for signature by any State which has signed the Covenant.

2. The present Protocol is subject to ratification by any State which has ratified or acceded to the Covenant. Instruments of ratification shall be deposited with the Secretary-General of the United Nations.

3. The present Protocol shall be open to accession by any State which has ratified or acceded to the Covenant.

4. Accession shall be effected by the deposit of an instrument of accession with the Secretary-General of the United Nations.

5. The Secretary-General of the United Nations shall inform all States which have signed the present Protocol or acceded to it of the deposit of each instrument of ratification or accession.

Article 9

1. Subject to the entry into force of the Covenant, the present Protocol shall enter into force three months after the date of the deposit with the Secretary-General of the United Nations of the tenth instrument of ratification or instrument of accession.

2. For each State ratifying the present Protocol or acceding to it after the deposit of the tenth instrument of ratification or instrument of accession, the present Protocol shall enter into force three months after the date of the deposit of its own instrument of ratification or instrument of accession.

Article 10

The provisions of the present Protocol shall extend to all parts of federal States without any limitations or exceptions.

Article 11

1. Any State Party to the present Protocol may propose an amendment and file it with the Secretary-General of the United Nations. The Secretary-General shall thereupon communicate any proposed amendments to the States Parties to the present Protocol with a request that they notify him whether they favour a conference of States Parties for the purpose of considering and voting upon the proposal. In

the event that at least one third of the States Parties favours such a conference, the Secretary-General shall convene the conference under the auspices of the United Nations. Any amendment adopted by a majority of the States Parties present and voting at the conference shall be submitted to the General Assembly of the United Nations for approval.

2. Amendments shall come into force when they have been approved by the General Assembly of the United Nations and accepted by a two-thirds majority of the States Parties to the present Protocol in accordance with their respective constitutional processes.

3. When amendments come into force, they shall be binding on those States Parties which have accepted them, other States Parties still being bound by the provisions of the present Protocol and any earlier amendment which they have accepted.

Article 12

1. Any State Party may denounce the present Protocol at any time by written notification addressed to the Secretary-General of the United Nations. Denunciation shall take effect three months after the date of receipt of the notification by the Secretary-General.

2. Denunciation shall be without prejudice to the continued application of the provisions of the present Protocol to any communication submitted under article 2 before the effective date of denunciation.

Article 13

Irrespective of the notifications made under article 8, paragraph 5, of the present Protocol, the Secretary-General of the United Nations shall inform all States referred to in article 48, paragraph 1, of the Covenant of the following particulars:

(a) Signatures, ratifications and accessions under article 8;

(b) The date of the entry into force of the present Protocol under article 9 and the date of the entry into force of any amendments under article 11;

(c) Denunciations under article 12.

Article 14

1. The present Protocol, of which the Chinese, English, French, Russian and Spanish texts are equally authentic, shall be deposited in the archives of the United Nations.

2. The Secretary-General of the United Nations shall transmit certified copies of the present Protocol to all States referred to in article 48 of the Covenant.

Appendix E

*International Covenant on
Economic, Social and Cultural Rights*

dopted and opened for signature, ratification and accession by General Assembly resolution 2200A (XXI) of 16 December 1966 entry into force 3 January 1976, in accordance with article 27

Preamble

The States Parties to the present Covenant,

Considering that, in accordance with the principles proclaimed in the Charter of the United Nations, recognition of the inherent dignity and of the equal and inalienable rights of all members of the human family is the foundation of freedom, justice and peace in the world,

Recognizing that these rights derive from the inherent dignity of the human person,

Recognizing that, in accordance with the Universal Declaration of Human Rights, the ideal of free human beings enjoying freedom from fear and want can only be achieved if conditions are created whereby everyone may enjoy his economic, social and cultural rights, as well as his civil and political rights,

Considering the obligation of States under the Charter of the United Nations to promote universal respect for, and observance of, human rights and freedoms,

Realizing that the individual, having duties to other individuals and to the community to which he belongs, is under a responsibility to strive for the promotion and observance of the rights recognized in the present Covenant,

Agree upon the following articles:

Part I

Article 1

1. All peoples have the right of self-determination. By virtue of that right they freely determine their political status and freely pursue their economic, social and cultural development.

2. All peoples may, for their own ends, freely dispose of their natural wealth and resources without prejudice to any obligations arising out of international economic co-operation, based upon the principle of mutual benefit, and international law. In no case may a people be deprived of its own means of subsistence.

3. The States Parties to the present Covenant, including those having responsibility for the administration of Non-Self-Governing and Trust Territories, shall promote the realization of the right of self-determination, and shall respect that right, in conformity with the provisions of the Charter of the United Nations.

Part II

Article 2

1. Each State Party to the present Covenant undertakes to take steps, individually and through international assistance and co-operation, especially economic and technical, to the maximum of its available resources, with a view to achieving progressively the full realization of the rights recognized in the present Covenant by all appropriate means, including particularly the adoption of legislative measures.

2. The States Parties to the present Covenant undertake to guarantee that the rights enunciated in the present Covenant will be exercised without discrimination of any kind as to race, colour, sex, language, religion, political or other opinion, national or social origin, property, birth or other status.

3. Developing countries, with due regard to human rights and their national economy, may determine to what extent they would guarantee the economic rights recognized in the present Covenant to non-nationals.

Article 3

The States Parties to the present Covenant undertake to ensure the equal right of men and women to the enjoyment of all economic, social and cultural rights set forth in the present Covenant.

Article 4

The States Parties to the present Covenant recognize that, in the enjoyment of those rights provided by the State in conformity with the present Covenant, the

State may subject such rights only to such limitations as are determined by law only in so far as this may be compatible with the nature of these rights and solely for the purpose of promoting the general welfare in a democratic society.

Article 5

1. Nothing in the present Covenant may be interpreted as implying for any State, group or person any right to engage in any activity or to perform any act aimed at the destruction of any of the rights or freedoms recognized herein, or at their limitation to a greater extent than is provided for in the present Covenant.

2. No restriction upon or derogation from any of the fundamental human rights recognized or existing in any country in virtue of law, conventions, regulations or custom shall be admitted on the pretext that the present Covenant does not recognize such rights or that it recognizes them to a lesser extent.

Part III

Article 6

1. The States Parties to the present Covenant recognize the right to work, which includes the right of everyone to the opportunity to gain his living by work which he freely chooses or accepts, and will take appropriate steps to safeguard this right.

2. The steps to be taken by a State Party to the present Covenant to achieve the full realization of this right shall include technical and vocational guidance and training programmes, policies and techniques to achieve steady economic, social and cultural development and full and productive employment under conditions safeguarding fundamental political and economic freedoms to the individual.

Article 7

The States Parties to the present Covenant recognize the right of everyone to the enjoyment of just and favourable conditions of work which ensure, in particular:

(a) Remuneration which provides all workers, as a minimum, with:
    (i) Fair wages and equal remuneration for work of equal value without distinction of any kind, in particular women being guaranteed conditions of work not inferior to those enjoyed by men, with equal pay for equal work;
    (ii) A decent living for themselves and their families in accordance with the provisions of the present Covenant;

(b) Safe and healthy working conditions;
(c) Equal opportunity for everyone to be promoted in his employment to an appropriate higher level, subject to no considerations other than those of seniority and competence;

(d) Rest, leisure and reasonable limitation of working hours and periodic holidays with pay, as well as remuneration for public holidays.

Article 8

1. The States Parties to the present Covenant undertake to ensure:
   (a) The right of everyone to form trade unions and join the trade union of his choice, subject only to the rules of the organization concerned, for the promotion and protection of his economic and social interests. No restrictions may be placed on the exercise of this right other than those prescribed by law and which are necessary in a democratic society in the interests of national security or public order or for the protection of the rights and freedoms of others;
   (b) The right of trade unions to establish national federations or confederations and the right of the latter to form or join international trade-union organizations;
   (c) The right of trade unions to function freely subject to no limitations other than those prescribed by law and which are necessary in a democratic society in the interests of national security or public order or for the protection of the rights and freedoms of others;
   (d) The right to strike, provided that it is exercised in conformity with the laws of the particular country.

2. This article shall not prevent the imposition of lawful restrictions on the exercise of these rights by members of the armed forces or of the police or of the administration of the State.

3. Nothing in this article shall authorize States Parties to the International Labour Organisation Convention of 1948 concerning Freedom of Association and Protection of the Right to Organize to take legislative measures which would prejudice, or apply the law in such a manner as would prejudice, the guarantees provided for in that Convention.

Article 9

The States Parties to the present Covenant recognize the right of everyone to social security, including social insurance.

Article 10

The States Parties to the present Covenant recognize that:

1. The widest possible protection and assistance should be accorded to the family, which is the natural and fundamental group unit of society, particularly for its establishment and while it is responsible for the care and education of dependent children. Marriage must be entered into with the free consent of the intending spouses.

2. Special protection should be accorded to mothers during a reasonable period before and after childbirth. During such period working mothers should be accorded paid leave or leave with adequate social security benefits.

3. Special measures of protection and assistance should be taken on behalf of all children and young persons without any discrimination for reasons of parentage or other conditions. Children and young persons should be protected from economic and social exploitation. Their employment in work harmful to their morals or health or dangerous to life or likely to hamper their normal development should be punishable by law. States should also set age limits below which the paid employment of child labour should be prohibited and punishable by law.

Article 11

1. The States Parties to the present Covenant recognize the right of everyone to an adequate standard of living for himself and his family, including adequate food, clothing and housing, and to the continuous improvement of living conditions. The States Parties will take appropriate steps to ensure the realization of this right, recognizing to this effect the essential importance of international co-operation based on free consent.

2. The States Parties to the present Covenant, recognizing the fundamental right of everyone to be free from hunger, shall take, individually and through international co-operation, the measures, including specific programmes, which are needed:
    (a) To improve methods of production, conservation and distribution of food by making full use of technical and scientific knowledge, by disseminating knowledge of the principles of nutrition and by developing or reforming agrarian systems in such a way as to achieve the most efficient development and utilization of natural resources;
    (b) Taking into account the problems of both food-importing and food-exporting countries, to ensure an equitable distribution of world food supplies in relation to need.

Article 12

1. The States Parties to the present Covenant recognize the right of everyone to the enjoyment of the highest attainable standard of physical and mental health.

2. The steps to be taken by the States Parties to the present Covenant to achieve the full realization of this right shall include those necessary for:
    (a) The provision for the reduction of the stillbirth-rate and of infant mortality and for the healthy development of the child;
    (b) The improvement of all aspects of environmental and industrial hygiene;
    (c) The prevention, treatment and control of epidemic, endemic, occupational and other diseases;
    (d) The creation of conditions which would assure to all medical service and medical attention in the event of sickness.

Article 13

1. The States Parties to the present Covenant recognize the right of everyone to education. They agree that education shall be directed to the full development of the human personality and the sense of its dignity, and shall strengthen the respect for human rights and fundamental freedoms. They further agree that education shall enable all persons to participate effectively in a free society, promote understanding, tolerance and friendship among all nations and all racial, ethnic or religious groups, and further the activities of the United Nations for the maintenance of peace.

2. The States Parties to the present Covenant recognize that, with a view to achieving the full realization of this right:
   (a) Primary education shall be compulsory and available free to all;
   (b) Secondary education in its different forms, including technical and vocational secondary education, shall be made generally available and accessible to all by every appropriate means, and in particular by the progressive introduction of free education;
   (c) Higher education shall be made equally accessible to all, on the basis of capacity, by every appropriate means, and in particular by the progressive introduction of free education;
   (d) Fundamental education shall be encouraged or intensified as far as possible for those persons who have not received or completed the whole period of their primary education;
   (e) The development of a system of schools at all levels shall be actively pursued, an adequate fellowship system shall be established, and the material conditions of teaching staff shall be continuously improved.

3. The States Parties to the present Covenant undertake to have respect for the liberty of parents and, when applicable, legal guardians to choose for their children schools, other than those established by the public authorities, which conform to such minimum educational standards as may be laid down or approved by the State and to ensure the religious and moral education of their children in conformity with their own convictions.

4. No part of this article shall be construed so as to interfere with the liberty of individuals and bodies to establish and direct educational institutions, subject always to the observance of the principles set forth in paragraph I of this article and to the requirement that the education given in such institutions shall conform to such minimum standards as may be laid down by the State.

Article 14

Each State Party to the present Covenant which, at the time of becoming a Party, has not been able to secure in its metropolitan territory or other territories under its jurisdiction compulsory primary education, free of charge, undertakes, within two years, to work out and adopt a detailed plan of action for the progressive implementation, within a reasonable number of years, to be fixed in the plan, of the principle of compulsory education free of charge for all.

Article 15

1. The States Parties to the present Covenant recognize the right of everyone:
   (a) To take part in cultural life;
   (b) To enjoy the benefits of scientific progress and its applications;
   (c) To benefit from the protection of the moral and material interests resulting from any scientific, literary or artistic production of which he is the author.

2. The steps to be taken by the States Parties to the present Covenant to achieve the full realization of this right shall include those necessary for the conservation, the development and the diffusion of science and culture.

3. The States Parties to the present Covenant undertake to respect the freedom indispensable for scientific research and creative activity.

4. The States Parties to the present Covenant recognize the benefits to be derived from the encouragement and development of international contacts and co-operation in the scientific and cultural fields.

Part IV

Article 16

1. The States Parties to the present Covenant undertake to submit in conformity with this part of the Covenant reports on the measures which they have adopted and the progress made in achieving the observance of the rights recognized herein.

2. (a) All reports shall be submitted to the Secretary-General of the United Nations, who shall transmit copies to the Economic and Social Council for consideration in accordance with the provisions of the present Covenant;
   (b) The Secretary-General of the United Nations shall also transmit to the specialized agencies copies of the reports, or any relevant parts there from, from States Parties to the present Covenant which are also members of these specialized agencies in so far as these reports, or parts there from, relate to any matters which fall within the responsibilities of the said agencies in accordance with their constitutional instruments.

Article 17

1. The States Parties to the present Covenant shall furnish their reports in stages, in accordance with a programme to be established by the Economic and Social Council within one year of the entry into force of the present Covenant after consultation with the States Parties and the specialized agencies concerned.

2. Reports may indicate factors and difficulties affecting the degree of fulfillment of obligations under the present Covenant.

3. Where relevant information has previously been furnished to the United Nations or to any specialized agency by any State Party to the present Covenant, it will not be necessary to reproduce that information, but a precise reference to the information so furnished will suffice.

Article 18

Pursuant to its responsibilities under the Charter of the United Nations in the field of human rights and fundamental freedoms, the Economic and Social Council may make arrangements with the specialized agencies in respect of their reporting to it on the progress made in achieving the observance of the provisions of the present Covenant falling within the scope of their activities. These reports may include particulars of decisions and recommendations on such implementation adopted by their competent organs.

Article 19

The Economic and Social Council may transmit to the Commission on Human Rights for study and general recommendation or, as appropriate, for information the reports concerning human rights submitted by States in accordance with articles 16 and 17, and those concerning human rights submitted by the specialized agencies in accordance with article 18.

Article 20

The States Parties to the present Covenant and the specialized agencies concerned may submit comments to the Economic and Social Council on any general recommendation under article 19 or reference to such general recommendation in any report of the Commission on Human Rights or any documentation referred to therein.

Article 21

The Economic and Social Council may submit from time to time to the General Assembly reports with recommendations of a general nature and a summary of the information received from the States Parties to the present Covenant and the specialized agencies on the measures taken and the progress made in achieving general observance of the rights recognized in the present Covenant.

Article 22

The Economic and Social Council may bring to the attention of other organs of the United Nations, their subsidiary organs and specialized agencies concerned with furnishing technical assistance any matters arising out of the reports referred to in this part of the present Covenant which may assist such bodies in deciding, each within its field of competence, on the advisability of international measures likely to contribute to the effective progressive implementation of the present Covenant.

Article 23

The States Parties to the present Covenant agree that international action for the achievement of the rights recognized in the present Covenant includes such methods as the conclusion of conventions, the adoption of recommendations, the furnishing of technical assistance and the holding of regional meetings and technical meetings for the purpose of consultation and study organized in conjunction with the Governments concerned.

Article 24

Nothing in the present Covenant shall be interpreted as impairing the provisions of the Charter of the United Nations and of the constitutions of the specialized agencies which define the respective responsibilities of the various organs of the United Nations and of the specialized agencies in regard to the matters dealt with in the present Covenant.

Article 25

Nothing in the present Covenant shall be interpreted as impairing the inherent right of all peoples to enjoy and utilize fully and freely their natural wealth and resources.

Part V

Article 26

1. The present Covenant is open for signature by any State Member of the United Nations or member of any of its specialized agencies, by any State Party to the Statute of the International Court of Justice, and by any other State which has been invited by the General Assembly of the United Nations to become a party to the present Covenant.

2. The present Covenant is subject to ratification. Instruments of ratification shall be deposited with the Secretary-General of the United Nations.

3. The present Covenant shall be open to accession by any State referred to in paragraph 1 of this article.

4. Accession shall be effected by the deposit of an instrument of accession with the Secretary-General of the United Nations.

5. The Secretary-General of the United Nations shall inform all States which have signed the present Covenant or acceded to it of the deposit of each instrument of ratification or accession.

Article 27

1. The present Covenant shall enter into force three months after the date of the deposit with the Secretary-General of the United Nations of the thirty-fifth instrument of ratification or instrument of accession.

2. For each State ratifying the present Covenant or acceding to it after the deposit of the thirty-fifth instrument of ratification or instrument of accession, the present Covenant shall enter into force three months after the date of the deposit of its own instrument of ratification or instrument of accession.

Article 28

The provisions of the present Covenant shall extend to all parts of federal States without any limitations or exceptions.

Article 29

1. Any State Party to the present Covenant may propose an amendment and file it with the Secretary-General of the United Nations. The Secretary-General shall thereupon communicate any proposed amendments to the States Parties to the present Covenant with a request that they notify him whether they favour a conference of States Parties for the purpose of considering and voting upon the proposals. In the event that at least one third of the States Parties favours such a conference, the Secretary-General shall convene the conference under the auspices of the United Nations. Any amendment adopted by a majority of the States Parties present and voting at the conference shall be submitted to the General Assembly of the United Nations for approval.

2. Amendments shall come into force when they have been approved by the General Assembly of the United Nations and accepted by a two-thirds majority of the States Parties to the present Covenant in accordance with their respective constitutional processes.

3. When amendments come into force they shall be binding on those States Parties which have accepted them, other States Parties still being bound by the provisions of the present Covenant and any earlier amendment which they have accepted.

Article 30

Irrespective of the notifications made under article 26, paragraph 5, the Secretary-General of the United Nations shall inform all States referred to in paragraph 1 of the same article of the following particulars:

(a) Signatures, ratifications and accessions under article 26;

(b) The date of the entry into force of the present Covenant under article 27 and the date of the entry into force of any amendments under article 29.

Article 31

1. The present Covenant, of which the Chinese, English, French, Russian and Spanish texts are equally authentic, shall be deposited in the archives of the United Nations.

2. The Secretary-General of the United Nations shall transmit certified copies of the present Covenant to all States referred to in article 26.

Appendix F

Convention on the Elimination of All Forms of Discrimination Against Women

> *. . . the full and complete development of a country, the welfare of the world and the cause of peace require the maximum participation of women on equal terms with men in all fields[.]*

Introduction

On 18 December 1979, the Convention on the Elimination of All Forms of Discrimination against Women was adopted by the United Nations General Assembly. It entered into force as an international treaty on 3 September 1981 after the twentieth country had ratified it. By the tenth anniversary of the Convention in 1989, almost one hundred nations have agreed to be bound by its provisions.

The Convention was the culmination of more than thirty years of work by the United Nations Commission on the Status of Women, a body established in 1946 to monitor the situation of women and to promote women's rights. The Commission's work has been instrumental in bringing to light all the areas in which women are denied equality with men. These efforts for the advancement of women have resulted in several declarations and conventions, of which the Convention on the Elimination of All Forms of Discrimination against Women is the central and most comprehensive document.

Among the international human rights treaties, the Convention takes an important place in bringing the female half of humanity into the focus of human rights concerns. The spirit of the Convention is rooted in the goals of the United Nations: to reaffirm faith in fundamental human rights, in the dignity and worth of the human person, in the equal rights of men and women. The present document spells out the meaning of equality and how it can be achieved. In so doing, the

Convention establishes not only an international bill of rights for women, but also an agenda for action by countries to guarantee the enjoyment of those rights.

In its preamble, the Convention explicitly acknowledges that "extensive discrimination against women continues to exist," and emphasizes that such discrimination "violates the principles of equality of rights and respect for human dignity." As defined in article 1, discrimination is understood as "any distinction, exclusion or restriction made on the basis of sex . . . in the political, economic, social, cultural, civil or any other field." The Convention gives positive affirmation to the principle of equality by requiring States parties to take "all appropriate measures, including legislation, to ensure the full development and advancement of women, for the purpose of guaranteeing them the exercise and enjoyment of human rights and fundamental freedoms on a basis of equality with men" (article 3).

The agenda for equality is specified in fourteen subsequent articles. In its approach, the Convention covers three dimensions of the situation of women. Civil rights and the legal status of women are dealt with in great detail. In addition, and unlike other human rights treaties, the Convention is also concerned with the dimension of human reproduction as well as with the impact of cultural factors on gender relations.

The legal status of women receives the broadest attention. Concern over the basic rights of political participation has not diminished since the adoption of the Convention on the Political Rights of Women in 1952. Its provisions, therefore, are restated in article 7 of the present document, whereby women are guaranteed the rights to vote, to hold public office and to exercise public functions. This includes equal rights for women to represent their countries at the international level (article 8). The Convention on the Nationality of Married Women—adopted in 1957—is integrated under article 9 providing for the statehood of women, irrespective of their marital status. The Convention, thereby, draws attention to the fact that often women's legal status has been linked to marriage, making them dependent on their husband's nationality rather than individuals in their own right. Articles 10, 11 and 13, respectively, affirm women's rights to non-discrimination in education, employment and economic and social activities. These demands are given special emphasis with regard to the situation of rural women, whose particular struggles and vital economic contributions, as noted in article 14, warrant more attention in policy planning. Article 15 asserts the full equality of women in civil and business matters, demanding that all instruments directed at restricting women's legal capacity "shall be deemed null and void." Finally, in article 16, the Convention returns to the issue of marriage and family relations, asserting the equal rights and obligations of women and men with regard to choice of spouse, parenthood, personal rights and command over property.

Aside from civil rights issues, the Convention also devotes major attention to a most vital concern of women, namely their reproductive rights. The preamble sets the tone by stating that "the role of women in procreation should not be a basis for discrimination." The link between discrimination and women's reproductive role is a matter of recurrent concern in the Convention. For example, it advocates, in article 5, "a proper understanding of maternity as a social function," demanding fully shared responsibility for child-rearing by both sexes. Accordingly, provisions for maternity protection and child-care are proclaimed as essential rights and are incorporated into all areas of the Convention, whether dealing with employment, family law, health care or education. Society's obligation extends to offering social services, especially child-care facilities, that allow individuals to combine family responsibilities with work and participation in public life. Special measures for maternity protection are recommended and "shall not be considered discriminatory" (article 4). The Convention also affirms women's right to reproductive choice. Notably, it is the only human rights treaty to mention family planning. States parties are obliged to include advice on family planning in the education process (article 10.h) and to develop family codes that guarantee women's rights "to decide freely and responsibly on the number and spacing of their children and to have access to the information, education and means to enable them to exercise these rights" (article 16.e).

The third general thrust of the Convention aims at enlarging our understanding of the concept of human rights, as it gives formal recognition to the influence of culture and tradition on restricting women's enjoyment of their fundamental rights. These forces take shape in stereotypes, customs and norms which give rise to the multitude of legal, political and economic constraints on the advancement of women. Noting this interrelationship, the preamble of the Convention stresses "that a change in the traditional role of men as well as the role of women in society and in the family is needed to achieve full equality of men and women." States parties are therefore obliged to work towards the modification of social and cultural patterns of individual conduct in order to eliminate "prejudices and customary and all other practices which are based on the idea of the inferiority or the superiority of either of the sexes or on stereotyped roles for men and women" (article 5). And Article 10.c mandates the revision of textbooks, school programmes and teaching methods with a view to eliminating stereotyped concepts in the field of education. Finally, cultural patterns which define the public realm as a man's world and the domestic sphere as women's domain are strongly targeted in all of the Convention's provisions that affirm the equal responsibilities of both sexes in family life and their equal rights with regard to education and employment. Altogether, the Convention provides a comprehensive framework for challenging the various forces that have created and sustained discrimination based upon sex.

The implementation of the Convention is monitored by the Committee on the Elimination of Discrimination against Women (CEDAW). The Committee's mandate and the administration of the treaty are defined in the Articles 17 to 30 of the Convention. The Committee is composed of 23 experts nominated by their Governments and elected by the States parties as individuals "of high moral standing and competence in the field covered by the Convention."

At least every four years, the States parties are expected to submit a national report to the Committee, indicating the measures they have adopted to give effect to the provisions of the Convention. During its annual session, the Committee members discuss these reports with the Government representatives and explore with them areas for further action by the specific country. The Committee also makes general recommendations to the States parties on matters concerning the elimination of discrimination against women.

The full text of the Convention is set out herein.

Convention on the Elimination of All Forms of Discrimination Against Women

The States Parties to the present Convention,

Noting that the Charter of the United Nations reaffirms faith in fundamental human rights, in the dignity and worth of the human person and in the equal rights of men and women,

Noting that the Universal Declaration of Human Rights affirms the principle of the inadmissibility of discrimination and proclaims that all human beings are born free and equal in dignity and rights and that everyone is entitled to all the rights and freedoms set forth therein, without distinction of any kind, including distinction based on sex,

Noting that the States Parties to the International Covenants on Human Rights have the obligation to ensure the equal rights of men and women to enjoy all economic, social, cultural, civil and political rights,

Considering the international conventions concluded under the auspices of the United Nations and the specialized agencies promoting equality of rights of men and women,

Noting also the resolutions, declarations and recommendations adopted by the United Nations and the specialized agencies promoting equality of rights of men and women,

Concerned, however, that despite these various instruments extensive discrimination against women continues to exist,

Recalling that discrimination against women violates the principles of equality of rights and respect for human dignity, is an obstacle to the participation of women, on equal terms with men, in the political, social, economic and cultural life of their countries, hampers the growth of the prosperity of society and the family and makes more difficult the full development of the potentialities of women in the service of their countries and of humanity,

Concerned that in situations of poverty women have the least access to food, health, education, training and opportunities for employment and other needs,

Convinced that the establishment of the new international economic order based on equity and justice will contribute significantly towards the promotion of equality between men and women,

Emphasizing that the eradication of apartheid, all forms of racism, racial discrimination, colonialism, neo-colonialism, aggression, foreign occupation and domination and interference in the internal affairs of States is essential to the full enjoyment of the rights of men and women,

Affirming that the strengthening of international peace and security, the relaxation of international tension, mutual co-operation among all States irrespective of their social and economic systems, general and complete disarmament, in particular nuclear disarmament under strict and effective international control, the affirmation of the principles of justice, equality and mutual benefit in relations among countries and the realization of the right of peoples under alien and colonial domination and foreign occupation to self-determination and independence, as well as respect for national sovereignty and territorial integrity, will promote social progress and development and as a consequence will contribute to the attainment of full equality between men and women,

Convinced that the full and complete development of a country, the welfare of the world and the cause of peace require the maximum participation of women on equal terms with men in all fields,

Bearing in mind the great contribution of women to the welfare of the family and to the development of society, so far not fully recognized, the social significance of maternity and the role of both parents in the family and in the upbringing of children, and aware that the role of women in procreation should not be a basis for discrimination but that the upbringing of children requires a sharing of responsibility between men and women and society as a whole,

Aware that a change in the traditional role of men as well as the role of women in society and in the family is needed to achieve full equality between men and women,

Determined to implement the principles set forth in the Declaration on the Elimination of Discrimination against Women and, for that purpose, to adopt the measures required for the elimination of such discrimination in all its forms and manifestations,

Have agreed on the following:

Part I

Article 1

For the purposes of the present Convention, the term "discrimination against women" shall mean any distinction, exclusion or restriction made on the basis of sex which has the effect or purpose of impairing or nullifying the recognition, enjoyment or exercise by women, irrespective of their marital status, on a basis of equality of men and women, of human rights and fundamental freedoms in the political, economic, social, cultural, civil or any other field.

Article 2

States Parties condemn discrimination against women in all its forms, agree to pursue by all appropriate means and without delay a policy of eliminating discrimination against women and, to this end, undertake:

(a) To embody the principle of the equality of men and women in their national constitutions or other appropriate legislation if not yet incorporated therein and to ensure, through law and other appropriate means, the practical realization of this principle;

(b) To adopt appropriate legislative and other measures, including sanctions where appropriate, prohibiting all discrimination against women;

(c) To establish legal protection of the rights of women on an equal basis with men and to ensure through competent national tribunals and other public institutions the effective protection of women against any act of discrimination;

(d) To refrain from engaging in any act or practice of discrimination against women and to ensure that public authorities and institutions shall act in conformity with this obligation;

(e) To take all appropriate measures to eliminate discrimination against women by any person, organization or enterprise;

(f) To take all appropriate measures, including legislation, to modify or abolish existing laws, regulations, customs and practices which constitute discrimination against women;

(g) To repeal all national penal provisions which constitute discrimination against women.

Article 3

States Parties shall take in all fields, in particular in the political, social, economic and cultural fields, all appropriate measures, including legislation, to ensure the full development and advancement of women, for the purpose of guaranteeing them the exercise and enjoyment of human rights and fundamental freedoms on a basis of equality with men.

Article 4

1. Adoption by States Parties of temporary special measures aimed at accelerating de facto equality between men and women shall not be considered discrimination as defined in the present Convention, but shall in no way entail as a consequence the maintenance of unequal or separate standards; these measures shall be discontinued when the objectives of equality of opportunity and treatment have been achieved.

2. Adoption by States Parties of special measures, including those measures contained in the present Convention, aimed at protecting maternity shall not be considered discriminatory.

Article 5

States Parties shall take all appropriate measures:

(a) To modify the social and cultural patterns of conduct of men and women, with a view to achieving the elimination of prejudices and customary and all other practices which are based on the idea of the inferiority or the superiority of either of the sexes or on stereotyped roles for men and women;

(b) To ensure that family education includes a proper understanding of maternity as a social function and the recognition of the common responsibility of men and women in the upbringing and development of their children, it being understood that the interest of the children is the primordial consideration in all cases.

Article 6

States Parties shall take all appropriate measures, including legislation, to suppress all forms of traffic in women and exploitation of prostitution of women.

Part II

Article 7

States Parties shall take all appropriate measures to eliminate discrimination against women in the political and public life of the country and, in particular, shall ensure to women, on equal terms with men, the right:

(a) To vote in all elections and public referenda and to be eligible for election to all publicly elected bodies;

(b) To participate in the formulation of government policy and the implementation thereof and to hold public office and perform all public functions at all levels of government;

(c) To participate in non-governmental organizations and associations concerned with the public and political life of the country.

Article 8

States Parties shall take all appropriate measures to ensure to women, on equal terms with men and without any discrimination, the opportunity to represent their Governments at the international level and to participate in the work of international organizations.

Article 9

1. States Parties shall grant women equal rights with men to acquire, change or retain their nationality. They shall ensure in particular that neither marriage to an alien nor change of nationality by the husband during marriage shall automatically change the nationality of the wife, render her stateless or force upon her the nationality of the husband.

2. States Parties shall grant women equal rights with men with respect to the nationality of their children.

Part III

Article 10

States Parties shall take all appropriate measures to eliminate discrimination against women in order to ensure to them equal rights with men in the field of education and in particular to ensure, on a basis of equality of men and women:

(a) The same conditions for career and vocational guidance, for access to studies and for the achievement of diplomas in educational establishments of all categories in rural as well as in urban areas; this equality shall be ensured in pre-school, general, technical, professional and higher technical education, as well as in all types of vocational training;

(b) Access to the same curricula, the same examinations, teaching staff with qualifications of the same standard and school premises and equipment of the same quality;

(c) The elimination of any stereotyped concept of the roles of men and women at all levels and in all forms of education by encouraging coeducation and other types of education which will help to achieve this aim and, in particular, by the revision of textbooks and school programmes and the adaptation of teaching methods;

(d) The same opportunities to benefit from scholarships and other study grants;

(e) The same opportunities for access to programmes of continuing education, including adult and functional literacy programmes, particularly those aimed at reducing, at the earliest possible time, any gap in education existing between men and women;

(f) The reduction of female student drop-out rates and the organization of programmes for girls and women who have left school prematurely;

(g) The same opportunities to participate actively in sports and physical education;

(h) Access to specific educational information to help to ensure the health and well-being of families, including information and advice on family planning.

Article 11

1. States Parties shall take all appropriate measures to eliminate discrimination against women in the field of employment in order to ensure, on a basis of equality of men and women, the same rights, in particular:

(a) The right to work as an inalienable right of all human beings;

(b) The right to the same employment opportunities, including the application of the same criteria for selection in matters of employment;

(c) The right to free choice of profession and employment, the right to promotion, job security and all benefits and conditions of service and the right to receive vocational training and retraining, including apprentice-ships, advanced vocational training and recurrent training;

(d) The right to equal remuneration, including benefits, and to equal treat-ment in respect of work of equal value, as well as equality of treatment in the evaluation of the quality of work;

(e) The right to social security, particularly in cases of retirement, unem-ployment, sickness, invalidity and old age and other incapacity to work, as well as the right to paid leave;

(f) The right to protection of health and to safety in working conditions, including the safeguarding of the function of reproduction.

2. In order to prevent discrimination against women on the grounds of mar-riage or maternity and to ensure their effective right to work, States Parties shall take appropriate measures:

(a) To prohibit, subject to the imposition of sanctions, dismissal on the grounds of pregnancy or of maternity leave and discrimination in dis-missals on the basis of marital status;

(b) To introduce maternity leave with pay or with comparable social bene-fits without loss of former employment, seniority or social allowances;

(c) To encourage the provision of the necessary supporting social services to enable parents to combine family obligations with work responsibilities and participation in public life, in particular through promoting the esta-blishment and development of a network of child-care facilities;

(d) To provide special protection to women during pregnancy in types of work proved to be harmful to them.

3. Protective legislation relating to matters covered in this article shall be reviewed periodically in the light of scientific and technological knowledge and shall be revised, repealed or extended as necessary.

Article 12

1. States Parties shall take all appropriate measures to eliminate discrimination against women in the field of health care in order to ensure, on a basis of equality of men and women, access to health care services, including those related to family planning.

2. Notwithstanding the provisions of paragraph 1 of this article, States Parties shall ensure to women appropriate services in connection with pregnancy, confine-ment and the post-natal period, granting free services where necessary, as well as adequate nutrition during pregnancy and lactation.

Article 13

States Parties shall take all appropriate measures to eliminate discrimination against women in other areas of economic and social life in order to ensure, on a basis of equality of men and women, the same rights, in particular:

(a) The right to family benefits;

(b) The right to bank loans, mortgages and other forms of financial credit;

(c) The right to participate in recreational activities, sports and all aspects of cultural life.

Article 14

1. States Parties shall take into account the particular problems faced by rural women and the significant roles which rural women play in the economic survival of their families, including their work in the non-monetized sectors of the economy, and shall take all appropriate measures to ensure the application of the provisions of the present Convention to women in rural areas.

2. States Parties shall take all appropriate measures to eliminate discrimination against women in rural areas in order to ensure, on a basis of equality of men and women, that they participate in and benefit from rural development and, in particular, shall ensure to such women the right:

(a) To participate in the elaboration and implementation of development planning at all levels;

(b) To have access to adequate health care facilities, including information, counselling and services in family planning;

(c) To benefit directly from social security programmes;

(d) To obtain all types of training and education, formal and non-formal, including that relating to functional literacy, as well as, inter alia, the benefit of all community and extension services, in order to increase their technical proficiency;

(e) To organize self-help groups and co-operatives in order to obtain equal access to economic opportunities through employment or self employment;

(f) To participate in all community activities;

(g) To have access to agricultural credit and loans, marketing facilities, appropriate technology and equal treatment in land and agrarian reform as well as in land resettlement schemes;

(h) To enjoy adequate living conditions, particularly in relation to housing, sanitation, electricity and water supply, transport and communications.

Part IV

Article 15

1. States Parties shall accord to women equality with men before the law.

2. States Parties shall accord to women, in civil matters, a legal capacity identical to that of men and the same opportunities to exercise that capacity. In particular, they shall give women equal rights to conclude contracts and to administer property and shall treat them equally in all stages of procedure in courts and tribunals.

3. States Parties agree that all contracts and all other private instruments of any kind with a legal effect which is directed at restricting the legal capacity of women shall be deemed null and void.

4. States Parties shall accord to men and women the same rights with regard to the law relating to the movement of persons and the freedom to choose their residence and domicile.

Article 16

1. States Parties shall take all appropriate measures to eliminate discrimination against women in all matters relating to marriage and family relations and in particular shall ensure, on a basis of equality of men and women:

   (a) The same right to enter into marriage;
   (b) The same right freely to choose a spouse and to enter into marriage only with their free and full consent;
   (c) The same rights and responsibilities during marriage and at its dissolution;
   (d) The same rights and responsibilities as parents, irrespective of their marital status, in matters relating to their children; in all cases the interests of the children shall be paramount;
   (e) The same rights to decide freely and responsibly on the number and spacing of their children and to have access to the information, education and means to enable them to exercise these rights;
   (f) The same rights and responsibilities with regard to guardianship, wardship, trusteeship and adoption of children, or similar institutions where these concepts exist in national legislation; in all cases the interests of the children shall be paramount;
   (g) The same personal rights as husband and wife, including the right to choose a family name, a profession and an occupation;
   (h) The same rights for both spouses in respect of the ownership, acquisition, management, administration, enjoyment and disposition of property, whether free of charge or for a valuable consideration.

2. The betrothal and the marriage of a child shall have no legal effect, and all necessary action, including legislation, shall be taken to specify a minimum age for marriage and to make the registration of marriages in an official registry compulsory.

Part V

Article 17

1. For the purpose of considering the progress made in the implementation of the present Convention, there shall be established a Committee on the Elimination of Discrimination against Women (hereinafter referred to as the Committee) consisting, at the time of entry into force of the Convention, of eighteen and, after

ratification of or accession to the Convention by the thirty-fifth State Party, of twenty-three experts of high moral standing and competence in the field covered by the Convention. The experts shall be elected by States Parties from among their nationals and shall serve in their personal capacity, consideration being given to equitable geographical distribution and to the representation of the different forms of civilization as well as the principal legal systems.

2. The members of the Committee shall be elected by secret ballot from a list of persons nominated by States Parties. Each State Party may nominate one person from among its own nationals.

3. The initial election shall be held six months after the date of the entry into force of the present Convention. At least three months before the date of each election the Secretary-General of the United Nations shall address a letter to the States Parties inviting them to submit their nominations within two months. The Secretary-General shall prepare a list in alphabetical order of all persons thus nominated, indicating the States Parties which have nominated them, and shall submit it to the States Parties.

4. Elections of the members of the Committee shall be held at a meeting of States Parties convened by the Secretary-General at United Nations Headquarters. At that meeting, for which two thirds of the States Parties shall constitute a quorum, the persons elected to the Committee shall be those nominees who obtain the largest number of votes and an absolute majority of the votes of the representatives of States Parties present and voting.

5. The members of the Committee shall be elected for a term of four years. However, the terms of nine of the members elected at the first election shall expire at the end of two years; immediately after the first election the names of these nine members shall be chosen by lot by the Chairman of the Committee.

6. The election of the five additional members of the Committee shall be held in accordance with the provisions of paragraphs 2, 3 and 4 of this article, following the thirty-fifth ratification or accession. The terms of two of the additional members elected on this occasion shall expire at the end of two years, the names of these two members having been chosen by lot by the Chairman of the Committee.

7. For the filling of casual vacancies, the State Party whose expert has ceased to function as a member of the Committee shall appoint another expert from among its nationals, subject to the approval of the Committee.

8. The members of the Committee shall, with the approval of the General Assembly, receive emoluments from United Nations resources on such terms and conditions as the Assembly may decide, having regard to the importance of the Committee's responsibilities.

9. The Secretary-General of the United Nations shall provide the necessary staff and facilities for the effective performance of the functions of the Committee under the present Convention.

Article 18

1. States Parties undertake to submit to the Secretary-General of the United Nations, for consideration by the Committee, a report on the legislative, judicial, administrative or other measures which they have adopted to give effect to the provisions of the present Convention and on the progress made in this respect:

(a) Within one year after the entry into force for the State concerned;

(b) Thereafter at least every four years and further whenever the Committee so requests.

2. Reports may indicate factors and difficulties affecting the degree of fulfillment of obligations under the present Convention.

Article 19

1. The Committee shall adopt its own rules of procedure.

2. The Committee shall elect its officers for a term of two years.

Article 20

1. The Committee shall normally meet for a period of not more than two weeks annually in order to consider the reports submitted in accordance with article 18 of the present Convention.

2. The meetings of the Committee shall normally be held at United Nations Headquarters or at any other convenient place as determined by the Committee (amendment, status of ratification).

Article 21

1. The Committee shall, through the Economic and Social Council, report annually to the General Assembly of the United Nations on its activities and may make suggestions and general recommendations based on the examination of reports and information received from the States Parties. Such suggestions and general recommendations shall be included in the report of the Committee together with comments, if any, from States Parties.

2. The Secretary-General of the United Nations shall transmit the reports of the Committee to the Commission on the Status of Women for its information.

Article 22

The specialized agencies shall be entitled to be represented at the consideration of the implementation of such provisions of the present Convention as fall within the scope of their activities. The Committee may invite the specialized agencies to submit reports on the implementation of the Convention in areas falling within the scope of their activities.

Part VI

Article 23

Nothing in the present Convention shall affect any provisions that are more conducive to the achievement of equality between men and women which may be contained:

(a) In the legislation of a State Party; or

(b) In any other international convention, treaty or agreement in force for that State.

Article 24

States Parties undertake to adopt all necessary measures at the national level aimed at achieving the full realization of the rights recognized in the present Convention.

Article 25

1. The present Convention shall be open for signature by all States.

2. The Secretary-General of the United Nations is designated as the depositary of the present Convention.

3. The present Convention is subject to ratification. Instruments of ratification shall be deposited with the Secretary-General of the United Nations.

4. The present Convention shall be open to accession by all States. Accession shall be effected by the deposit of an instrument of accession with the Secretary-General of the United Nations.

Article 26

1. A request for the revision of the present Convention may be made at any time by any State Party by means of a notification in writing addressed to the Secretary-General of the United Nations.

2. The General Assembly of the United Nations shall decide upon the steps, if any, to be taken in respect of such a request.

Article 27

1. The present Convention shall enter into force on the thirtieth day after the date of deposit with the Secretary-General of the United Nations of the twentieth instrument of ratification or accession.

2. For each State ratifying the present Convention or acceding to it after the deposit of the twentieth instrument of ratification or accession, the Convention shall enter into force on the thirtieth day after the date of the deposit of its own instrument of ratification or accession.

Article 28

1. The Secretary-General of the United Nations shall receive and circulate to all States the text of reservations made by States at the time of ratification or accession.

2. A reservation incompatible with the object and purpose of the present Convention shall not be permitted.

3. Reservations may be withdrawn at any time by notification to this effect addressed to the Secretary-General of the United Nations, who shall then inform all States thereof. Such notification shall take effect on the date on which it is received.

Article 29

1. Any dispute between two or more States Parties concerning the interpretation or application of the present Convention which is not settled by negotiation shall, at the request of one of them, be submitted to arbitration. If within six months from the date of the request for arbitration the parties are unable to agree on the organization of the arbitration, any one of those parties may refer the dispute to the International Court of Justice by request in conformity with the Statute of the Court.

2. Each State Party may at the time of signature or ratification of the present Convention or accession thereto declare that it does not consider itself bound by paragraph I of this article. The other States Parties shall not be bound by that paragraph with respect to any State Party which has made such a reservation.

3. Any State Party which has made a reservation in accordance with paragraph 2 of this article may at any time withdraw that reservation by notification to the Secretary-General of the United Nations.

Article 30

The present Convention, the Arabic, Chinese, English, French, Russian and Spanish texts of which are equally authentic, shall be deposited with the Secretary-General of the United Nations.

IN WITNESS WHEREOF the undersigned, duly authorized, have signed the present Convention.

Appendix G

Convention on the Rights of the Child

dopted and opened for signature, ratification and accession by General Assembly resolution 44/25 of 20 November 1989 entry into force 2 September 1990, in accordance with article 49.

Preamble

The States Parties to the present Convention,

Considering that, in accordance with the principles proclaimed in the Charter of the United Nations, recognition of the inherent dignity and of the equal and inalienable rights of all members of the human family is the foundation of freedom, justice and peace in the world,

Bearing in mind that the peoples of the United Nations have, in the Charter, reaffirmed their faith in fundamental human rights and in the dignity and worth of the human person, and have determined to promote social progress and better standards of life in larger freedom,

Recognizing that the United Nations has, in the Universal Declaration of Human Rights and in the International Covenants on Human Rights, proclaimed and agreed that everyone is entitled to all the rights and freedoms set forth therein, without distinction of any kind, such as race, colour, sex, language, religion, political or other opinion, national or social origin, property, birth or other status,

Recalling that, in the Universal Declaration of Human Rights, the United Nations has proclaimed that childhood is entitled to special care and assistance,

Convinced that the family, as the fundamental group of society and the natural environment for the growth and well-being of all its members and particularly children, should be afforded the necessary protection and assistance so that it can fully assume its responsibilities within the community,

Recognizing that the child, for the full and harmonious development of his or her personality, should grow up in a family environment, in an atmosphere of happiness, love and understanding,

Considering that the child should be fully prepared to live an individual life in society, and brought up in the spirit of the ideals proclaimed in the Charter of the United Nations, and in particular in the spirit of peace, dignity, tolerance, freedom, equality and solidarity,

Bearing in mind that the need to extend particular care to the child has been stated in the Geneva Declaration of the Rights of the Child of 1924 and in the Declaration of the Rights of the Child adopted by the General Assembly on 20 November 1959 and recognized in the Universal Declaration of Human Rights, in the International Covenant on Civil and Political Rights (in particular in articles 23 and 24), in the International Covenant on Economic, Social and Cultural Rights (in particular in article 10) and in the statutes and relevant instruments of specialized agencies and international organizations concerned with the welfare of children,

Bearing in mind that, as indicated in the Declaration of the Rights of the Child, "the child, by reason of his physical and mental immaturity, needs special safeguards and care, including appropriate legal protection, before as well as after birth,"

Recalling the provisions of the Declaration on Social and Legal Principles relating to the Protection and Welfare of Children, with Special Reference to Foster Placement and Adoption Nationally and Internationally; the United Nations Standard Minimum Rules for the Administration of Juvenile Justice (The Beijing Rules); and the Declaration on the Protection of Women and Children in Emergency and Armed Conflict,

Recognizing that, in all countries in the world, there are children living in exceptionally difficult conditions, and that such children need special consideration,

Taking due account of the importance of the traditions and cultural values of each people for the protection and harmonious development of the child,

Recognizing the importance of international co-operation for improving the living conditions of children in every country, in particular in the developing countries,

Have agreed as follows:

Part I

Article 1

For the purposes of the present Convention, a child means every human being below the age of eighteen years unless under the law applicable to the child, majority is attained earlier.

Article 2

1. States Parties shall respect and ensure the rights set forth in the present Convention to each child within their jurisdiction without discrimination of any kind, irrespective of the child's or his or her parent's or legal guardian's race, colour,

sex, language, religion, political or other opinion, national, ethnic or social origin, property, disability, birth or other status.

2. States Parties shall take all appropriate measures to ensure that the child is protected against all forms of discrimination or punishment on the basis of the status, activities, expressed opinions, or beliefs of the child's parents, legal guardians, or family members.

Article 3

1. In all actions concerning children, whether undertaken by public or private social welfare institutions, courts of law, administrative authorities or legislative bodies, the best interests of the child shall be a primary consideration.

2. States Parties undertake to ensure the child such protection and care as is necessary for his or her well-being, taking into account the rights and duties of his or her parents, legal guardians, or other individuals legally responsible for him or her, and, to this end, shall take all appropriate legislative and administrative measures.

3. States Parties shall ensure that the institutions, services and facilities responsible for the care or protection of children shall conform with the standards established by competent authorities, particularly in the areas of safety, health, in the number and suitability of their staff, as well as competent supervision.

Article 4

States Parties shall undertake all appropriate legislative, administrative, and other measures for the implementation of the rights recognized in the present Convention. With regard to economic, social and cultural rights, States Parties shall undertake such measures to the maximum extent of their available resources and, where needed, within the framework of international co-operation.

Article 5

States Parties shall respect the responsibilities, rights and duties of parents or, where applicable, the members of the extended family or community as provided for by local custom, legal guardians or other persons legally responsible for the child, to provide, in a manner consistent with the evolving capacities of the child, appropriate direction and guidance in the exercise by the child of the rights recognized in the present Convention.

Article 6

1. States Parties recognize that every child has the inherent right to life.

2. States Parties shall ensure to the maximum extent possible the survival and development of the child.

Article 7

1. The child shall be registered immediately after birth and shall have the right from birth to a name, the right to acquire a nationality and, as far as possible, the right to know and be cared for by his or her parents.

2. States Parties shall ensure the implementation of these rights in accordance with their national law and their obligations under the relevant international instruments in this field, in particular where the child would otherwise be stateless.

Article 8

1. States Parties undertake to respect the right of the child to preserve his or her identity, including nationality, name and family relations as recognized by law without unlawful interference.

2. Where a child is illegally deprived of some or all of the elements of his or her identity, States Parties shall provide appropriate assistance and protection, with a view to re-establishing speedily his or her identity.

Article 9

1. States Parties shall ensure that a child shall not be separated from his or her parents against their will, except when competent authorities subject to judicial review determine, in accordance with applicable law and procedures, that such separation is necessary for the best interests of the child. Such determination may be necessary in a particular case such as one involving abuse or neglect of the child by the parents, or one where the parents are living separately and a decision must be made as to the child's place of residence.

2. In any proceedings pursuant to paragraph 1 of the present article, all interested parties shall be given an opportunity to participate in the proceedings and make their views known.

3. States Parties shall respect the right of the child who is separated from one or both parents to maintain personal relations and direct contact with both parents on a regular basis, except if it is contrary to the child's best interests.

4. Where such separation results from any action initiated by a State Party, such as the detention, imprisonment, exile, deportation or death (including death arising from any cause while the person is in the custody of the State) of one or both parents or of the child, that State Party shall, upon request, provide the parents, the child or, if appropriate, another member of the family with the essential information concerning the whereabouts of the absent member(s) of the family unless the provision of the information would be detrimental to the well-being of the child. States Parties shall further ensure that the submission of such a request shall of itself entail no adverse consequences for the person(s) concerned.

Article 10

1. In accordance with the obligation of States Parties under article 9, paragraph 1, applications by a child or his or her parents to enter or leave a State Party for the purpose of family reunification shall be dealt with by States Parties in a positive, humane and expeditious manner. States Parties shall further ensure that the submission of such a request shall entail no adverse consequences for the applicants and for the members of their family.

2. A child whose parents reside in different States shall have the right to maintain on a regular basis, save in exceptional circumstances, personal relations and direct contacts with both parents. Towards that end and in accordance with the obligation of States Parties under article 9, paragraph 1, States Parties shall respect the right of the child and his or her parents to leave any country, including their own, and to enter their own country. The right to leave any country shall be subject only to such restrictions as are prescribed by law and which are necessary to protect the national security, public order (*ordre public*), public health or morals or the rights and freedoms of others and are consistent with the other rights recognized in the present Convention.

Article 11

1. States Parties shall take measures to combat the illicit transfer and non-return of children abroad.

2. To this end, States Parties shall promote the conclusion of bilateral or multilateral agreements or accession to existing agreements.

Article 12

1. States Parties shall assure to the child who is capable of forming his or her own views the right to express those views freely in all matters affecting the child, the views of the child being given due weight in accordance with the age and maturity of the child.

2. For this purpose, the child shall in particular be provided the opportunity to be heard in any judicial and administrative proceedings affecting the child, either directly, or through a representative or an appropriate body, in a manner consistent with the procedural rules of national law.

Article 13

1. The child shall have the right to freedom of expression; this right shall include freedom to seek, receive and impart information and ideas of all kinds, regardless of frontiers, either orally, in writing or in print, in the form of art, or through any other media of the child's choice.

2. The exercise of this right may be subject to certain restrictions, but these shall only be such as are provided by law and are necessary:

(a) For respect of the rights or reputations of others; or

(b) For the protection of national security or of public order (*ordre public*), or of public health or morals.

Article 14

1. States Parties shall respect the right of the child to freedom of thought, conscience and religion.

2. States Parties shall respect the rights and duties of the parents and, when applicable, legal guardians, to provide direction to the child in the exercise of his or her right in a manner consistent with the evolving capacities of the child.

3. Freedom to manifest one's religion or beliefs may be subject only to such limitations as are prescribed by law and are necessary to protect public safety, order, health or morals, or the fundamental rights and freedoms of others.

Article 15

1. States Parties recognize the rights of the child to freedom of association and to freedom of peaceful assembly.

2. No restrictions may be placed on the exercise of these rights other than those imposed in conformity with the law and which are necessary in a democratic society in the interests of national security or public safety, public order (*ordre public*), the protection of public health or morals or the protection of the rights and freedoms of others.

Article 16

1. No child shall be subjected to arbitrary or unlawful interference with his or her privacy, family, home or correspondence, nor to unlawful attacks on his or her honour and reputation.

2. The child has the right to the protection of the law against such interference or attacks.

Article 17

States Parties recognize the important function performed by the mass media and shall ensure that the child has access to information and material from a diversity of national and international sources, especially those aimed at the promotion of his or her social, spiritual and moral well-being and physical and mental health. To this end, States Parties shall:

(a) Encourage the mass media to disseminate information and material of social and cultural benefit to the child and in accordance with the spirit of article 29;

(b) Encourage international co-operation in the production, exchange and dissemination of such information and material from a diversity of cultural, national and international sources;

(c) Encourage the production and dissemination of children's books;

(d) Encourage the mass media to have particular regard to the linguistic needs of the child who belongs to a minority group or who is indigenous;

(e) Encourage the development of appropriate guidelines for the protection of the child from information and material injurious to his or her well-being, bearing in mind the provisions of articles 13 and 18.

Article 18

1. States Parties shall use their best efforts to ensure recognition of the principle that both parents have common responsibilities for the upbringing and development of the child. Parents or, as the case may be, legal guardians, have the primary responsibility for the upbringing and development of the child. The best interests of the child will be their basic concern.

2. For the purpose of guaranteeing and promoting the rights set forth in the present Convention, States Parties shall render appropriate assistance to parents and legal guardians in the performance of their child-rearing responsibilities and shall ensure the development of institutions, facilities and services for the care of children.

3. States Parties shall take all appropriate measures to ensure that children of working parents have the right to benefit from child-care services and facilities for which they are eligible.

Article 19

1. States Parties shall take all appropriate legislative, administrative, social and educational measures to protect the child from all forms of physical or mental violence, injury or abuse, neglect or negligent treatment, maltreatment or exploitation, including sexual abuse, while in the care of parent(s), legal guardian(s) or any other person who has the care of the child.

2. Such protective measures should, as appropriate, include effective procedures for the establishment of social programmes to provide necessary support for the child and for those who have the care of the child, as well as for other forms of prevention and for identification, reporting, referral, investigation, treatment and follow-up of instances of child maltreatment described heretofore, and, as appropriate, for judicial involvement.

Article 20

1. A child temporarily or permanently deprived of his or her family environment, or in whose own best interests cannot be allowed to remain in that environment, shall be entitled to special protection and assistance provided by the State.

2. States Parties shall in accordance with their national laws ensure alternative care for such a child.

3. Such care could include, inter alia, foster placement, kafalah of Islamic law, adoption or if necessary placement in suitable institutions for the care of children. When considering solutions, due regard shall be paid to the desirability of continuity in a child's upbringing and to the child's ethnic, religious, cultural and linguistic background.

Article 21

States Parties that recognize and/or permit the system of adoption shall ensure that the best interests of the child shall be the paramount consideration and they shall:

(a) Ensure that the adoption of a child is authorized only by competent authorities who determine, in accordance with applicable law and procedures and on the basis of all pertinent and reliable information, that the adoption is permissible in view of the child's status concerning parents, relatives and legal guardians and that, if required, the persons concerned have given their informed consent to the adoption on the basis of such counselling as may be necessary;

(b) Recognize that inter-country adoption may be considered as an alternative means of child's care, if the child cannot be placed in a foster or an adoptive family or cannot in any suitable manner be cared for in the child's country of origin;

(c) Ensure that the child concerned by inter-country adoption enjoys safeguards and standards equivalent to those existing in the case of national adoption;

(d) Take all appropriate measures to ensure that, in inter-country adoption, the placement does not result in improper financial gain for those involved in it;

(e) Promote, where appropriate, the objectives of the present article by concluding bilateral or multilateral arrangements or agreements, and endeavour, within this framework, to ensure that the placement of the child in another country is carried out by competent authorities or organs.

Article 22

1. States Parties shall take appropriate measures to ensure that a child who is seeking refugee status or who is considered a refugee in accordance with applicable

international or domestic law and procedures shall, whether unaccompanied or accompanied by his or her parents or by any other person, receive appropriate protection and humanitarian assistance in the enjoyment of applicable rights set forth in the present Convention and in other international human rights or humanitarian instruments to which the said States are Parties.

2. For this purpose, States Parties shall provide, as they consider appropriate, co-operation in any efforts by the United Nations and other competent intergovernmental organizations or non-governmental organizations co-operating with the United Nations to protect and assist such a child and to trace the parents or other members of the family of any refugee child in order to obtain information necessary for reunification with his or her family. In cases where no parents or other members of the family can be found, the child shall be accorded the same protection as any other child permanently or temporarily deprived of his or her family environment for any reason, as set forth in the present Convention.

Article 23

1. States Parties recognize that a mentally or physically disabled child should enjoy a full and decent life, in conditions which ensure dignity, promote self-reliance and facilitate the child's active participation in the community.

2. States Parties recognize the right of the disabled child to special care and shall encourage and ensure the extension, subject to available resources, to the eligible child and those responsible for his or her care, of assistance for which application is made and which is appropriate to the child's condition and to the circumstances of the parents or others caring for the child.

3. Recognizing the special needs of a disabled child, assistance extended in accordance with paragraph 2 of the present article shall be provided free of charge, whenever possible, taking into account the financial resources of the parents or others caring for the child, and shall be designed to ensure that the disabled child has effective access to and receives education, training, health care services, rehabilitation services, preparation for employment and recreation opportunities in a manner conducive to the child's achieving the fullest possible social integration and individual development, including his or her cultural and spiritual development.

4. States Parties shall promote, in the spirit of international cooperation, the exchange of appropriate information in the field of preventive health care and of medical, psychological and functional treatment of disabled children, including dissemination of and access to information concerning methods of rehabilitation, education and vocational services, with the aim of enabling States Parties to improve their capabilities and skills and to widen their experience in these areas. In this regard, particular account shall be taken of the needs of developing countries.

Article 24

1. States Parties recognize the right of the child to the enjoyment of the highest attainable standard of health and to facilities for the treatment of illness and rehabilitation of health. States Parties shall strive to ensure that no child is deprived of his or her right of access to such health care services.

2. States Parties shall pursue full implementation of this right and, in particular, shall take appropriate measures:
   (a) To diminish infant and child mortality;
   (b) To ensure the provision of necessary medical assistance and health care to all children with emphasis on the development of primary health care;
   (c) To combat disease and malnutrition, including within the framework of primary health care, through, inter alia, the application of readily available technology and through the provision of adequate nutritious foods and clean drinking-water, taking into consideration the dangers and risks of environmental pollution;
   (d) To ensure appropriate pre-natal and post-natal health care for mothers;
   (e) To ensure that all segments of society, in particular parents and children, are informed, have access to education and are supported in the use of basic knowledge of child health and nutrition, the advantages of breast-feeding, hygiene and environmental sanitation and the prevention of accidents;
   (f) To develop preventive health care, guidance for parents and family planning education and services.

3. States Parties shall take all effective and appropriate measures with a view to abolishing traditional practices prejudicial to the health of children.

4. States Parties undertake to promote and encourage international co-operation with a view to achieving progressively the full realization of the right recognized in the present article. In this regard, particular account shall be taken of the needs of developing countries.

Article 25

States Parties recognize the right of a child who has been placed by the competent authorities for the purposes of care, protection or treatment of his or her physical or mental health, to a periodic review of the treatment provided to the child and all other circumstances relevant to his or her placement.

Article 26

1. States Parties shall recognize for every child the right to benefit from social security, including social insurance, and shall take the necessary measures to achieve the full realization of this right in accordance with their national law.

2. The benefits should, where appropriate, be granted, taking into account the resources and the circumstances of the child and persons having responsibility for the maintenance of the child, as well as any other consideration relevant to an application for benefits made by or on behalf of the child.

Article 27

1. States Parties recognize the right of every child to a standard of living adequate for the child's physical, mental, spiritual, moral and social development.

2. The parent(s) or others responsible for the child have the primary responsibility to secure, within their abilities and financial capacities, the conditions of living necessary for the child's development.

3. States Parties, in accordance with national conditions and within their means, shall take appropriate measures to assist parents and others responsible for the child to implement this right and shall in case of need provide material assistance and support programmes, particularly with regard to nutrition, clothing and housing.

4. States Parties shall take all appropriate measures to secure the recovery of maintenance for the child from the parents or other persons having financial responsibility for the child, both within the State Party and from abroad. In particular, where the person having financial responsibility for the child lives in a State different from that of the child, States Parties shall promote the accession to international agreements or the conclusion of such agreements, as well as the making of other appropriate arrangements.

Article 28

1. States Parties recognize the right of the child to education, and with a view to achieving this right progressively and on the basis of equal opportunity, they shall, in particular:
   (a) Make primary education compulsory and available free to all;
   (b) Encourage the development of different forms of secondary education, including general and vocational education, make them available and accessible to every child, and take appropriate measures such as the introduction of free education and offering financial assistance in case of need;
   (c) Make higher education accessible to all on the basis of capacity by every appropriate means;
   (d) Make educational and vocational information and guidance available and accessible to all children;
   (e) Take measures to encourage regular attendance at schools and the reduction of drop-out rates.

2. States Parties shall take all appropriate measures to ensure that school discipline is administered in a manner consistent with the child's human dignity and in conformity with the present Convention.

3. States Parties shall promote and encourage international cooperation in matters relating to education, in particular with a view to contributing to the elimination of ignorance and illiteracy throughout the world and facilitating access to scientific and technical knowledge and modern teaching methods. In this regard, particular account shall be taken of the needs of developing countries.

Article 29

1. States Parties agree that the education of the child shall be directed to:
   (a) The development of the child's personality, talents and mental and physical abilities to their fullest potential;
   (b) The development of respect for human rights and fundamental freedoms, and for the principles enshrined in the Charter of the United Nations;
   (c) The development of respect for the child's parents, his or her own cultural identity, language and values, for the national values of the country in which the child is living, the country from which he or she may originate, and for civilizations different from his or her own;
   (d) The preparation of the child for responsible life in a free society, in the spirit of understanding, peace, tolerance, equality of sexes, and friendship among all peoples, ethnic, national and religious groups and persons of indigenous origin;
   (e) The development of respect for the natural environment.

2. No part of the present article or article 28 shall be construed so as to interfere with the liberty of individuals and bodies to establish and direct educational institutions, subject always to the observance of the principle set forth in paragraph 1 of the present article and to the requirements that the education given in such institutions shall conform to such minimum standards as may be laid down by the State.

Article 30

In those States in which ethnic, religious or linguistic minorities or persons of indigenous origin exist, a child belonging to such a minority or who is indigenous shall not be denied the right, in community with other members of his or her group, to enjoy his or her own culture, to profess and practise his or her own religion, or to use his or her own language.

Article 31

1. States Parties recognize the right of the child to rest and leisure, to engage in play and recreational activities appropriate to the age of the child and to participate freely in cultural life and the arts.

2. States Parties shall respect and promote the right of the child to participate fully in cultural and artistic life and shall encourage the provision of appropriate and equal opportunities for cultural, artistic, recreational and leisure activity.

Article 32

1. States Parties recognize the right of the child to be protected from economic exploitation and from performing any work that is likely to be hazardous or to interfere with the child's education, or to be harmful to the child's health or physical, mental, spiritual, moral or social development.

2. States Parties shall take legislative, administrative, social and educational measures to ensure the implementation of the present article. To this end, and having regard to the relevant provisions of other international instruments, States Parties shall in particular:

    (a) Provide for a minimum age or minimum ages for admission to employment;

    (b) Provide for appropriate regulation of the hours and conditions of employment;

    (c) Provide for appropriate penalties or other sanctions to ensure the effective enforcement of the present article.

Article 33

States Parties shall take all appropriate measures, including legislative, administrative, social and educational measures, to protect children from the illicit use of narcotic drugs and psychotropic substances as defined in the relevant international treaties, and to prevent the use of children in the illicit production and trafficking of such substances.

Article 34

States Parties undertake to protect the child from all forms of sexual exploitation and sexual abuse. For these purposes, States Parties shall in particular take all appropriate national, bilateral and multilateral measures to prevent:

    (a) The inducement or coercion of a child to engage in any unlawful sexual activity;

    (b) The exploitative use of children in prostitution or other unlawful sexual practices;

    (c) The exploitative use of children in pornographic performances and materials.

Article 35

States Parties shall take all appropriate national, bilateral and multilateral measures to prevent the abduction of, the sale of or traffic in children for any purpose or in any form.

Article 36

States Parties shall protect the child against all other forms of exploitation prejudicial to any aspects of the child's welfare.

Article 37

States Parties shall ensure that:

(a) No child shall be subjected to torture or other cruel, inhuman or degrading treatment or punishment. Neither capital punishment nor life imprisonment without possibility of release shall be imposed for offences committed by persons below eighteen years of age;

(b) No child shall be deprived of his or her liberty unlawfully or arbitrarily. The arrest, detention or imprisonment of a child shall be in conformity with the law and shall be used only as a measure of last resort and for the shortest appropriate period of time;

(c) Every child deprived of liberty shall be treated with humanity and respect for the inherent dignity of the human person, and in a manner which takes into account the needs of persons of his or her age. In particular, every child deprived of liberty shall be separated from adults unless it is considered in the child's best interest not to do so and shall have the right to maintain contact with his or her family through correspondence and visits, save in exceptional circumstances;

(d) Every child deprived of his or her liberty shall have the right to prompt access to legal and other appropriate assistance, as well as the right to challenge the legality of the deprivation of his or her liberty before a court or other competent, independent and impartial authority, and to a prompt decision on any such action.

Article 38

1. States Parties undertake to respect and to ensure respect for rules of international humanitarian law applicable to them in armed conflicts which are relevant to the child.

2. States Parties shall take all feasible measures to ensure that persons who have not attained the age of fifteen years do not take a direct part in hostilities.

3. States Parties shall refrain from recruiting any person who has not attained the age of fifteen years into their armed forces. In recruiting among those persons who have attained the age of fifteen years but who have not attained the age of eighteen years, States Parties shall endeavour to give priority to those who are oldest.

4. In accordance with their obligations under international humanitarian law to protect the civilian population in armed conflicts, States Parties shall take all

feasible measures to ensure protection and care of children who are affected by an armed conflict.

Article 39

States Parties shall take all appropriate measures to promote physical and psychological recovery and social reintegration of a child victim of: any form of neglect, exploitation, or abuse; torture or any other form of cruel, inhuman or degrading treatment or punishment; or armed conflicts. Such recovery and reintegration shall take place in an environment which fosters the health, self-respect and dignity of the child.

Article 40

1. States Parties recognize the right of every child alleged as, accused of, or recognized as having infringed the penal law to be treated in a manner consistent with the promotion of the child's sense of dignity and worth, which reinforces the child's respect for the human rights and fundamental freedoms of others and which takes into account the child's age and the desirability of promoting the child's reintegration and the child's assuming a constructive role in society.

2. To this end, and having regard to the relevant provisions of international instruments, States Parties shall, in particular, ensure that:

(a) No child shall be alleged as, be accused of, or recognized as having infringed the penal law by reason of acts or omissions that were not prohibited by national or international law at the time they were committed;

(b) Every child alleged as or accused of having infringed the penal law has at least the following guarantees:

   (i)   To be presumed innocent until proven guilty according to law;

   (ii) To be informed promptly and directly of the charges against him or her, and, if appropriate, through his or her parents or legal guardians, and to have legal or other appropriate assistance in the preparation and presentation of his or her defence;

   (iii) To have the matter determined without delay by a competent, independent and impartial authority or judicial body in a fair hearing according to law, in the presence of legal or other appropriate assistance and, unless it is considered not to be in the best interest of the child, in particular, taking into account his or her age or situation, his or her parents or legal guardians;

   (iv) Not to be compelled to give testimony or to confess guilt; to examine or have examined adverse witnesses and to obtain the participation and examination of witnesses on his or her behalf under conditions of equality;

   (v)   If considered to have infringed the penal law, to have this decision and any measures imposed in consequence thereof reviewed by a higher competent, independent and impartial authority or judicial body according to law;

     (vi) To have the free assistance of an interpreter if the child cannot understand or speak the language used;

     (vii) To have his or her privacy fully respected at all stages of the proceedings.

3. States Parties shall seek to promote the establishment of laws, procedures, authorities and institutions specifically applicable to children alleged as, accused of, or recognized as having infringed the penal law, and, in particular:

    (a) The establishment of a minimum age below which children shall be presumed not to have the capacity to infringe the penal law;

    (b) Whenever appropriate and desirable, measures for dealing with such children without resorting to judicial proceedings, providing that human rights and legal safeguards are fully respected.

4. A variety of dispositions, such as care, guidance and supervision orders; counselling; probation; foster care; education and vocational training programmes and other alternatives to institutional care shall be available to ensure that children are dealt with in a manner appropriate to their well-being and proportionate both to their circumstances and the offence.

Article 41

Nothing in the present Convention shall affect any provisions which are more conducive to the realization of the rights of the child and which may be contained in:

(a) The law of a State party; or

(b) International law in force for that State.

Part II

Article 42

States Parties undertake to make the principles and provisions of the Convention widely known, by appropriate and active means, to adults and children alike.

Article 43

1. For the purpose of examining the progress made by States Parties in achieving the realization of the obligations undertaken in the present Convention, there shall be established a Committee on the Rights of the Child, which shall carry out the functions hereinafter provided.

2. The Committee shall consist of ten experts of high moral standing and recognized competence in the field covered by this Convention. The members of the Committee shall be elected by States Parties from among their nationals and shall

serve in their personal capacity, consideration being given to equitable geographical distribution, as well as to the principal legal systems (amendment).

3. The members of the Committee shall be elected by secret ballot from a list of persons nominated by States Parties. Each State Party may nominate one person from among its own nationals.

4. The initial election to the Committee shall be held no later than six months after the date of the entry into force of the present Convention and thereafter every second year. At least four months before the date of each election, the Secretary-General of the United Nations shall address a letter to States Parties inviting them to submit their nominations within two months. The Secretary-General shall subsequently prepare a list in alphabetical order of all persons thus nominated, indicating States Parties which have nominated them, and shall submit it to the States Parties to the present Convention.

5. The elections shall be held at meetings of States Parties convened by the Secretary-General at United Nations Headquarters. At those meetings, for which two thirds of States Parties shall constitute a quorum, the persons elected to the Committee shall be those who obtain the largest number of votes and an absolute majority of the votes of the representatives of States Parties present and voting.

6. The members of the Committee shall be elected for a term of four years. They shall be eligible for re-election if renominated. The term of five of the members elected at the first election shall expire at the end of two years; immediately after the first election, the names of these five members shall be chosen by lot by the Chairman of the meeting.

7. If a member of the Committee dies or resigns or declares that for any other cause he or she can no longer perform the duties of the Committee, the State Party which nominated the member shall appoint another expert from among its nationals to serve for the remainder of the term, subject to the approval of the Committee.

8. The Committee shall establish its own rules of procedure.

9. The Committee shall elect its officers for a period of two years.

10. The meetings of the Committee shall normally be held at United Nations Headquarters or at any other convenient place as determined by the Committee. The Committee shall normally meet annually. The duration of the meetings of the Committee shall be determined, and reviewed, if necessary, by a meeting of the States Parties to the present Convention, subject to the approval of the General Assembly.

11. The Secretary-General of the United Nations shall provide the necessary staff and facilities for the effective performance of the functions of the Committee under the present Convention.

12. With the approval of the General Assembly, the members of the Committee established under the present Convention shall receive emoluments from United Nations resources on such terms and conditions as the Assembly may decide.

Article 44

1. States Parties undertake to submit to the Committee, through the Secretary-General of the United Nations, reports on the measures they have adopted which give effect to the rights recognized herein and on the progress made on the enjoyment of those rights:

(a) Within two years of the entry into force of the Convention for the State Party concerned;

(b) Thereafter every five years.

2. Reports made under the present article shall indicate factors and difficulties, if any, affecting the degree of fulfillment of the obligations under the present Convention. Reports shall also contain sufficient information to provide the Committee with a comprehensive understanding of the implementation of the Convention in the country concerned.

3. A State Party which has submitted a comprehensive initial report to the Committee need not, in its subsequent reports submitted in accordance with paragraph 1 (b) of the present article, repeat basic information previously provided.

4. The Committee may request from States Parties further information relevant to the implementation of the Convention.

5. The Committee shall submit to the General Assembly, through the Economic and Social Council, every two years, reports on its activities.

6. States Parties shall make their reports widely available to the public in their own countries.

Article 45

In order to foster the effective implementation of the Convention and to encourage international co-operation in the field covered by the Convention:

(a) The specialized agencies, the United Nations Children's Fund, and other United Nations organs shall be entitled to be represented at the consideration of the implementation of such provisions of the present Convention as fall within the scope of their mandate. The Committee may invite the specialized agencies, the United Nations Children's Fund and other competent bodies as it may consider appropriate to provide expert advice on the implementation of the Convention in areas falling within the scope of their respective mandates. The Committee may invite the specialized agencies, the United Nations Children's Fund, and other United Nations organs to submit reports on the implementation of the Convention in areas falling within the scope of their activities;

(b) The Committee shall transmit, as it may consider appropriate, to the specialized agencies, the United Nations Children's Fund and other competent bodies, any reports from States Parties that contain a request, or indicate a need, for technical advice or assistance, along with the Committee's observations and suggestions, if any, on these requests or indications;

(c) The Committee may recommend to the General Assembly to request the Secretary-General to undertake on its behalf studies on specific issues relating to the rights of the child;

(d) The Committee may make suggestions and general recommendations based on information received pursuant to articles 44 and 45 of the present Convention. Such suggestions and general recommendations shall be transmitted to any State Party concerned and reported to the General Assembly, together with comments, if any, from States Parties.

Part III

Article 46

The present Convention shall be open for signature by all States.

Article 47

The present Convention is subject to ratification. Instruments of ratification shall be deposited with the Secretary-General of the United Nations.

Article 48

The present Convention shall remain open for accession by any State. The instruments of accession shall be deposited with the Secretary-General of the United Nations.

Article 49

1. The present Convention shall enter into force on the thirtieth day following the date of deposit with the Secretary-General of the United Nations of the twentieth instrument of ratification or accession.

2. For each State ratifying or acceding to the Convention after the deposit of the twentieth instrument of ratification or accession, the Convention shall enter into force on the thirtieth day after the deposit by such State of its instrument of ratification or accession.

Article 50

1. Any State Party may propose an amendment and file it with the Secretary-General of the United Nations. The Secretary-General shall thereupon communicate the proposed amendment to States Parties, with a request that they indicate

whether they favour a conference of States Parties for the purpose of considering and voting upon the proposals. In the event that, within four months from the date of such communication, at least one third of the States Parties favour such a conference, the Secretary-General shall convene the conference under the auspices of the United Nations. Any amendment adopted by a majority of States Parties present and voting at the conference shall be submitted to the General Assembly for approval.

2. An amendment adopted in accordance with paragraph 1 of the present article shall enter into force when it has been approved by the General Assembly of the United Nations and accepted by a two-thirds majority of States Parties.

3. When an amendment enters into force, it shall be binding on those States Parties which have accepted it, other States Parties still being bound by the provisions of the present Convention and any earlier amendments which they have accepted.

Article 51

1. The Secretary-General of the United Nations shall receive and circulate to all States the text of reservations made by States at the time of ratification or accession.

2. A reservation incompatible with the object and purpose of the present Convention shall not be permitted.

3. Reservations may be withdrawn at any time by notification to that effect addressed to the Secretary-General of the United Nations, who shall then inform all States. Such notification shall take effect on the date on which it is received by the Secretary-General.

Article 52

A State Party may denounce the present Convention by written notification to the Secretary-General of the United Nations. Denunciation becomes effective one year after the date of receipt of the notification by the Secretary-General.

Article 53

The Secretary-General of the United Nations is designated as the depositary of the present Convention.

Article 54

The original of the present Convention, of which the Arabic, Chinese, English, French, Russian and Spanish texts are equally authentic, shall be deposited with the Secretary-General of the United Nations.

IN WITNESS THEREOF the undersigned plenipotentiaries, being duly authorized thereto by their respective governments, have signed the present Convention.

References

Achebe, C. (1987). *Anthills of the savannah*. New York: Doubleday.

Alexander, F., Isaacs, A., Law, J., & Lewis, P. (Eds.). (1998). *Encyclopedia of world history*. New York: Oxford University Press.

Alexander, T. (1996). *Unravelling global apartheid: An overview of world politics*. Cambridge, England: Polity Press.

Allen, M., & Baker, P. (2005, February 7). $2.5 trillion budget plan cuts many programs: Domestic spending falls; defense, security rise. *Washington Post*, p. A1.

Amnesty International. (2005). *Indian Ocean earthquake & tsunami: Human rights as risk in the aftermath*. Retrieved November 29, 2005, from http://web.amnesty.org/pages/tsunami2-eng

Appleby, G., Colon, E., & Hamilton, J. (2001). *Diversity, oppression and social functioning: Person in environment and assessment and intervention*. Boston: Allyn & Bacon.

The Beijing Declaration and the Platform for Action. (1995, September 4–15). 4th World Conference on Women, Beijing, China. New York: UN Department of Public Information.

Black, H. Campbell. (1968). *Black's law dictionary, abridged: Definitions of the terms and phrases of American and English jurisprudence, ancient and modern* (Rev. 4th ed.). St. Paul, MN: West Publishing.

Bricker-Jenkins, M., Hooeyman, N., & Gottlieb, N. (Eds.). (1991). *Feminist social work practice in clinical settings*. Newbury Park, CA: Sage.

Brown, D. (1970). *Bury my heart at Wounded Knee: An Indian history of the American west*. New York: Holt, Rinehart and Winston.

Brown, D. (2004, December 8). Iraq abuse witnesses were told not to talk, memo says. *St. Louis Post-Dispatch*, pp. A1, A11.

Buergenthal, T. (1988). *International human rights law*. St. Paul, MN: West Publishing.

Bunch, C. (1991). Women's rights as human rights: Toward a re-vision of human rights. In C. Bunch & R. Carrillo (Eds.), *Gender violence: A development and human rights issue* (pp. 3–18). New Brunswick, NJ: Center for Women's Global Leadership.

Center for Global Development. (2004). Retrieved December 3, 2004, from www.cgdev.org/

Center for Human Rights. (1994). *Human rights and social work: A manual for schools of social work and the social work profession*. Training Series no. 1. Geneva: United Nations.

Chesler, E. (2004, October). International holdout. *American Prospect*, A27–A28.

Congress, E. (1999). *Social work values and ethics: Identifying and resolving professional dilemmas*. Chicago: Nelson Hall.

Cook, R. (1995). Gender, health and human rights. *Health and Human Rights: An International Quarterly Journal, 1*(4), 350–366.

Council on Social Work Education. (2003). *Handbook of accreditation standards and procedures* (5th ed.). Alexandria, VA: CSWE Press.

Davis, M. (2000, October 11). Bring international law into domestic courtrooms. *Christian Science Monitor, 11,* 9.

Dershowitz, Alan M. (2002). *Shouting fire: Civil liberties in a turbulent age.* New York: Little Brown.

Devore, W., & Schlesinger, E. (1996). *Ethnic sensitive social work practice* (5th ed.). Boston: Allyn & Bacon.

Dippel, J. (1996). *Bound upon a wheel of fire.* New York: Basic Books.

Ehrenreich, B. (2001). *Nickel and dimed: On (not) getting by in America.* New York: Metropolitan Books, Henry Holt and Company.

European Court of Human Rights. (2005). Retrieved November 15, 2005, from www.echr .coe.int/

Farer, T. (1989). The United Nations and human rights: More than a whimper. In R. P. Claude & B. H. Weston (Eds.), *Human rights in the world community* (pp. 194–208). Philadelphia: University of Pennsylvania Press.

Gangjian, D., & Gang, S. (1995). Relating human rights to Chinese culture: The four paths of the Confucian *analects* and the four principles of a new theory of benevolence. In F. Davis (Ed.), *Human rights and Chinese values* (pp. 35–55). Hong Kong: Oxford University Press.

German unemployment passes 5 million mark: Highest since World War II. (2005, February 2). *Finfacts Team.* Retrieved November 19, 2005, from www.finfacts.com/irelandbusiness news/publish/printer

Giris, U. (2005, February 9). For India's daughters, a dark birthday, infanticide and sex selective abortion yield a more skewed gender ratio. *Christian Science Monitor,* p. 11.

Gold, D. (2004). *Tower of babble: How the United Nations has fueled global chaos.* New York: Crown Forum.

Goldhagen, D. (1996). *Hitler's willing executioners: Ordinary Germans and the holocaust.* New York: Alfred A. Knopf.

Gutierrez, L. M. (1990). Working with women of color: An empowerment perspective. *Social Work: Journal of the National Association of Social Workers, 35,* 149–153.

Hall, K. (Ed.). (1992). *The Oxford companion to the Supreme Court of the United States.* Oxford: Oxford University Press.

Hansen E. (1991). *Wohlfahrtspolitik im NS-Staat: Motivationen, konflikte und machtstrukturen im "Solialismus der Tat" des dritten reiches.* Augsburg: Maro.

Healy, L. (2001). *International social work.* New York: Oxford University Press.

Holtzman, E. (2005, July 18–25). Torture and accountability. *The Nation,* pp. 20–24.

Hughes, R. (1987). *The fatal shore: The epic of Australia's founding.* New York: Knopf.

Human-rights law. (1998, December 15). *The Economist,* pp. 4–16.

Human Rights Resource Center, University of Minnesota Law School. (2005). Retrieved January 25, 2005, from www.hrusa.org

Human Rights Watch. (2000). *Human rights world report 2001: Events of 2000.* New York: Author.

Ife, J. (2001). *Human rights and social work: Towards rights-based practice.* Cambridge: Cambridge University Press.

Inter Action Council. (1997). *A universal declaration of human responsibilities.* Retrieved November 21, 2005, from www.asiawide.or.jp/iac/contents.htm

International Federation of Social Workers. (2005). *Code of ethics.* Retrieved November 19, 2005, from www.ifsw.org/en/p38000324.html

Ishay, M. (2004). *History of human rights, from ancient times to the globalization era.* Berkeley: University of California Press.

Kramer, J. (2004, November 22). Letter from Europe: Taking the veil. *The New Yorker*, pp. 59–71.

Lederer, W, & Burdick, E. (1958). *The ugly American*. New York: W. W. Norton.

Lee, J. (1994). *The empowerment approach to social work practice*. New York: Columbia University Press.

Loewenberg, F. M., & Dolgoff, R. (1992). *Ethical decisions for social work practice*. Itasca, IL: Peacock.

Mannig, S. (1997). The social worker as a moral citizen: Ethics in action. *Social Work: Journal of the National Association of Social Workers, 42*(3), 223–230.

Marks, A. (2004, October 8). The prison that Martha Stewart will call home. *Christian Science Monitor*, p. 1.

Mattison, M. (2000). Ethical decision making: The person in the process. *Social Work: Journal of the National Association of Social Workers, 45*(3), 201–212.

McDougall, G. (2004). Shame in our own house: How segregation and racism have fed U.S. resistance to international human-rights treaties. *American Prospect Special Report: U.S. Human Rights*, A21–A23.

McGoldrick, M., Giordano, J., & Pearce, J. (1996). *Ethnicity and family therapy* (2nd ed.). New York: Guilford.

Mink, E. (2005, February 9). Moral values test. *St .Louis Post-Dispatch*, B7.

Mintz, M. (2004, November 15). Single-payer: Good for business. *The Nation*, pp. 18–24.

Moravcsik, A. (2005, January 31). Dream on America. *Newsweek International*. Retrieved November 20, 2005, from www.newsweek.com, article ID #nwov10520050131

Morsink, J. (1999). *The universal declaration of human rights: Origins. drafting, and intent*. Philadelphia: University of Pennsylvania Press.

Namazie, M. (1998) *Cultural relativism: This era's fascism*. Retrieved October 30, 2003, from www.hambastegi.org/english/selectedarticles.culturalr.htm

National Association of Social Workers. (1999). *Code of ethics* (Rev. ed.). Washington, DC: NASW Press.

National Association of Social Workers. (2003). *Social work speaks: National Association of Social Workers Policy Statements, 2003–2006* (6th ed.). Washington, DC: NASW Press.

Neuffer, E. (2001, June 28). Anti-AIDS plan sets out a strategy, but "the real work, starts only now." *St. Louis Post-Dispatch*, p. B8.

The New Face of AIDS. (2004, November 27). *The Economist*, p. 82.

Newman, F., & Weisbrodt, D. (1996). *International human rights: Law, policy, and process* (2nd ed.). Cincinnati, OH: Anderson Publishing.

Oliver, M. (2005, February 15). McLibel Two win legal aid case. *Guardian Unlimited*. Retrieved November 13, 2005, from www.guardian.co.uk/print0,3858,5127360-103526,00.html

Otto, H. U., & Sunker, H. (1991). *Politische formierung und soziale erziehung im nationall-sozialismus*. Frankfurt: Suhrkamp.

Parker, A. (2004, October). Inalienable rights. *American Prospect*, A11–A13.

Pinderhughes, E. (1989). *Understanding race, ethnicity and power: The key to efficacy in clinical practice*. New York: Free Press.

Press, E. (2000, December 25). Human rights: The next step. *The Nation*, pp. 13–18.

Reamer, F. (1995). *Social work values and ethics*. New York: Columbia University Press.

Reamer, F. (1998). *Ethical standards in social work: A critical review of the NASW code of ethics*. Washington, DC: NASW Press.

Reamer, F. (1999). *Social work values and ethics* (2nd ed.). New York: Columbia University Press.

Reichert, E. (1996). Keep on moving forward: NGO forum on women, Beijing, China. *Social Development Issues, 18*(1), 61–71.

Reichert, E. (1998). Women's rights are human rights: A platform for action. *International Social Work, 41*(3), 371–385.

Reichert, E. (2003). *Social work and human rights: A foundation for policy and practice.* New York: Columbia University Press.

Reichert, E., & McCormick, R. (1997). Different approaches to child welfare: United States and Germany. *Journal of Law and Social Work, 7*(1), 17–33.

Reichert, E., & McCormick, R. (1998). U.S. welfare law violates human rights of immigrants. *Migration World, 26,* 15–18.

Rice-Oxley, M. (2004, July 7). Britain examines "honor killings." *Christian Science Monitor, 96,* 6.

Rifkin, J. (2004). *The European dream: How Europe's vision of the future is quickly eclipsing the American dream.* New York: Jeremy P. Tarcher/Penguin.

Roosevelt, E. (1948, December 10). Presentation of the Universal Declaration of Human Rights to the General Assembly. Quote retrieved November 9, 2005, from www.unac.org/rights/actguide/intor.html

Roper v. Simmons, 543 U.S., 125 S.Ct 1183, 161 L.Ed.2nd (2005).

Saleebey, D. (2002). *The strengths perspective in social work practice* (3rd ed.). Boston: Allyn & Bacon.

Salomon, B. (1976). *Black empowerment: Social work in oppressed communities.* New York: Columbia University Press.

Schnurr, S. (1997). Why did social workers accept the new order? In H. Sunker & H. U. Otto (Eds.), *Education and fascism* (pp. 326–388). London: Falmer Press.

Schulman, L. (1999). *Skills of helping individual and groups* (4th ed.). Itasca, IL: Peacock.

Shirer, W. (1959, 1960). *The rise and fall of the third reich.* Greenwich, CT: Fawcett Publications.

Simon, B. (1994). *The empowerment tradition in American social work.* New York: Columbia University Press.

Sklar, H. (1997, July/August). Cross currents: Imagine a country. *Z Magazine.* Retrieved November 22, 2005, from http://zena.secureforum.com/Znet/zmag/allarticles1.cfm

Staub-Bernasconi, S. (1998). Soziale Arbeit als Menschenrechtsprofession. In A. Woehrle (Ed.), *Profession und Wissenschaft Sozialer Arbeit: Positionen in einerPhase der generellen Neuverortung und Spezifika* (pp. 305–332). Pfaffenweilern, Germany: Cenaurus.

Sunstein, C. (2004). *The second bill of rights: FDR's unfinished revolution and why we need it more than ever.* New York: Basic Books.

Swarns, R. (2001, September 9). Conference calls for reversing consequences of slavery: UN meeting on racism ends in controversy. *St. Louis Post-Dispatch,* pp. A1, A10.

Swenson, C. (1998). Clinical social work's contribution to a social justice perspective. *Social Work: Journal of the National Association of Social Workers, 43*(6), 527–537.

UNICEF. (2005). *Convention on the rights of the child.* Retrieved November 15, 2005, from www.unicef.org/crc/crc.htm

United Nations. (1948). *Universal declaration of human rights.* Adopted December 10, 1948. GA Res. 217 AIII (UN Doc. a/810).

United Nations. (1966a, March 7). International convention on the elimination of all forms of racial discrimination. Retrieved November 21, 2005, from http://law-ref.org/DISCRIMINATION/index.html

United Nations. (1966b). *International covenant on economic, social and cultural rights.* Adopted December 16, 1966. GA Res. 2200A XXI. Retrieved January 14, 2004, from www.unhchr.ch/html/menu3/b/a_cescr.htm

United Nations. (1975). *Declaration on the rights of disabled persons.* GA Res. 3447 XXX.

United Nations. (1978, November 27). *Declaration on race and racial prejudice* (E/CN.4/Sub.2/1982/2/Add.1, annex V). Adopted and proclaimed by the General

Conference of the United Nations Educational, Scientific and Cultural Organization at its twentieth session.

United Nations. (1980, July 14–30). Report of the World Conference of the United Nations Decade for Women: Equality, development, and peace, Copenhagen (U.N. Pub. no. E. 80. IV-3, A/CONF.94/35). New York: Author.

United Nations. (1981). *Convention on the elimination of all forms of discrimination against women.* Adopted September 3, 1981. GA Res. 34/180, U.N. GAOR, 34th Sess., Supp. No. 46 at 193 (U.N. Doc. A/34/46). New York: Author.

United Nations. (1986). *Declaration on the right to development.* Retrieved November 28, 2005, from www.un.org

United Nations. (1987). *Human rights: Questions and answers.* New York: Author.

United Nations. (1989). *Convention on the rights of the child* (UN Doc. A/Res/44/23). New York: Author.

United Nations. (1991). *Principles for the protection of persons with mental illness and the improvement of mental health care.* Adopted December 17, 1991. GA Res. 46/119. Retrieved November 28, 2005, from www.peoplewho.org/documents/unprinciples.doc

United Nations. (1995). *Platform for action.* Retrieved November 15, 2004, from www.un.org/womenwatch/daw/beijing/platform/plat1.htm

United Nations. (1996). *International covenant on civil and political rights.* Retrieved November 14, 2004, from www.unhchr.ch/html/menu3/b/a_ccpr.htm

United Nations. (1999). *Principles for the older person.* Retrieved January 24, 2005, from www.un.org/esa/socdev/iyop/iyoppop.htm

United Nations. (2004). *Report on global AIDS epidemic.* Retrieved November 13, 2004, from www.unaids.org/bangkok2004/report.html

United States Peace Corps. (2005). *History.* Retrieved November 21, 2005, from www.peace corps.gov

Van Den Bergh, N., & Cooper, L. B. (1986). *Feminist visions for social work.* Silver Spring, MD: NASW.

Van Wormer, K. (1997). *Social welfare: A world view.* Chicago: Nelson Hall.

Van Wormer, K. (2001). *Counseling female offenders and victims: A strengths-restorative approach.* New York: Springer.

Van Wormer, K. (2004a). *Confronting oppression, restoring justice: From policy analysis to social action.* Alexandria, VA: Council of Social Work Education.

Van Wormer, K. (2004b). *Introduction to social welfare and social work: The U.S. in global perspective.* Pacific Grove, CA: Thompson Brooks/Cole.

Vienna Convention on the Law of Treaties. (1969). Retrieved November 21, 2005, from www.un.org/law/ilc/texts/treaties.htm

Who is running the show? (2004, August 8). *St. Louis Post-Dispatch,* p. 1.

Witkin, S. (2000). Ethics-R-Us. *Social Work: Journal of the National Association of Social Workers, 45*(3), 197–201.

The World Factbook. (2004). Retrieved December 8, 2004, from www.cia.gov/cia/publica tions/factbook/index.html

Wronka, J. (1998). *Human rights and social policy in the 21st century: A history of the idea of human rights and comparison of the United Nations universal declaration of human rights with United States federal and state constitutions* (Rev. ed.). Lanham, MD: University Press of America.

Index

Note: Page numbers in *italic* type refer to figures or tables.

Aceh, 168
Activists, exercises on, 36–37
Addams, Jane, 1, 28
AIDS, 87
American Dream, 27, 161–162
Amnesty International, 167–169
Analysis of human rights, exercises in
    local circumstances, 74–75
    Spain and Taino, 33–35
    statistics, 73–74
    United States history, 35–36
Arrest, 43
Asylum from persecution, 44

Best interests principle, 83
Bill of Rights, 22
Biographies, exercises using, 36–37
Blunt, Matt, 126
Bolivar, Simon, 24
Brando, Marlon, 159
Bush, George W., 125, 161

Capital punishment, 63
Carter, Jimmy, 60, 65, 68, 81
Cassin, Rene, 25
Catastrophes, exercise on, 167–169
CEDAW. *See* Convention on the
    Elimination of All Forms of
    Discrimination Against Women
Charters. *See* Human rights charters
Children
    child prostitution exercise, 166
    child soldier exercise, 166

Convention on the Rights of the
    Child (1989), 82–84, 92–96
    definition of, 83
    exercises, 92–96, 166
    protections for, 48, 82
Chile, 25
China, 24, 116–117
Civil and political rights, ix, 3, 42–46
    exercise, 69–70
    See also International Covenant on
        Civil and Political Rights
Clinton, Bill, 83
Code of Hammurabi, 28
Collective rights. *See* Solidarity and
    international rights
Colonialism, 40
Commission on Human Rights, 23, 25
Common humanity, definition of, 2
Communist Manifesto (Marx and
    Engels), 22
Community assessment, exercise on, 54–58
Community development, 159
Confucius, 24, 29
Convention, definition of, 12
    See also specific conventions
Convention on the Elimination of All
    Forms of Discrimination Against
    Women (CEDAW) (1979)
    exercise, 92
    gender discrimination defined by, 80
    overview, 221–223
    provisions, 79–81
    social work practice and, 138

text of, 224–235
United States and, 81–82
Convention on the Elimination of All
Forms of Racism (1966), 86
Convention on the Rights of the Child
(1989), 82–84
exercise, 92–96
social work practice and, 138
text of, 237–256
Council of Social Work Education
(CSWE), vii
Courts. *See* Human rights courts
Covenants
definition of, 12
ratification process for, in U.S., 60
See also specific covenants
Cultural competence, 143
Cultural relativism, 103–111
analysis of, 104–109
case studies, 104–109
case study exercises, 112–117
challenge of, 171
continuum, *105*
defining, 104, 111–112
exercises, 111–117
fascism and, 109–110
universality principle and, 10–12, 104
Cultural rights, ix, 3, 46, 48–49
Culture
customs exercise, 165–166
ethics exercise, 132
human rights in conflict with, 6
non-Western contributions to
human rights, 24
participation in, 49, 67
superiority feelings based on, 20–21,
85–86, 160
See also terms beginning with Cultural
Customs of culture, exercise on, 165–166

Declaration, definition of, 12
See also Universal Declaration of
Human Rights
Declaration of Independence (1776), 22,
30–31
Declaration of the Rights of Man and the
Citizen (1789), 31
Declaration on the Rights of the Child
(1989), 82

Declaration on the Right to Development
(1986), 157–158
Defining human rights
actors involved in, 7–9
beneficiaries, 9
cultural relativism, 10–12
definition, 2–3
disadvantaged, 9–10
exercise, 52
important questions, *8*
indivisibility, 6–7
social work and, 5
terminology, 12–13
three sets, 3–4
universality, 5–6
voices heard in, 10
Detention, 43
Development
Declaration on the Right to
Development (1986), 157–158
U.S. Peace Corps, 158–160
Dignity, 40
exercise, 13–15
Disabilities, 86–87
exercise, 97
Discrimination
chief principle of, 20
gender, 80
human rights narrowed to, 77
International Covenant on Civil and
Political Rights and, 61–62
protection against, 43
racial, 107
Domestic violence, 82

Economic rights, cultural relativism and,
104–109
Economic, social, and cultural rights,
ix, 3, 46, 48–49
cultural relativism analysis, 104–109
exercise, 70
See also International Covenant on
Economic, Social, and Cultural
Rights
Education, 48–49, 67
Elderly. *See* Older persons
Emancipation Proclamation (1863), 31–32
Employment. *See* Work
Empowerment, 140–141

Enforcement
    approaches to, 13
    conventions and, 12–13
    covenants and, 12–13
    exercise, 16–17
    importance of, 171
    Universal Declaration and, 59
Engels, Friedrich, 22
English Bill of Rights (1689), 30
Environment for human rights, exercises
        on, 52–54, 129–130
Equality, 40, 42
Ethics, 119–127
    case study exercises, 132–134
    decision-making exercise, 134–135
    dilemma exercises, 128–129
    exercises, 127–135
    human rights and, 122–127
    responsibilities, 122
    social work codes of, 119–122, *123*, 153
Ethnic-sensitive practice, 141–142
European Court of Human Rights, 13, 64

Family, 45, 67
Fascism, cultural relativism
        and, 109–110
Feminist social work practice, 142
First set of human rights, 3
France, 113
Free Aceh Movement, 168
Freedom, 42
Freedom from fear, 40
Freedom from want, 40
Freedom of association, 45
Freedom of belief, 40
Freedom of movement, 44
Freedom of speech, ix, 40, 45
Freedom of thought, 45

Gandhi, Mohandas Karamchand, 32
Gays, 88–89
exercise, 99–101
Gender. *See* Women
Gender discrimination, 80
Geneva Conventions (1864, 1949), 12, 32
Germany. *See* Nazi Germany
GLBT (Gay, lesbian, bisexual, and
        transgender) rights, exercise on,
        99–101

Globalization, 161
Gouges, Olyme de, 22

Hammurabi, Code of, 28
Health care coverage
indivisibility principle and, 6–7
    universality principle and, 6
    U.S. policy on, 8–9, 162
Helms, Jesse, 81
Historical foundation of human
        rights, 21–23
    exercise in, 28–33
Hitler, Adolf, 20, 23
HIV-AIDS, 87
    exercises, 91–92, 98, 167
Holocaust, 19–20
Homeland security, 125
Homosexuality, 88–89
    exercise, 99–101
Honor killings, 11
Human existence, principles of, 40–41
Human nature, definition of, 2
Human rights
    actors involved in defining, 7–9
    analysis exercise, 33–35
    broad meaning of, 77
    comparisons or rankings of, 7, 60, 65
    culture and, 6
    defining, 2–12, 52, 77
    fragility of, 172
    historical foundation of, 21–23, 28–33
    implementing, table for, *47*
    important questions in, *8*
    influences on defining, 10
    international issues, 155–162
    law and, ix–x, 1, 40
    limitation of, 66
    obligations and, 2, 50, *69*
    origin of, 19–21
    politics and, 1
    religion and, 6
    significance of, for social work, vii–ix, 5
    teaching, xiii–xiv
    terminology for, 12–13
    winners and losers in defining, 9–10
Human rights charters, exercise on,
        164–165
Human rights commission, exercise on,
        71–72

Human Rights Committee, 64
Human rights courts, exercise on, 164–165
Human Rights Squares Handout, *156*
Hussein, Saddam, 10, 155

Immigration
 exercise, 165
 U.S. attitudes toward, 143
Indigenous peoples, 24
Indivisibility, 6–7, 60
 exercise, 17–18
Indonesia, 168
Innocence, presumption of, 43
Inter Action Council, 124
International Association of Schools of
 Social Work, 27
International Committee of Schools of
 Social Work, 22
International Covenant on Civil and
 Political Rights (1966)
 adoption of, 59
 Optional Protocol, 205–208
 social work and, 65
 summary of, 60–64
 text of, 185–203
International Covenant on Economic,
 Social, and Cultural Rights (1966)
 adoption of, 59
 social work and, 68
 social work practice and, 138
 summary of, 65–68
 text of, 209–219
International Declaration of Ethical
 Principles of Social Work, 120–121
International Ethical Standards for Social
 Workers, 120–121
International Federation of Social Workers
 (IFSW), 5, 119, 153
 code of ethics, 120–122, 179–183
 code of ethics exercise, 165
International Labor Organization, 22
International Permanent Secretariat of
 Social Workers, 22
International Red Cross, 32
International rights. *See* Solidarity and
 international rights
International social work, 153–162
 case study exercises, 165–167
 definition of, 153

guidelines, 160–161
human rights issues, 155–162
skill development exercise, 162–163
social problems, 154
Interview, exercise using, 38
Iraq, 10, 155, 161

James II, King of England, 30
Jefferson, Thomas, 31
Jesus, 29
Jews, 20
John, King of England, 21, 30

Language, and discrimination, 62
Law
 adversarial nature of, ix
 expense of, ix–x
 human rights and, ix–x, 1, 40
 right to trial, 43
 selective character of, ix
League of Nations, 22–23
Leisure, 48
Lesbians, 88–89
 exercise, 99–101
Liberation Tigers of Tamil Eelam, 168–169
Life, right to, 42
Lincoln, Abraham, 32

Magna Carta (1215), 21, 30
Marriage rights, 45
Marx, Karl, 22
Mary II, Queen of England, 30
McCormick, Robert J., 158–160
McDonalds, 64
McLibel Two, 64
Media, exercises on, 17, 51–52
Mink, Eric, 126–127
Missouri, 126–127
Moravcsik, Andrew, 161–162
Motherhood, 48

Namazie, Maryam, 109–110
National Association of Social Workers
 (NASW), vii, 14, 138
 code of ethics, 119–120, 122, *123*, 153
 code of ethics exercise, 165
Nationality, right to, 44
Natural law, 22
Natural rights, 22

Nazi Germany, 19–20, 39
Negative rights, 3, 65
New Testament, 29
Nongovernmental organizations
    (NGOs), 25
Non-Western peoples, human rights
    contributions by, 24

Obligations, 2, 50, *69*
Older persons, 88
    exercise, 98–99
Old Testament, 29
Oppression, 139–140
Optional Protocol to the International
    Covenant on Civil and Political
    Rights (1966), text of, 205–208

Palestinians, 61
Paul (apostle), 29
Pen game exercise, 130–131
Plato, 21
Political participation, 46
Political rights. *See* Civil and
    political rights
Politics, 1
Positive rights, 3, 65
Principles for the Older
    Person (1999), 88
Privacy, 44
Property, 45

Race, 26
Racism, 85–86
    exercise, 96–97
Religion
    freedom of, 45
    human rights in conflict with, 6
Reports, on human rights progress, 67–68
Reservations, 63
Responsibilities
    ethical, 122–124
    exercises, 132, 135
    Universal Declaration of Human
        Responsibilities, 124–125
    See also Obligations
Rights
    inalienable, 40
    natural, 22
    negative versus positive, 3, 65

See also Civil and political rights;
    Economic, social, and cultural
    rights; Human rights; Solidarity
    and international rights
Roosevelt, Eleanor, 13, 25
Roosevelt, Franklin, 108

Salomon, Alice, 1
Saudi Arabia, 25–26
Science, participation in, 49, 67
Second set of human rights, 3
Security, homeland, 125
Security of person, 42
Segregation, 107
Self-determination, 60–61, 66
Sexual slavery, exercise on, 166–167
Slavery
    prohibition of, 42
    U.S. Civil War and, 31–32
Social justice, vagueness of, 5
Social programs, 125–127
Social rights. *See* Economic, social,
    and cultural rights
Social security, 46, 67
Social work
    activists exercise, 37
    code of ethics, 119
    human rights' significance for, vii–ix, 5
    international, 153–162
    International Covenant on Civil and
        Political Rights and, 65
    International Covenant
        on Economic, Social, and
        Cultural Rights and, 68
    women's rights and, 82
    See also Social work practice
Social workers, 27–28
    exercise, 16
    international counterpart exercise,
        163–164
    international organization exercise, 164
Social work practice, 137–144
    case study exercises, 144–152
    cultural competence, 142
    empowerment, 140–141
    ethnic-sensitive practice, 141–142
    feminist practice, 142
    human rights applications,
        139–143, *144*

NASW policy statement, 138–139
oppression, 139–140
strengths perspective, 141
Socrates, 21
Solidarity and international rights,
3–4, 49–50
South Africa, 25–26
South America, 24
Soviet Constitution (1936), 24
Soviet Union, 24–26
Spain, 33–35
Sri Lanka, 168–169
Standard of living, 48
Statistics, exercise on, 73–74
Stewart, Martha, 140
Strengths perspective, 141

Taino, 33–35
Thailand, 169
Third set of human rights, 3–4
Torture, 11–12, 42
Treaty of Westphalia (1648), 30
Trial, right to, 43

The Ugly American, 159
UN Charter (1945), 33
United Nations
Charter (1945), 33
Commission on Human Rights, 23, 25
Educational, Scientific, and Cultural
Organization (UNESCO), 85
formation of, 23
U.S. view of, 103
See also Universal Declaration of
Human Rights
United States
CEDAW, 81–82
Convention on the Rights of the Child,
83, 84
cultural superiority and, 21, 85–86, 160
discrimination as defined by, 80
economic rights and cultural
relativism, 104–109
enforcement of human rights in, 13
health care system, 8–9, 162
historical analysis exercise, 35–36
human rights shortcomings of, 27,
65–66, 82

immigration, 143
International Covenant on Civil and
Political Rights, 60
International Covenant on Economic,
Social, and Cultural Rights,
65–66, 68
international effects of, 155
opposition to, 161–162
self-perception of, 161–162
torture and, 11–12
United Nations as viewed by, 103
Universal Declaration, 25–26
Universal Declaration of Human
Responsibilities, 124–125
Universal Declaration of Human Rights
(1948), 39–50
debate over, 25
economic, social, and cultural rights in,
46, 48–49
free speech as issue in, ix
health care as issue in, ix, 8
international order promotion,
153, 156–157
NASW code of ethics compared to, *123*
opening statement of, 40–41
origin of, xiii, 23–26, 33, 39–40
political/civil rights in, 42–46
significance of, 12, 26
social work practice and, 138
text of, 173–178
Universality
as basic principle, 5–6, 42
cultural relativism and, 10–12, 104
exercise, 17
local challenges to, 7, 103–104
U.S. Constitution (1787), 22, 31
U.S. Peace Corps, 158–160

Vulnerable groups
children, 82–84
definition of, 78
disabilities, 86–87
exercise, 89
gays and lesbians, 88–89
HIV-AIDS, 87
older persons, 88
racism victims, 85–86
women, 78–82

Welfare reform, viii
William III, King of England, 30
Women
    CEDAW, 79–82
    exercises, 90–91, 116
    feminist social work practice, 142
    gender discrimination, 80
    human rights for, 79, *80*
    social work and rights of, 82
    subordination of, 78–79
Work, 46, 48, 67
World War II, 19, 23

About the Author

Elisabeth Reichert, LCSW, PhD received her degree in social work from the University of Tennessee in 1985 with the aid of a Fulbright Scholarship. She also holds an equivalent degree in Germany. After receiving her social work degree, she practiced clinical social work until 1994, when she began teaching social work policy and practice. She is a professor at Southern Illinois University at Carbondale and has previously published a book on social work and human rights titled *Social Work and Human Rights: A Foundation for Policy and Practice.*